MOHAWK
INTERRUPTUS

MOHAWK
INTERRUPTUS

{ POLITICAL LIFE ACROSS THE BORDERS OF SETTLER STATES }

Audra Simpson

Duke University Press   Durham and London   2014

Printed in the United States of America on acid-free paper ∞
Designed by Heather Hensley
Typeset in Warnock Pro by Copperline Book Services, Inc.

Library of Congress Cataloging-in-Publication Data
Simpson, Audra.
Mohawk interruptus : political life across the borders of settler
states / Audra Simpson.
p. cm.
Includes bibliographical references and index.
ISBN 978–0–8223–5643–1 (cloth : alk. paper)
ISBN 978–0–8223–5655–4 (pbk. : alk. paper)
1. Mohawk Indians–Quebec (Province)–Kahnawake Indian
Reserve–Ethnic identity. 2. Mohawk Indians–Quebec
(Province)–Kahnawake Indian Reserve–History. I. Title.
E99.M8556 2014
971.4004'975542–dc23
2013042833

IN LOVING MEMORY:

Danielle N. Terrance,

1973–2013

A best friend to all of us.

Contents

Acknowledgments

Much of this book is about the labor to live a good life. The people of the Mohawk nation at Kahnawà:ke do this work with great verve and equanimity, while enduring and pushing against the ongoing stress and structure of settler colonialism. Their commitment to the principle of a good mind and to the struggle to maintain and then assert that principle has inspired and forms the core questions of this book. I am deeply, deeply grateful to them for this, and for holding on to everything.

Kahnawà:ke, the Mohawk Nation, and the Haudenosaunee are embedded conceptually and in different ways politically in the global category of "Indigeneity" and of course, by extension, Indigenous peoples. I owe an ongoing debt—a general one that is so broad and simultaneously categorical as to seem abstract, to those whose lives and lands brought forth the questions that animate this book. Indigenous peoples within and beyond Kahnawà:ke continue to strive and in so doing sustain questions of profound theoretical and political importance—questions of persistence, vigor, and dignity in the face of grinding power—as well as the disavowal of staggering wrongdoing.

I am fortunate to be around people who care deeply and think very hard about these sorts of things. I am especially grateful to Beth Povinelli, Roz Morris, Lila Abu-Lughod, Brinkley Messick, and Nadia Abu El-Haj for their careful readings, before which this was a different book. I am grateful to the entire Anthropology

Department at Columbia. Mellie Ivy, John Pemberton, and Mick Taussig are not only great thinkers and ethnographers; they are my neighbors. I am grateful to them and every single one of the scholars for their collegiality, their support, their acuity of vision, and their analysis. Brian Boyd, Zoe Crossland, Terry D'Altroy, Cassie Fennell, Severin Fowles, Brian Larkin, Hlonipha Mokoena, Lesley Sharp, and Paige West are intellectually and interpersonally, and quite simply, great colleagues.

This book has had a long life to fruition and so has traveled with me from place to place. It started as a dissertation that was written in the Department of Anthropology at McGill University. There it had the good fortune to be directed by Colin Scott and the late Bruce Trigger. During the final revisions of this book, the enormity of Bruce Trigger's loss to this field and to my own thinking was felt acutely, and over and over again. I wish very much that he were still with us. My first job was at Cornell University, where I had wonderful colleagues. I am indebted to the Department of Anthropology there, where my thinking was supported and my days well spent.

For years I have been in conversation with individuals who have helped this work along immensely. They have come to the fore to help to figure things out, read drafts, convene panels, push arguments, and tend to queries over e-mail and on the phone. Jessica Cattelino, Mishuana Goeman, and Andrea Smith have been key thinking partners through the course of this book. They have stopped everything at certain points in their own writing and lives and helped me to puzzle through matters pertaining to this work—this is collegiality that is rare and is precious. While I was revising this book, Robert Nichols was on fellowship at Columbia, and I was able to talk to him about its argumentation and claims. I am grateful to him for his intellectual generosity during a crucial time.

My dear old friend (and former favorite sparring partner) is Gerald (Taiaiake) Alfred, who wrote the first political analysis of our community in 1995. In doing so, he implicitly and explicitly prompted me to write another. He has been a great mentor and friend. Here the list is long, and it is not detailed enough. Each of these great people deserve paragraphs upon paragraphs of praise: Chris Andersen, Joanne Barker, Ned Blackhawk, Kevin Bruyneel, Bruno Cornellier, Glen Coulthard, Jennifer Denetdale, Vince Diaz, Alyosha Goldstein, Sandy Grande, Kēhaulani Kauanui, Scott Lyons, Dian Million, Aileen Moreton-Robinson, Scott Morgensen, Michael

Orsini, Michelle Raheja, Jackie Rand, Justin Richland, Mark Rifkin and Dale Turner are scholars, colleagues, and more often than not, truly outstanding friends whose thinking, work, and example have had a profound effect upon my own.

Similarly, but very specifically, acknowledgments just fall apart when I am confronted with thanks for my friends and colleagues in Haudenosaunee studies. Sue Hill, Kurt Jordan, Theresa McCarthy, Rick Monture, Vera Palmer, Jon Parmenter, and Jolene Rickard have been conversation partners through the years (good, long years now), and are also people whose work I greatly require and enjoy. Rob Odawi Porter and Carrie Garrow have been wonderful, from afar, as has Martin Cannon. Although Deborah Doxtator is on the other side of the sky, her work has been critical to my own. I would be remiss if I did not mark her deep importance in the field of Indigenous history and, most specifically, to the project of renewing Haudenosaunee studies. Ellen Gabriel has been a rock among our people but also a steady and elegant friend to my thinking and research.

Jasmin Habib is a scholar whose industry, grace, and ethical standard has been important to my own; she is also a person with whom I love to laugh. I am so grateful to her for this. Profuse thanks go as well to Whitney Battle-Baptiste, Sean Brotherton, June Kitanaka, Kristin Norget, Jessica Winegar, and Vinh-Kim Nguyen, great friends and colleagues who have shared conversations about this work. Sora Han, Nadine Naber, and Jodi Kim have engaged with the argumentation, and are scholars whose work serve as models of critical ethical posture and rigor for my own. I will never forget the early support and advice of Karen Blu, as I started my cross-border research, nor the late Robert Paine, as well as the late and still deeply missed Gail Guthrie-Valaskakis. Fred Myers and Faye Ginsburg have been supportive of this project since before "day one."

Frances Negrón-Muntaner has helped to make Columbia a place where Indigenous studies can flourish through her early and ongoing efforts through the Center for the Study of Ethnicity and Race (soon to be Center for the Study of Race, Ethnicity, and Indigeneity). I thank her for her institutional flexibility, her enthusiasm, her ongoing support of all that is done in our field. Aaron Fox is also a terrific colleague whose own scholarship and effort and does much for Indigenous studies (and people!) at Columbia.

I have presented earlier and greatly redacted versions of this work at University of Victoria, Northwestern University, McGill University, Université de Montréal, University of California (Riverside), Wilfrid Laurier University, University of Illinois (Champaign), University of Chicago, Kanien'kehá:ka Onkwawén:na Raotitióhkwa Language & Cultural Center, University of Michigan, Syracuse University, McMaster University, Tufts University, Williams College, Columbia University, Harvard University, New York University, Cornell University, and the State University of New York, Buffalo. I am grateful for the incisive comments and suggestions of the scholars at these talks, all of which greatly improved the following book.

The research and writing for this book project were supported by several fellowships and awards. I am grateful to the Social Sciences and Humanities Research Council of Canada (internal grants—McGill University), the Fulbright Foundation, the American Anthropological Association (Minority Dissertation Write Up Fellowship), Dartmouth College (the Charles Eastman Fellowship), Cornell University (Provost's Diversity Post-Doctoral Fellowship) and the School for Advanced Research, Santa Fe (Katrin H. Lamon Fellowship). These fellowships were crucial for the fieldwork and write-up of this project, both as a dissertation and then as a book. I am also grateful to James Brooks at the School for Advanced Research (SAR) as well as to Rebecca Allahyari and Cam Cocks, who were terrific to talk to during my tenure there. Among my cohort at SAR Tim Pauketat, Susan Alt, and Danny Hoffman were fun, smart friends and colleagues.

Graduate students at Cornell and Columbia have been subjected to thinking that is found in the following pages in the "Governmentality, Citizenship and Indigenous Political Critique" (formerly "theory") and "Settler Colonialism in North America" seminars. I acknowledge and thank these excellent minds for their engagement. Jay Hammond and Alexandra Wagner were keen (and former) students who wound up researching for me. I thank them for their great labor. At Duke University Press, Courtney Berger has been a dream of an editor: patient and so smart. I am grateful to her for this and to the great copyediting of Anitra Grisales—who kept me on tack, on track, and also from great grammatical and conceptual embarrassment. Deborah Guterman was terrific with the details. I am hugely indebted and grateful to the excellent anonymous reviewers whose readings sharpened the book. An earlier version of chapter 4 appeared in *Junctures: A Journal of Thematic Dialogue* (2007) and was reprinted in *Racism, Colonialism, and Indigeneity in Canada* (2011). An earlier version of chapter 5 appeared in *Law and Contemporary Problems* (2008).

Every year Kahnawà:ke calls me home to present elements from this book or comment on the work of others. For one month Kwatokent TV televised an earlier version of the "border" chapter, chapter 5 after a "Meet the Authors" event at Kanien'kehá:ka Onkwawén:na Raotitióhkwa Language & Cultural Center. I thank Donna Goodleaf and Martin Loft for these invitations, and I thank them for calling me an author long before I was published. Not only did they honor this work tremendously by doing so; they animated, inspired, and made less painful the work of revision. I thank Teyowisonte (Tommy) Deer, Carla Hemlock, Kanentokon Hemlock, Tekanerahtaneken (Greg) Horn, Stephanie Waterman, Percy Abrams, and the 207 Longhouse for their help tracking down permissions and then for their permission to use the images within. Teyowisonte also helped me with my spelling in Mohawk, which is hugely needed (and appreciated!). Any mistakes are my own, of course.

My immediate and extended family have been relentless in their support of this work and the strange project of having a scholar in the family—a project that has required prolonged absences, borderline disappearances, and their infinite patience. My parents, Ronny and Gloria Simpson, and my sister, Cori Simpson, are models of industry, patience, intellectual curiosity, and support. They were somehow patient and fun throughout all of this, I less so. Chuck Barnett and Tracee Diabo are friends who are like family and so have stayed the course, through thick and thin. And like my family, they also make me laugh—a lot. I am so grateful to them for this. My aunties, cousins, and other friends in Kahnawà:ke, Ahkwesáhsne, and Kanehsatà:ke still care about me even though I am more of an absence than a presence in their lives. For this I am forever grateful and bound. P. J. Herne has read portions this work and offered his advice, helping me in the later stages of revision.

It is because of these very people that I am a person in debt, or simply in deep, wondrous gratitude. So I come up against the limit of language—as these people embody, in so many ways, the theoretical, the methodological, and the affective properties and desires of this project. I find it impossible to express in these moments their profound influence, their worth, and their value to me. I hope that this book is a start.

Niawen ko:wa akwek:on.

ONE

Indigenous Interruptions

Mohawk Nationhood, Citizenship, and the State

Unless you are one of the first Americans, a Native American, we are all descended from folks who came from somewhere else. The story of immigrants in America isn't a story of them. It's a story of us. . . . For just as we remain a nation of laws, we have to remain a nation of immigrants.
—**US President Barack Obama, July 4, 2012**

We are representing a nation, and we are not going to travel on the passport of a competitor.
—**Tonya Gonella Frichner, Iroquois Nationals Lacrosse Team spokesperson and negotiator, World Lacrosse Championships, July 19, 2010**

What does it mean to refuse a passport—what some consider to be a gift or a right, the freedom of mobility and residency? What does it mean to say no to these things, or to wait until your terms have been met for agreement, for a reversal of recognition, or a conferral of rights? What happens when we refuse what all (presumably) "sensible" people perceive as good things? What does this refusal do to politics, to sense, to reason? When we add Indigenous peoples to this question, the assumptions and the *histories* that structure what is perceived to be "good" (and utilitarian goods themselves) shift and stand in stark relief. The positions assumed by people who refuse "gifts" may seem reasoned, sensible, and in fact deeply correct. Indeed, from this perspective, we see that a good is not a good for everyone.

The Mohawks of Kahnawà:ke are nationals of a precontact Indigenous polity that simply refuse to stop being themselves.[1] In other words, they insist on being and acting as peoples who belong to a nation other than the United States or Canada. Their political form predates and survives "conquest"; it is tangible (albeit strangulated by colonial governmentality) and is tied to sovereign practices. This architecture is not fanciful; it is in place because the Mohawks of Kahnawà:ke share a genealogical kin-ship relationship with other native peoples in North America and they *know this*. They refuse to *let go of this knowledge*. In fact, they enact this knowledge through marriage practices, political engagements, and the way they live their lives. Their genealogical and political connectedness is part of a covenant—the decision-making Iroquois Confederacy called Haudenosaunee—which is made up of clans that spread across territory. As Indigenous peoples they have survived a great, transformative process of settler occupation, and they continue to live under the conditions of this occupation, its disavowal, and its ongoing life, which has required and still requires that they give up their lands and give up themselves.

What is the self that I speak of that they will not give up? The course of this book will unpack this for us, but most commonly that self is conflated with the figure of the ironworker and understood, in largely celebratory terms, through this image. Ironworkers are (usually) men who put up the infrastructure for skyscrapers, bridges, and all sorts of other large-scale construction jobs all over the United States and Canada,[2] but Kahnawà:ke labor is most associated with cities in the northeastern United States. They are famous for traveling from Kahnawà:ke on Sunday night to get to New York City (or Buffalo, or Ithaca, or as far as Detroit) by Monday morning.[3] This is a life of difficult, dangerous labor, and intense travel, and a life that returns, the literature of various sorts tells us, back to the "reserve" as much as the job and drive time can allow. In his very popular *New Yorker* piece, Joseph Mitchell started his article on ironwork and Kahnawà:ke in the following way: "The most footloose Indians in North America are a band of mixed-blood Mohawks whose home, the Caughnawaga Reser-vation, is on the St. Lawrence River in Quebec" (1959).[4]

This popular notion of the ironworking Mohawk, specifically from Kahnawà:ke, will not be lost because it is tied up with capital and the ma-terial reproduction of the community as well as postindustrial skylines.

But much of this book charts out the other labor that these people have undertaken and still undertake to maintain themselves in the face of a force that is imperial, legislative, ideological, and territorial and that has made them more than men who walk on beams. Their masculinized labor on iron matters to them, and to others, and I suspect will continue to matter as long as there is a market for construction. Yet the community is more than that form of labor can signal.

This community is now a reservation, or "reserve," located in what is now southwestern Quebec, a largely Francophone province in Canada. It is a reserved territory of approximately 18.55 miles. However, it belongs to people who have moved through the past four hundred years from the Mohawk Valley in what is now New York State to the northern part of their hunting territory—partially where they are now. Present-day Kahnawà:ke was a seigniorial land grant that became a reserve held in trust for the use and benefit of these "footloose" mixed-blood Mohawks—Mohawks, who, I will demonstrate through the course of this book, are not "mixed blood." In fact, they are Indigenous nationals of a strangulated political order who do all they can to live a political life robustly, with dignity *as* Nationals. In holding on to this, they interrupt and fundamentally challenge stories that have been told about them and about others like them, as well as the structure of settlement that strangles their political form and tries to take their land and their selves from them. As with all Indigenous people, they were supposed to have stepped off the beam that they walked on and plummeted to the ground several times through the course of their historical lives. Staying on top of a beam has involved effort and labor that extends beyond even the hard work of putting up steel. Since the time of Lewis Henry Morgan, this is the labor of living in the face of an expectant and a *foretold* cultural and political death. As such it is the hard labor of hanging on to territory, defining and fighting for your rights, negotiating and maintaining governmental and gendered forms of power.

Much of this labor I am talking about is tied up with a care for and defense of territory—so I will tell you first about this place and its institutions. If one desires a sociological sketch, the community has, as a federally recognized First Nation, accepted transfer funds from the government of Canada to build these institutions; other times they are completely self-funded. There is a Band Council, or "tribal government"; an in-patient hospital; a community services center with an economic development office; a bank with tellers; an ATM; a post office. Thus they have their own postal code, a sports arena, an Elders Lodge, a police force with a negotiated power to issue warrants and tickets for arrest (The Kahnawà:ke Peacekeepers). They have an AAA junior hockey team (the Condors), online gaming, an adult male lacrosse team (the Kahnawake Mohawks),[5] a community court, grocery stores (two with fresh produce and a butcher), gas stations, golf courses, two children's schools, a middle school, a high school (the Kahnawà:ke Survival School), a Catholic church, a Protestant church, two Longhouses, between five to ten sit-down restaurants, an Internet provider, a bilingual (Mohawk-English) TV station, a radio station, an offshore gaming host site (Mohawk Internet Technologies), poker houses, smoke shacks, cigarette manufacturing factories, a bingo hall, a tae kwon do gym, poker houses, a fabulous restaurant to get mixed drinks: "The Rail." There is a funeral home, a bakery shop, an education center, an optometrist with expensive, designer frames. There is a flower shop; antique stores; a shop that sells hypoallergenic and handcrafted soaps and bath salts; craft shops that sell moccasins, blankets, and objects for community members and tourists. In its economic past, there have been chip stands (selling French fries and pickled eggs) lining the highway, a dance hall, pizza parlor, a taco stand, beloved and now closed convenience stores such as Evelyn's, sit-down and takeout restaurants such as Rabaska's—closed due to fire and mourned as the passing of truly great pizza. There was a great bookstore, Mohawk Nation Books. The one public, coin-operated telephone is defunct but still in front of Rabaska's, on Highway 120, which connects Kahnawà:ke to Chateauguay, the south shore of Montreal and routes leading to the United States and north into Montreal and beyond, Oka, Quebec City, and so forth.

Indeed, there are many ironworkers, along with office workers; teachers; band councilors (called "chiefs" by the Indian Act); scholars;[6] three lawyers; one professional, retired hockey player; at least two who were semipro; many lacrosse players; fast-pitch softball players; two Olympians; several journalists (and two award-winning newspapers); musicians; filmmakers (two specifically are documentarians); actors; actresses; two former professional wrestlers, one who has now passed (his son is a conductor). There are people on social assistance and people who refuse social assistance and medical coverage because they do not recognize Canada.

There are veterans of every branch of the US armed forces, veterans of every war or conflict the United States has been in, even though this is on the Canadian side of the International Boundary Line. There are also veterans of the Canadian armed forces, members of the traditional Warrior Society who were en pointe during the "Oka Crisis," clan mothers, traditional people who live according to the precepts of the Kaianere'kó:wa, or Great Law of Peace, only. I have interviewed one person (out of thirty-six) who voted in a Canadian election. The Catholic Church at Kahnawà:ke houses the partial, bodily remains of the "first" Mohawk saint, and second Indigenous saint in church history, Kateri Tekakwitha, who was canonized in 2012.

That is the institutional face of the reserve. Its geographical limits are marked by two steel crosses, illuminated at night, that commemorate the passing of thirty-three (out of ninety-six) ironworkers who fell to their deaths when the Victoria bridge collapsed in 1907. There is now another memorial to their passing.[7] The riverfront of this community was expropriated by an order in Canadian Parliament in 1954 to construct a seaway that would facilitate commercial transport from the Port of Montreal to Lake Erie through the construction of a "deep draft waterway" through the St. Lawrence River, so it seems today as if ocean liners and freights move through it or in front of it or in back of the reserve, depending on how you see things. There is a train bridge that cuts through the reserve and over it along with the Mercier Bridge. This is a bridge that is perpetually under construction—travel on it is slow, tedious, and feels dangerous as it is decrepit. It connects this reserve to Montreal, across the St. Lawrence River and the aforementioned seaway. You can drive to Chateauguay in the opposite direction in five to ten minutes. When traffic is right you can get to LaSalle (Montreal) in 10, downtown Montreal in 15, and Pierre Elliot Trudeau airport in 20 minutes to 25 minutes; Vermont in 2 hours; Plattsburgh, New York, in 1.5 hours; Oka or Kanehsatà:ke, in 2 hours; Ahkwesáhsne in 1 hour; Toronto in 4 to 5 hours; New York City in 6 to 8 hours; and Ithaca, New York, as I did regularly for three years, in 6.5 hours. There are people who have walked the train bridge to Lachine, took boats to cross the seaway to Montreal.

As with the territorial body that was just described, the content of the corporeal bodies that inhabit and care for the place, are also crossed by markers and other histories of intent. With settler colonialism came "reservationization" and a radical shift in Indigenous diets and their bodies. As a result their blood is excessively "sweet" and has a high prevalence of diabetes—a bodily indicator of these spatial and dietary transitions. Rates in Kahnawà:ke are high,[8] and there are people who have had to have their toes and sometimes their feet and legs removed (Montour, Macaulay, and Adelson 1989). There is an aggressive campaign to educate the community on the perils of obesity and the importance of nutrition and exercise in order to prevent and control this condition (Potvin et al. 2003). Nonetheless, "bad carbs" have a great taste and take a traditional turn on Sundays, when it is common to make the savory, filling, sleep-inducing meal "cornbread and steak." This is cornbread bathed in thick gravy, sometimes served with sausages as well as or in place of steak. Long before the Internet, you could find people reading the *New York Post* or the *New York Daily News* in restaurants, on porches. One woman used to ask me to bring her the *New York Times* from the city, and when I lived in Montreal, I brought it for her from "Multimags"[9] whenever I came home. Older women tend to wear their hair in tight, short perms, and speak in Mohawk; ironworkers retire, go home, and amble arthritically and from the looks painfully behind their wives. My earliest memories of Kahnawà:ke were of my own grandmother, the late Margaret K. Diabo (née Phillips) fixing people's bones in her kitchen and switching back and forth from English and Mohawk with everyone who came into her home. She spoke this way with the man I call my grandfather, Eddie "Cantor" Diabo,[10] who switches back and forth from Mohawk to English to everyone, whether they are Indian or not. Most emphatically, it seems, when there is talk of the Boston Bruins or the border. Ten percent of the community now speaks Mohawk, but there is an aggressive campaign to educate everyone to speak the language. There is an adult immersion program with a graduating class of approximately fifteen to twenty people every year. There is a Catholic cemetery and a Protestant cemetery, and traditional people are buried according to Longhouse custom. There is also a pet cemetery. There are no addresses.

For those who are familiar with reserves, this sociological and historical sketch is both familiar and very different. There are no traplines mentioned; nor is there an emphasis or mention even of commodity cheese or of exorbitant poverty. There are institutions, professionals, the righteous. . . . There is a lot that goes unsaid. . . . There are those who drive "hummers" and gas guzzlers, Cadillacs, and Volkswagens; people who ride bikes or jog; young mothers who walk with strollers; one man who pushes a cart with great purpose every day in warm weather. There are highways, paved roads, train tracks, two bridges that cut through and connect this community to every place, if you want. There is relentless discussion of how things should be, relentless critique and engagement about what some would call "politics," of again, how things are, how they should be. There are unprompted, monologic "state of the nation" addresses. All of this exceeds the simplified figure of the ironworker. And yes, there are a lot of ironworkers there and, now, in Bay Ridge, Brooklyn. But the story that I am telling in this book is of a place and people through time and their labor to live a good life and, in this, their imperative to live upon and move through their territory in the teeth of constraint—constraint of various forms but that we may gloss as settler colonialism. Although ironwork is a part of their story, one that we all seem to like and admire, other things I will talk and not talk about are less easy to like, such as refusal.

Like many other Iroquois people, the Mohawks of Kahnawà:ke refuse to walk on some beams, and through this gesture they refuse to be Canadian or American. They refuse the "gifts" of American and Canadian citizenship; they insist upon the integrity of Haudenosaunee governance. Moreover, some in this study answer only to that governmental authority. So the bestowal of settler citizenship has been received with a certain "awkwardness" if not outright refusal—a refusal to vote, to pay taxes, to stop *politically* being Iroquois. The language that this book uses to tell this story of refusal is the language that people use to talk about themselves. They speak in terms of nationhood, which stages a fundamental difficulty given that "Indigenous" and "nation" are two terms that seem incommensurable.[11] "Indigenous" is embedded conceptually in a geographic alterity and a radical past as the Other in the history of the West. Although seemingly unable to be both things at once, the Mohawks of Kahnawà:ke strive to articulate these modalities as they live and move within a territorial space that is overlaid with settler regimes that regulate or circumscribe their way of life. Their struggle with the state is manifest in their ongoing debate and discussion around a membership law within their community. This registers as a conflict and a crisis, as something eventful rather than structural. My argument is that it is a sign, also, of colonialism's ongoing existence and simultaneous failure. Colonialism survives in a settler form. In this form, it fails at what it is supposed to do: eliminate Indigenous people; take all their land; absorb them into a white, property-owning body politic. Kahnawà:ke's debates over membership index colonialism's life as well its failure and their own life through their grip on this failure.

When I started this work formally in 1996, much of the political energy of Kahnawà:ke was focused on the "question of membership." The criteria for political membership and formal recognition within their community remained contentious, as did the need and desire to come up with a formal code to define political rights independent of the Canadian state. A reservation, or reserve, consisted of 6,154 (on the band list) and 9,531 (on the Federal Registry list, or "roll").[12] Membership was then and still is considered deeply fundamental; it affords someone "the rights that matter": to live on the reserve, to vote if you want in band council or tribal elections, and to be buried on the reservation. Yet their diminished land base, the imposition of the Indian Act—*colonization*—has made this an issue, a divisive, lacerating one, within the community. The terms of this fundamental question are underscored by existential ones: Who are we? Who shall we be for the future? Who belongs here, and why do they belong here? The discussion of "membership"—the formation of a code—was (and still is) something over which nearly every community member agrees to disagree. Conversations are weighted by previous and ongoing miscarriages of justice, lacunae, misrecognitions, and animosities, and the list goes on.

Here, summarized, recalled, taken from notes, overheard, engaged in, processed, flipped back to—different moments from research, different moments abstracted from my own life as a part of this community[13]—are fragments taken from careening and breakneck moments of conversation:

"I know someone who is listed as 48 percent and the sister is 100 percent—they have the same parents . . ."

"What the hell happened there? . . ."

"I have no idea . . ."

"How can you be 48 percent Indian?"

"I have no idea."

"Why are we not going through the women?"

"We should go through the women."

"How is she on this list when she is white?"

"They were taken off the list because they are white."

"Who the hell is that?!"

"I don't know him—he is not from here!"

"I never heard of that person!"

"That man is full of shit!"

"I don't know him"

"Who is your mother?"

"I saw your mother yesterday."

Direct, pointed, fast: "Who are you?" There is always an answer with genealogic authority—"I am to you, this way . . ."; "this is my family, this is my mother, this is my father"; "thus, I am known to you this way"—which is sorted in those breakneck, fast, summarizing, and deeply important reckoning moments between people. The subtext seems to be "I want to know who you are. Tell me who you are. I will know who you are if you or someone else tells me who you are." But is there a supratext? Why *wouldn't* people know every single person they encounter in a reserve community of six thousand or more members? Because this is a space with entries and exits; it is not hermetic. People come and go and come back again. There have been legal impositions, and historically outsiders have acquired legal rights to reside there. More innocuously, there are visitors, friends from outside, friends from other reserves. Kahnawa'kehró:non are not always immediately discernible because of this;[14] the webs of kinship have to be made material through dialogue and discourse. The authority for this dialogue rests in knowledge of another's family, whether the members are (entirely) from the community or not. "I know who you are." *Pointe finale.* We are done; we can proceed. If you require more explanation, or cannot explain yourself, or be explained (or claimed) by others, then there is a problem.

"Membership talk" conditions such people as problems—unknowable, illegitimate—and also determines the conditions of belonging, the legitimacy of legal personhood outside of official or state law. Here the axis is in memory, in conversation, in sociality; by talking to other people you understand who someone is, how she is connected, and thus she is socially and affectively legitimized with or without official recognition. This knowledge archive, however, is structured through prior languages and experiences of exclusion and inclusion that are tethered, sometimes with venom, to historical processes: from the movement of Mohawk people in the seventeenth century from what is now New York State into their northern hunting territory, what is now southwestern Quebec (Canada). This moved Mohawks territorially into the first Catholic mission in the

Northeast, into an emergent reservation (the oldest in the Northeast), and into new sites of permanence and ongoing mobility.[15] The Indian Act of 1876, the overarching "law" of Indians in Canada, legally "made" and "unmade" Indians and their rights in a Western, specifically Victorian, model of patrilineal descent (and rule) that attempted to order their winnowed territories. This foreign authority and government has competed with and continues to compete with the life of Iroquois "tradition"—the ongoing philosophical system and governmental structure that connects them through clan and ceremony to other Haudenosaunee peoples.

These seemingly antagonistic processes of "tradition," "modernity," and "settlement" are what made forming an agreed-upon membership code in Kahnawà:ke deeply challenging, not to mention vexed, and biting. They open "the problem" of membership to much larger historical and political processes and questions—such as the context for rights, their meanings on the ground—quite simply, how to be a nation, when much of one's territory has been taken. These processes also bring into question how to proceed as a nation if the right to determine the terms of legal belonging, a crucial component of sovereignty, has been dictated by a foreign government. The question emerges of how to do this—procedurally, ethically—if the certainty of its means are opaque or hidden and you are also viewed not as a people with a governmental system, a philosophical order, but as a remnant, a "culture," a minority within an ethnocultural mosaic of differences. This speaks of settler manageability in biopolitical states of care, or abandonment on land reserved for your "use and benefit," with regulations on how you use that land, who gets to use it, what the terms of that use are. This does not speak of sovereign political orders with authority over land and life. How can you proceed, then, under these conditions as if you are sovereign, as if you are a nation? Nationhood, one might think, hangs on the brink. But this story starts with a grounded refusal, not a precipice.

In this book I make three claims that are drawn from ethnographic research with the Mohawks of Kahnawà:ke. First, sovereignty may exist within sovereignty. One does not entirely negate the other, but they necessarily stand in terrific tension and pose serious jurisdictional and normative challenges to each other: Whose citizen are you? What authority do you answer to? One challenges the very legitimacy of the other. As Indigenous nations are enframed by settler states that call themselves nations and appear to have a monopoly on institutional and military power, this is a significant assertion. There is more than one *political* show in town. If a Haudenosaunee person is to travel internationally, for example, on a Confederacy passport, then the very boundaries and lawfulness of the original territorial referent is called into question. The entire United States may then be "international," which, some would argue, it was prior to contact and still is. Like Indigenous bodies, Indigenous sovereignties and Indigenous political orders prevail within and apart from settler governance. This form of "nested sovereignty" has implications for the sturdiness of nation-states over all, but especially for formulations of political membership as articulated and fought over within these nested sovereignties.

Second, there is a political alternative to "recognition," the much sought-after and presumed "good" of multicultural politics. This alternative is "refusal," and it is exercised by people within this book. They deploy it as a political and ethical stance that stands in stark contrast to the desire to have one's distinctiveness as a culture, as a people, recognized. Refusal comes with the requirement of having one's *political* sovereignty acknowledged and upheld, and raises the question of legitimacy for those who are usually in the position of recognizing: What is their authority to do so? Where does it come from? Who are they to do so? Those of us writing about these issues can also "refuse"; this is a distinct form of ethnographic refusal and is tied inextricably to my final claim.[16]

Third, the way that we come to know the politics and culture of "Indigenous" peoples requires an accounting that neither anthropology nor political science has done robustly.[17] One field of inquiry—anthropology—has dealt almost exclusively with Indigenous peoples in an ahistorical and depoliticized sense, innocent or dismissive of the strains of colonization and then settler colonialism on their politics, looking instead for pure culture and pure interlocutors of that culture.[18] Political science, government, and political theory are relatively new to questions of Indigenous politics and life and deal with them as a "case" that is wholly documentary or an ethical and practical test to the limits of Western norms of acknowledgment. Because of their Western, institutional, and statist focus, none of these disciplines have dealt evenhandedly, robustly, or *critically* with Indigenous politics and how they challenge what most perceive as settled. By "settled" I mean "done," "finished," "complete." This is the presumption that the colonial project has been realized: land has been dispossessed; its owners have been eliminated or absorbed. This clean-slate settlement is now considered a "nation of immigrants" (except the Indians). But this belief demonstrates a blindness to the structure of settler-colonial nation-statehood—of its labor, its pain, and its agonies—which get glossed and celebrated by the likes of US president Barack Obama as progressive acknowledgment of the exceptional status of Indigenous people.

These three claims force us to an argument about political form, positioning, and strategy. We see that rooted in the Iroquois case broadly—and Kahnawà:ke specifically—under the conditions of settler colonialism, multiple sovereignties cannot proliferate robustly or equally. The ongoing conditions of settler colonialism have forced Kahnawa'kehró:non to take an offensive position not just against the settler nation, but in some ways against themselves. This position then manifests in calculated refusals of the "gifts" of the state, and in vexed determinations of "membership" and belonging in that state. To understand this situation and perhaps move to a more productive place of refusal, we need to look at the history of this community within a larger matrix of relatedness (to territory, to other Iroquois peoples, to the politics that enframe them) and, in making these more robust forms of inquiry, change the ways we study and write about Indigenous politics.

In situations in which sovereignties are nested and embedded, one proliferates at the other's expense; the United States and Canada can only come into political being because of Indigenous dispossession. Under these conditions there cannot be two perfectly equal, robust sovereignties. Built into "sovereignty" is a jurisdictional dominion over territory, a notion of singular law, and singular authority (the king, the state, the band council, tribal council, and even the notion of the People). But this ongoing and structural project to acquire and maintain land, and to eliminate those on it, did not work completely. There are still Indians, some still know this, and some will defend what they have left. They will persist, robustly.

There has been and, we can infer, will continue to be push back on the settler logics of elimination. Those who still live this struggle with different political authorities find themselves in a "nested" form of sovereignty and in politics of refusal. Ethnography in such settings requires a historical and ethnologic accounting of why politics take this form. How is it that Indigenous people, and their politics, have come to be known in particular ways? These are politics that narrow to a point of irrational, unexplainable, seemingly illiberal expulsion and exclusion: "the problem of membership."

Signpost 1: Membership

On February 1, 2010, twenty-six non-Natives cohabitating with residents and members of Kahnawà:ke were issued eviction notices by the Mohawk Council of Kahnawà:ke (MCK), the council of elected officials that is authorized by the Indian Act, and thus Canada, to govern the community. They were told that they must leave the territory because as non-Indians residing in Kahnawà:ke without any form of recognition from the band council, they were living in contravention to the Kahnawà:ke Membership Law, enacted in 2003 and amended in 2007 and then in 2008.

Now, what kind of law would propose that couples be split up, that governance extend to love itself? What kind of law would seek to regulate the arrangement of families? All state law does this, but this particular one acknowledges the residue of the Indian Act, with its divisive, patrilineal bias, and attempts to correct it by making it unlawful for either a man or a woman to marry out, by being equally (some would say) discriminatory. The 2003 membership law was a gender-neutral, "heterosexed,"[19] discriminatory law that recognized only heterosexual marriages between status Indians, but offered "allowances" for the possibility of non-Native or unrecognized Indian individuals to marry "in" and reside legally on the reservation. The prior law only recognized heterosexual marriages between status Indians and those possessing Mohawk blood.

Here it is helpful to turn to Mark Rifkin's (2010) book on the literary and anthropological history of sexuality and colonization, which demonstrates the complicity of ethnology, kinship rules, and literature with actual, settler governance. Essayists, fiction writers, and anthropologists imagined and imaged properties of personhood in their arrangements and representations of Indigenous life into discernible grids of governance and what Denise Ferreira da Silva (2007) calls "affectability" in her theory of racial formation. Affectability is the condition that makes some vulnerable to and, by the structuring reach of capital, entwined with racial logics of exclusion that condition inclusion in a Western, white racial order. This process, in Ferreira da Silva's understanding, readies people for particular states of subjecting and being subjected to force and to law. The Kahnawà:ke Membership Law is that process, remade and reformed. It uses the governing impetus of settlement—"recognition"—to regulate, administer, and discipline the subject through a notion of band polity.

Consider here the first three paragraphs of the Preamble to the amended Kahnawà:ke Membership Law (2008):

We are the Kanien'kehá:ka of Kahnawà:ke. We are a community within the Kanien'kehá:ka Nation and the Rotinonhsonnión:we and as such are Indigenous Peoples who possess a fundamental and inherent right of self-determination given to us by the Creator.

As Indigenous Peoples, we have the right to maintain and promote our Kanien'kehá:ka identity including our culture, traditions, language, laws and customs.

As Indigenous Peoples, we have the collective right to determine our own membership. This right is fundamental to our survival.

We recognize that we have been harmed by foreign governments' attempts to undermine our will and ability to survive by dividing our community. We *reject* the imposition of the Indian Act and other foreign laws that have presumed to define the principles upon which the membership of our community will be determined. We *reject* all efforts to assimilate and extinguish our community under the guise of absolute individualism.

By enacting this Law we are fulfilling our responsibility to defend our community and our Nation from external threat, and in doing so are securing for future generations the right to survive and to continue living—proudly—as Kanien'kehá:ka of Kahnawà:ke.[20]

With this passage from the law we can see that this technique of governance is articulating a fear of disappearance through the very means that would disappear this nation: Canadian-authorized governance. This is expressed in the values of individual rights over "collective" rights—the ahistorical and presumed evenhandedness of liberalism to determine and render justice, in part, through presumed shared values of freedom, justice, equality, individualism, even distribution, and free trade. Yet these are the same values that Kahnawà:ke find intrusive and forcible. What is it from their political ethos and history that would make for such a paradoxical position?

Who are these people? Consider this in a descriptive register: "This is a reserve community of Indigenous nationals that belong to a larger pre-contact political Confederacy in what is now understood to be the Northeastern United States and Southeastern Canada." They are known to themselves as Haudenosaunee, or "people of the Longhouse," in reference to their traditional living arrangement of clan-based houses and their governing structure. This political confederacy is what is known in anthropological and everyday understanding as the "Iroquois Confederacy." As a polity, the Mohawks of Kahnawà:ke are comprised of Turtle, Wolf, and Bear clans,[21] determined through matrilineal descent lines. They also then have a membership within a political corpus of the larger Longhouse, which spreads metaphorically across Iroquoia. This is a different descriptive window into the community at hand from that offered earlier, and one more in tune with the sensibilities of anthropologists of an earlier time.

Yet, the content of both descriptive accounts is what they, in part, will not let go of, or forget, or cease to enact: their relatedness to their place, to others, to a particular history, to their ongoing experiences because of this relatedness. These kin and reciprocal relationships extend throughout the fifteen other Iroquois reservations on either side of the border as well as the cities, suburbs, and nonreserve rural areas that Iroquois people move through and dwell within. Because of these spatial arrangements and spatial connections throughout Iroquoia, per settler colonialism's past and present requirements, there are many severed connections that owe their severance to the Indian Act and its required geographic and gendered displacements. Joseph Mitchell's "footloose" Indians have a deeper context than he will allow, or knew of.

As we saw above, membership talk is articulated through an archive of knowledge, identification, and beliefs about what is right, what *should* be done; its design and its execution both portend much for the present and for the future. "Who should be here? How should we do this?" "Is this fair?" are questions that instill an ongoing preoccupation, a set of normative questions that find no easy juridical answers. And yet, membership is simultaneously so simply explained as "this is how I am, to you." This very simple, stop-the-clock mode of identification and claiming of others reaches even beyond recognition into a deeper archive of knowledge, drawing from sociality and genealogical and narrative relatedness. This archive of social and genealogic knowledge operates as an authorizing nexus of identification that also can and sometimes does refuse logics of the state. This is because formal recognition sometimes belongs to those *not* genealogically recognized: those who are non-Indian, married in, and obtained status (white women who married Indian men and now have Indian status) and those who have status and have never been to Kahnawà:ke (these people are few and far between). The truly foreign, those who are somehow outside of the space of social and genealogic reckoning—the indecipherable—may be refused in spite of their formal recognition by the state.

Along with the ideas of "Indigenous" and "nationhood," I use the Hegelian term "recognition" and its inverse, "misrecognition," to tell this story. No matter how deeply Kahnawa'kehró:non and other Indigenous nations understand themselves to be of their own philosophical systems and, simultaneously, no matter how deeply they understand the scene of their objectification as "Indians" or, even more ghastly, as "minoritized peoples," they are rarely seen or then treated in the eye of the settler as that which they are and wish to be recognized as: nationals with sovereign authority over their lives and over their membership and living within their own space, which has been "held for them" in the form of reservations.

Although homelands of a sort, reservations owe their lives to state power; thus, the grounded fields of belonging, recognition, misrecognition, and refusal that I am mapping out are tied up with state power and its primary technique of distributing rights and protections: citizenship (Beiner 1995). As well as producing affectively structured citizens (Berlant 1997), the state produces the conditions for what I want to suggest are "distantiations," "disaffiliations," or outright refusals—a willful distancing from state-driven forms of recognition and sociability in favor of others. The genealogy for this is deep, but I will give a very cursory overview and condition this for settler-colonial settings. In the case of settler societies, there is an old Aristotelian problem of how to govern alterity, how to order it, how to make sense of that which is not yours—a question that is not normative but rather tactical, and it reemerges, violently. The ideal of transcendent principles, still divine and sometimes democratically inflected, animate the governance of these territories. Yet the problem of governance itself remains. This is because the category and construct (and institutional apparatus) of the nation-state and its presumed homogeneity endure in spite of their fundamental inability to be resolved with the complexity and force that animate the territorial histories and horizons of settler-colonial nation-states. Indigenous dispossession caused by settler emplacement exacerbates the problem of rule, of governance, and of legitimacy itself. In this, people got and still get moved about and they survive eliminations, but the state projects of political homogeneity and the ideal correspondence of "ethnicity" and territorial boundaries remain irresolvable. The modern order itself is entwined with capital as this accumulative and acquisitive force further detaches people from places and moves them into other zones for productivity, accumulation, and territorial settlement.

This relationship is understood in part from literatures that have looked within presumably "postcolonial" or postrevolutionary/independent political orders to understand how nations come into being and how states emerge to manage that story of their beginnings and administer those populations. Thus, we have the importance in the literature on the iconic power of "nation" for governance. Within the literature on nationalism in anthropology, the state creates the image; this is Benedict Anderson's "re-presentation" of the nation (1991). The mediated, printed sense of relatedness to others (those who one does not know intimately, personally) was achieved in Anderson's account across vast territories because of communicable writing, because of newspaper. One would imagine now, in extending Anderson's argument, that that relatedness may be further instantiated and redefined through the Internet, telecommunications, and the immense popularity of social networking sites on the web. This representational and communicative process of "we"-ness, of relatedness, was accelerated in the earlier literature by rituals of the state—national parades, coronations, museums, exhibits, and, most importantly in Anderson's analysis, print media—all of which communicate in some way the essence of the nation, and who one's relations were, sort of. In this literature that proliferated around Anderson, it was more than simply suggesting, through iconic imagery, who its people are; the state also had a crucial role in the classification and definition of those people through its monopoly over territorial boundaries. In this way, the state provided the inspiration for nationalism, as it possesses a monopoly on institutions of control and influence that may not cohere with those within these territories. If nationalism is generated under conditions of this disconnect between state institutions and histories of force, then what does consent do? Or how does consent matter?

The issue of consent drives to the centrality of the state in the location of settler-colonial power and bureaucratic largesse. Part of the energy of nationalism issues from the question of state authority and its legitimacy (Jusdanis 2001). Thus the literature on nationalism has difficulty *viewing* Indigeneity as possibly nationalist, and something able to be theorized.[22]

Rather, Indigeneity is imagined as something entrapped within the analytics of "minoritization," a statistical model for the apprehension of (now) racialized populations "within" nation-states (Simpson 2011, 211). This is owing in part to the manner in which nationalism has been theorized, as something occurring within reified states in this formulation (and the formulations of Robert Foster, etc.), a reified state that is unresponsive and ahistorical.[23] Nationalism expresses a particular form of collective identity that embeds desire for sovereignty and justice. However, it does so only because of the deep impossibility of representation and consent within governance systems that are predicated upon dispossession and disavowal of the political histories that govern the populations now found within state regimes. When we add further nuance to this discussion within settler colonialist regimes, we have the problem of prior occupancy and ownership—Iroquois people with their own "constitution," for example.

The primary way in which the state's power is made real and personal, affective in its capacity, is through the granting of citizenship and, in this, the structural and legal preconditions for intimacy, forms of sociability, belongings, and affections (Berlant 1997). The bureaucratized state is one frame in which visibility is produced, creating the conditions under which difference becomes apparent; political aspirations are articulated; and culture, authenticity, and tradition (Verdery 1993, 42) become politically expedient resources. The state, in framing what is official, creates the conditions of affiliation or distance. These disaffiliations arise from the state's project of *homogenizing heterogeneity,* "the construction of homogeneity out of the realities of heterogeneity that characterise all nation building" (R. Foster 1991, 249; B. Williams 1989, 429), which they have failed to do in the case of Kahnawà:ke Mohawks. It is this process of homogenizing that Kahnawà:ke's own statelike apparatus of tribal governance (band council) also undertakes and that the community struggles with and against.

Signpost 2: Detention and Recognition

On April 28, 2010, three Mohawks of Kahnawà:ke were detained in El Salvador for seventeen days. They were flying back from the International Climate Change Conference in Bolivia and were traveling on Haudenosaunee passports. They refused to allow Canada to issue them "emergency travel documents" (which amounts to a passport).[24] They waited instead for ten more days, and they were permitted reentry into Canada via Iroquois Confederacy passports.

This detention is not an anomaly. Like the evictions described under the first signpost, this event is part of something larger, a set of assertions by Haudenosaunee peoples through time. They make these assertions based upon the validity and vitality of their own philosophical and governmental systems, systems that *predate* the advent of the settler state. Their arguments and actions regarding these systems, and the systems themselves, move discursively and materially into the face of the settler logic of dispossession and occupation. It is this same logic that informs Kahnawà:ke's reservation-based preoccupations and assertions regarding membership. Membership, passports, and evictions are of a piece with each other, as they all speak of a fear of disappearance but also from a form of sovereign authority: "I know you; I know who I am." "This is what I speak from, this treaty, this genealogic, this archive." "I refuse until you get it, or until I think you got it." Or, even, "I simply refuse."

In order to best give "refusal" as a political strategy its treads, it is helpful to turn directly to "colonialism" and to the work of Patrick Wolfe to contextualize the force that Kahnawa'kehró:non are up against. He argues that *settler* colonialism is defined by a territorial project—the accumulation of land—whose seemingly singular focus differentiates it from other forms of colonialism. Although the settler variety is acquisitive, unlike other colonialisms, it is not labor but territory that it seeks. Because "Indigenous" peoples are tied to the desired territories, they must be "eliminated"; in the settler-colonial model, "the settler never leaves" (1999, 2006). Their need for a permanent place to settle propels the process that Wolfe calls, starkly, "elimination."[25]

The desire for land produces "the problem" of the Indigenous life that is already living on that land. How, then, to manage that "Indian Problem," as it is known in American and Canadian administrative speak? Like the "Jewish Problem" posed by Jewish life and alterity, and now the "Palestinian Problem" posed by "overlapping claims" to territory, the "Indian Problem" is one of the existence of continued life (of any form) in the face of an acquisitional and territorial desire that then moves through time to become, in liberal parlance, the "problem" of difference. In the case of Indigeneity in North America, this became a question of what to do with their souls, their bodies, their culture, and their difference. Now the answer appears to be for settler states to apologize or to recognize Indigenous peoples and the historical wrong that they experienced.

Recognition is the gentler form, perhaps, or the least corporeally violent way of managing Indians and their difference, a multicultural solution to the settlers' Indian problem. The desires and attendant practices of settlers get rerouted, or displaced, in liberal argumentation through the trick of toleration, of "recognition," the performance postconquest of "seeing people as they ought to be seen," as they see themselves—an impossible and also tricky beneficence that actually may extend forms of settlement through the language and practices of, at times, nearly impossible but seemingly democratic inclusion (Wolfe 2011, 32). This inclusion, or juridical form of recognition, is only performed, however, *if* the problem of cultural difference and alterity does not pose too appalling a challenge to norms of the settler society, norms that are revealed largely through law in the form of decisions over the sturdiness, vitality, and purity of the cultural alterity before it (Povinelli 2002, Markell 2003, Coulthard 2007). This fixation on cultural difference and its purity occludes Indigenous sovereignty. Looking for "culture" instead of sovereignty (and defining culture in particularly exclusionist, nineteenth-century ways) is a tricky move, as sovereignty has not in fact been eliminated. It resides in the consciousness of Indigenous peoples, in the treaties and agreements they entered into between themselves and others and is tied to practices that do not solely mean making baskets as your ancestors did a hundred years ago, or hunting with the precise instruments your great grandfather did 150 years ago, in the exact same spot he did as well, when witnessed and textualized by a white person. This book will demonstrate how sovereignty and nationhood are expressed differently from these essentialized modes of expectation by the settler state and its law, and how this difference pushes up against these other extremely narrow forms of judicial interpretation.

If regimes of recognition narrow to the juridical, then why do they persist? In part because they are seen as invariably virtuous. Although political recognition is a technique of settler governance, it appears as a transcendent and universal human desire that becomes a political antidote to historical wrongdoing. Thus, it would seem to salve the wounds of settler colonialism. Charles Taylor offers a foundational and empirically driven moral formulation[26] and defense of recognition for those whose difference is of such culturally determined form that they cannot help *but* be different, and so must be recognized as having traditions that should be more than just "tolerated" (1994). The question of whether they should tolerate being tolerated, or tolerated in such a manner, does not arise for Taylor or others on his tail. However, "recognition" is a moral imperative, and, as Taylor argues, to be without it would cause harm—itself intolerable. In this context, then, people are not only deserving of recognition (a "courtesy"), but it is, he argues, a "vital human need" (26).

Kahnawà:ke Mohawks are caught up in the history of wrongdoing and disavowal from which Taylor's concerns speak. This is a historical attitude that supplants the ravages of settler colonialism with definitions of "difference." Tolerance, recognition, and the specific technique that is multicultural policy are but an elaboration of an older sequence of attitudes toward "the problem" of difference on acquired, some might argue *seized*, territories. Here I am talking about a latter-day move to techniques that are used to manage "the problem" of Indigenous people, rendered now as populations, to be administered to by the state. This moves Indigenous peoples and their polities in the settler imaginary from nations, to people, to populations—categories that have shifted through time and in relation to land and its dispossession. Most important for this discussion, these categorical shifts set Indigenous peoples up for governmental regulation (Morgensen 2011, 62).[27] These techniques—occupying, treating, forceful elimination, containment, assimilation, the coterminous logics and practices and languages of race and civilization, the practice of immigration (called such in the United States and Canada, rather than "settlement"), the legal notion of natal right, and presumptions of just occupancy—all form the fulcrum of settlement's labor (and its imaginary) as well as a whole host of other self-authorizing techniques and frameworks that *sustain* dispossession and occupation.[28]

It is in this imagined space of just settlement, of settler nationhood (and statehood), that the Iroquois assert the benchmarks of *Western* territorially based sovereignty discussed above: regulations over membership and jurisdictional authority over rights to residency; the issuing of Iroquois Confederacy passports; the insistence upon their validity according to prior agreements, prior recognitions; an insistence upon recognition and honorable relations *now* between nations. In these examples we see a prior recognition born from the political status of nationhood and an ongoing and unvanquished sovereignty. To assert this is to fundamentally interrupt the sovereignty and the monocultural aspirations of nation-states, but especially those that are rooted in Indigenous dispossession. It is in the assertion of these rights (which are being diminished and narrowly interpreted, if not completely abrogated, in the courts)[29] that Iroquois peoples *remind* nation-states such as the United States (and Canada) that they possess this very history, and within that history and seized space, they possess a *precarious* assumption that their boundaries are permanent, uncontestable, and entrenched. They possess a precarious assumption about their own (just) origins. And by extension, they possess a precarious assumption about themselves.

The settler precariousness that I speak of structures the story that I am telling in this book, of Mohawk life, the labor of principle and sovereignty, labor that begins with refusal. That refusal is simply to disappear, a refusal to be on the other end of Patrick Wolfe's critical, comparative history—to be "eliminated." In refusing to go away, to cease to be, in asserting something beyond difference, lies the position that requires one to "coexist" with others, with settlers, with "arrivants," in the parlance of Jodi Byrd (2011)[30]—meaning the formerly enslaved or the indentured who did not voluntarily come to North America—and to live tacitly and taciturnly in a "settled state." In this there is acceptance of the dispossession of your lands, of internalizing and believing the things that have been taught about you to you: that you are a savage, that your language is incoherent, that you are less than white people, not quite up to par, that you are then "different," with a different culture that is defined by others and will be accorded a protected space of legal recognition *if* your group evidences that "difference" in terms that are sufficient to the settlers' legal eye. To accept these conditions is an impossible project for some Indigenous people, not because it is impossible to achieve, but because it is politically untenable and thus normatively should be refused.

Contorting oneself in a fundamental space of misrecognition is not just about subject formation; it is about historical formation. And by refusing to agree to these terms and to be eliminated Mohawks are asserting *actual* histories and thus legislating interpretive possibilities in contestation—interpretations of treaty, possibilities of movement, electoral practices—not only individual *selves.* These are contesting systems of legitimacy and acknowledgment. The events of refusal we have seen in this introduction *enunciate,* in Pierre Bourdieu's sense, several processes. Most evident among these processes and accounts is their ability to signal Indigeneity and couple it with sovereignty. These stories of evictions, of Confederacy-issued passports, demonstrate Indigeneities comingling with sovereignty and their seemingly anomalous but insistent relation.

What does it mean to be unrecognized? What does it mean to not know what this means? These are fundamentally political questions, and thus require that I ask what it means to be recognized. Political recognition is, in its simplest terms, to be seen by another *as one wants to be seen*. Yet this regard is not merely for the sanctity of the self; it is to appear politically in formal and official forms, to have rights that protect you from harm, that provide you access to resources, or that protect certain resources. Patchen Markell describes this succinctly as, in its base form, "who we take ourselves and others to be" (2003, 1). One might specify this as "to have rights, to have an effectual capacity within a regime of power," as one should. This then means to have the recognition of the state and to have a passport that allows you as a formal member of the community to move, to travel, to receive, and exercise protections from harm. To be misrecognized, Markell also helpfully states in his discussion of the literature, is cast as a miscarriage of justice, a "failure whether out of malice or ignorance, to extend people the respect or esteem that is due to them in virtue of who they are" (2003, 2). To then be unrecognized would mean literally to be free from recognition and thus operate as a free-floating signifier, with politically unformed or unprotected identities—most important, as identities that are vulnerable to harm.[31] Here I want to argue that it is impossible to be free from an authorizing context, which means one is a slave, in some readings of Friedrich Hegel, and remains so until recognized in a system of mutuality ("I see you; you see me; this is reciprocal; this reciprocity signals justice"). We might, however, want to test this reading further through empiricism. Indigeneity and its imbrication with settler colonialism question the conditions of seeing (perhaps of writing) that are laid out in the master-bondsman allegory; this allows us to consider another vantage point in another perceptual and argumentative theater or space of recognition. Settler colonialism structures justice and injustice in particular ways, not through the conferral of recognition of the enslaved but by the conferral of disappearance in subject. This is *not seeing* that is so profound that mutuality cannot be achieved. "Recognition" in either a cognitive or juridical sense is impossible. It simply would require too much contortion from one protagonist and not the other to be considered just.

In order to further our understanding of the Iroquois case, I want to move the discussion to the theater of apprehension—the way in which we see and understand this scene of "recognition"/"nonrecognition"—into the materiality of current settler nation-states. This is a theater that is more than a neutral and performative dramaturgy; it is in fact a settler-colonial nation-state with particular optics, expectations, and possibilities for interpretation. Hegel's is a concern with the *position* of the slave, not the slave himself; that subjectivity is taken up by others. Frantz Fanon most forcefully argues in *Black Skin: White Masks* (1967) that the slave is the black man, and in this subjectifying allegory the black man comprehends the scene as one of objectification, and in this, the feeling of subjugation and the deep knowledge of its context. The black man sees an economy that is predicated upon the extraction of labor from specified bodies in order to annex territories and fuel the accumulation of surplus.[32] Recognition, in this reading of Hegel, is the basis for self-consciousness, and here taken to be a political self-consciousness that will translate into a revolutionary argument, a movement to unshackle oneself from this formula for self-perception. Glen Coulthard (2007) takes from Fanon's reading of Hegel the impetus to "turn away" from the oppressor, to avert one's gaze and refuse the recognition itself.[33] This moment of turning away can turn us toward Haudenosaunee assertions, which in different ways tell a story about a territory of willingness, a willingness to "stay enslaved." We could see this as a political strategy that is cognizant of an unequal relationship, understands the terms of bondage, and chooses to stay within them in order to assert a greater principle: nationhood, sovereignty, jurisdiction by those who are deemed to *lack* that power, a power that is rooted in historical precedent but is conveniently forgotten or legislated away.[34] Perhaps here we see a willingness to assert a greater principle and, in the assertion of this principle, to assert and be free whether this is apprehended as such or not. So in the Haudenosaunee political context it can mean recognition by another authoritative nexus (one's own?) and thereby call the other's into question. This negates the authority of the other's gaze.

Signpost 3: Refusing to Play the Game

On July 17, 2010, the Iroquois Nationals Lacrosse Team (INLT) "bowed out" of the World Lacrosse League Championship tournament in Manchester, England.[35] They did so because the United Kingdom refused to recognize the Haudenosaunee passport as secure and therefore legitimate. Their passports were signed and issued by the chiefs of the Iroquois Confederacy, a governance structure that predates the United States and the United Kingdom by at least three hundred years. The INLT had used this type of passport to travel to international competitions for the past thirty years. Numerous newspapers also reported that the Iroquois were the "creators of the very sport" they were to compete in.[36]

We could read this as a refusal to play the game of being American or Canadian, which for the lacrosse players would mean forgetting or abandoning the deep history, philosophy, and authority of Iroquois governance. This discourse of being and of *staying* Mohawk is articulated to notions of an Iroquois past, but also to the desire to stay distinct from nation-states, or states that are like nations (Canada, Quebec,[37] and, at times, the United States). These are states that are relatively new, that follow from distinctively colonial encounters, and are undertaking their own processes of self-fashioning. Patricia Seed argues in her book on the processes of colonization of the New World that this earlier acquisitional effort reads like a "pentimento," a watery imprint of earlier colonizing projects that surfaces on the texts that we inherit today (2001, 1–11). As such, for a particular colonial state, one possessing such spectacular power of self-definition and moral turpitude that it can define itself as a revolutionary (postcolonial) and simultaneously immigrant state—one that is innocent of the violence and dispossession that got it to its apparent point of newness—there is a need for an aggressive regulatory fixation on demarcating, through time, the boundaries and the content of the "we" of community. The move to administrative power and will is great, as these populations are to be tended to and also harmonized into a form of constructed, rights-bearing kin through citizenship.

In settler societies such as the United States and Canada, citizenship is key to this process of rationalizing dispossession and the rapid ascent of power for migrants; so, citizenship is also key to Kahnawà:ke's enunciation of self under conditions in which they would have to disappear. This issue of disappearance—and more particularly, *not* disappearing—has presented Kahnawa'kehró:non with a central problem: how to imagine themselves outside of the interstices of Empire while operating within it. They have to, because Empire is both everywhere and nowhere, ahistorical and endlessly performing a fast past; it is a place with a state, with imperatives, and with administrative power on top of Kahnawà:ke land. A turn to one of their own thinkers, the late Louis Karoniaktajeh Hall,[38] on just this question may help us to understand how Kahnawa'kehró:non approach questions of governance and the state. His is an approach and a position that many other Kahnawa'kehró:non take, and it informs the more militant stances on land expropriation that we will read about in this book. This position speaks from the particular interpretation of "tradition" within Kahnawà:ke as differentiated from other Confederacy reservations, which has made for a less conciliatory form of politics in dealing with settler occupation—an act of turning away, less willingness to "play the game."

> For the white race the nation is a recent concept. When the red and white races met, all the countries in Europe were kingdoms. In a kingdom, only the monarch has sovereignty. Everything and everyone belonged to the king. A true nation is where the authority flows upward from the people to the installed leaders, as in the case of the Six Nations "Iroquois" Confederacy, also known as the LongHouse [*sic*], world's first people's republic and the first to make a national constitution, a State far head [*sic*] of any then known. (Hall n.d.: 33)

For Hall, political authority vested in the people, in their past, and the past's aggressive articulation with the present.[39] Louis Hall's two influential pamphlets, *Rebuilding the Iroquois Confederacy* (n.d.) and the *Warrior's Handbook* (1979), evidence a critical, very non-Seneca (the ethnological core of Iroquois culture studies in anthropology), and decidedly anti–Handsome Lake (the dominant form of tradition in the literature) position for Iroquois people. His work deserves consideration for its critique of monarchical forms of sovereignty, for its position against the history of the Iroquois written by both outsiders and Iroquois themselves, and for the influence it wielded in communities such as Kahnawà:ke, Kanehsatà:ke, Ahkwesáhsne, and Tuscarora in reinterpreting and revitalizing more militant elements of traditional Iroquois politics and culture. Within the discursive tradition of writing on the Iroquois, which I detail in chapter 3,

Hall's thinking and writing is also important for its centering of the Kanien'kehá:ka, or Mohawk, as a clear cultural and political articulation of critique vis-à-vis monarchical and even traditional forms of power, for its remarkable hagiography of Handsome Lake, and for its historiography of the Confederacy itself. Hall engages with the notion of nationhood as both a traditional and contemporary form of political organization that is especially attractive to the Kanien'kehá:ka. Nationhood is a construct, in the *Warrior's Handbook*, that is a cultural and political "right" and a "good," and a matter of principle rather than procedure. This principled approach to tradition and culture is manifest most succinctly in his "Mohawk Ten Commandments." Quoted directly from the text:

1. BE BRAVE AND FEARLESS, as there can be no peace on earth for those who are in fear.

2. BE STRONG. In this hard cruel world, only the strong may know peace and happiness. To be weak is to invite aggression, oppression, tyranny, misery, and woe.

3. FIGHT FOR YOUR RIGHTS, for only those who fight for it can achieve human rights and respect. There is a right and wrong way to fight. Always propose to fight in a clever way, for he who fights in a clever way is equal to a thousand men.

4. MAINTAIN A STRONG NATIONAL INDEPENDENCE AND SOVEREIGNTY UNDER THE GREAT LAW OF PEACE—GAYANEREKOWA and let your slogan be PEACE, RIGHTEOUSNESS, AND POWER, for not one of these is possible without the other two. Let no power abolish your nation.

5. MAINTAIN YOUR OWN NATIONAL INITIATIVE and let no other nation control your destiny. Respect Nature's first law of SELF-PRESERVATION AND STOP TRAITOR [sic] SEEKING TO DESTROY YOU AND YOUR PEOPLE, for any nation which ignores this law stands condemned to extinction.

6. DEVELOP THE SPIRIT OF COOPERATION so that your nation can rely completely on its own efforts. To become a competitive state is to create tensions, strife, panic, frenzy, fear, hate, bigotry, weakness, and divisions.

7. THINK RIGHT SO THAT YOU SHALL DO RIGHT AND BE RIGHT, for only the purely justice minded can achieve peace and happiness for all.

8. RESPECT THE RIGHTS OF OTHERS so that your own rights may be respected, and these rights include the right to live and be free; the right to a nationality, territory, government, possessions, and freedom of speech, to

think and believe as one sees fit, to human rights and to the pursuit of peace and happiness.

9. ACQUIRE WISDOM AND KNOWLEDGE OF THE WORLD, FOR ONLY THROUGH UNDERSTANDING AMONG ALL PEOPLE WILL MISUNDER-STANDING AND WAR BE ELIMINATED. Let there be a special course of study on the subject of devising a proper moral government and let proper people be trained to operate this very important device to ensure the peace and happiness of mankind; and let a study be included to produce a most worthy economic system to eliminate poverty, misery, and wretchedness. Let only those who pass a most rigid test on the subjects of government and economic knowledge be allowed to run governments and nations.

10. ACQUIRE ADVANCED HUMAN RELATIONSHIP. Human birth is an act of Nature, and all humanity is equally subject to Nature's law of death. No one has the right of lordship over others. The more able only have the right to help those less able; the appointed leaders of governments only have the right to be the voice and will of the people that all may share in the bounties of Nature and know peace and happiness. (Hall 1979: 3–4)

Identifying Gayanerekowa[40] as the correct from of governance, Hall invokes traditional governance and philosophy as the just way of living, but then suggests an unusual dynamism and elasticity in that form when he calls for the development of a moral government as a *course of study* and uses the language of achievement ("let only those that pass a most rigid test on the subjects of government . . . be allowed to run governments and nations" for leadership). Perhaps most critically, in stating "No one has the right of lordship over others," he throws a direct jab at the hereditary chiefs of the Iroquois Confederacy and the hereditary process itself.

In Louis Hall's work, the Gayanerekowa is treated as a just and desirable model for governance, but one that may be revised and transformed according to its own democratic principles, rather than procedure. In the writing on the Iroquois (see especially Morgan, Beauchamp, and Shimony), the procedure becomes the principle; and in Kahnawà:ke, or rather, in Louis Hall's formulations, the principle *shall become* the procedure. Note the language of "shall" and "become": these formulations are both normative and future oriented and are premised upon the belief that the past shall be made dynamic by the demands of the present and the hopes of the future.

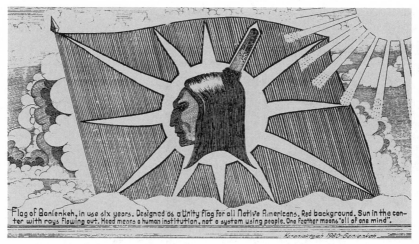

Flag of Ganienkeh, in use six years. Designed as a Unity Flag for all Native Americans. Red background. Sun in the center with rays flowing out. Head means a human institution, not a system using people. One feather means "all of one mind".

Karonaktyoh 1980-Ganienkeh

Fig 1.1 Warrior Flag with explanatory note by Louis Hall. Image courtesy of the 207 Longhouse.

Louis Hall is a critical voice in a Mohawk nation-building project, but for reasons that will become clear in chapter 3, it is marginal in the larger picture of Iroquois tradition and certainly in the textual project that is understood as "Iroquois studies," where his writing and artwork receive no attention whatsoever.[41] His work graces the cover of the now out-of-print ethnography *Sovereignty and Symbol* (Landsman 1988), but his teachings and writings have yet to receive scholarly attention.

I do not wish to suggest that I will be able to treat his work with the manuscript-length attention it deserves. I do want to discuss his writing as important for the effect it had on Kahnawa'kehró:non; it has a critical stance on matters that are both Iroquoian and very specific to Kahnawà:ke and yet has serious implications for the ways in which Indigeneity is written and thought about. Despite that his writings are outside of the authoritative domain of the Mohawk Council of Kahnawà:ke, and outside of the larger Confederacy Councils (at Six Nations and Onondaga), they are also absolutely caught up with questions of governance.

Hall is remarkable for thinking beyond the boundaries of the community. His interpretations present antipietistic critiques of the "new religion" of Handsome Lake—the religion and normative order that has governed Iroquois tradition in almost every community except Kahnawà:ke, Ahkwesáhsne, Kanehsatà:ke, and Tuscarora. Hall's critique and the position it

Fig 1.2 Warrior society defined by Louis Hall. Image courtesy of the 207 Longhouse.

articulates differentiate Kahnawà:ke traditionalism, or one iteration of it. Outsiders would associate his work and thinking with the "207 Longhouse" and the militant Warrior society by outsiders, although his work circulated more broadly than that (Horn-Miller 2003; see also Alfred 2005) and his critique of the proceduralism of the Confederacy may place him in a space perhaps of *excess* in the vein of Jacques Derrida, though it is an excess that refuses to sit still or stay put even in its state of difference between what it gestures for, what it hopes to signify: tradition. In this respect, Hall is speaking out of turn and he has no idea that he is outrageous. He *sounds* like a statesman, or maybe a pope, or maybe a democrat, and this is most important: he appears not to care that his ideas may be both marginal to the dominant ways of conceptualizing Iroquois tradition, history, or governance and yet be "familiar" to a Western, democratically tuned ear. He exceeds that with which he gestures. And he misses at times; but productively, I think. This excess lies, then, in a sign of nation. In this, he gestures before settler and state power itself, calling up traditional orthodoxy in Iroquoia, while installing himself to recruit for his mission of enlightened militancy, reformed living, and critical, democratically inflected *tradition.*

He is something like a metonym for Kahnawà:ke itself, the first reservation north of the United States–Mexico border, a reservation that predates Indian removals in the states, the "official" Indian wars, the Métis rebellion, and almost every formalized engagement with settlers that is deemed significant in Indigenous histories north of Mexico.[42] Founded in 1620 by Mohawks who moved out of the Mohawk Valley in what is now New York State, the families moved to the northernmost parts of their hunting territory and then three times up the St. Lawrence River until the first Longhouses were built in 1680, in what is now Kahnawà:ke. Like Louis Hall, Kahnawà:ke is deeply of and distanced from what is considered center. The largest concentration of speakers are there (10 percent of the community speak Mohawk, the highest concentration of Mohawk language speakers (and possibly any Iroquoian language in any Iroquois community), and yet Kahnawà:ke is considered "away from" the center of things—Tonawanda, Onondaga (where the central fire of the Confederacy was before the American Revolution), and the multinational Six Nations (population 23,294),[43] situated next to the white town of Brantford, Ontario. Kahnawà:ke is like the fringe on a boot of the Confederacy, a paradoxical version of the ideal type found in the literature and in traditional rhetoric. It is imperfect in ethnological terms, but definitely traditional; peace loving, but definitely ready to use force (consistently in defense of rights and of territory); deeply "matriarchal," but juridically disenfranchising of women.[44] The categories that are used to understand them, and to govern them, come apart when we try to "place" the community perfectly within a sociological grid of Iroquois or Indigenous ethnological categories. This is because of their assertiveness, their refusal to stay in an ethnological grid of apprehension and governance (Rifkin 2010), their aspirations to something else. This defiance of categorization causes them to stretch beyond and perhaps destroy what is a pre-given anthropological matrix, simply: "Iroquoian language group."

As a community of clans that formed a precontact nation, one that was recognized by other Confederacy nations,[45] and then by the political regimes of the Dutch, the English, and the French—and in their earliest stages, the United States and Canada—Kahnawà:ke has a serious investment in and memory of the history of political recognition in the Northeast. The people of Kahnawà:ke carry this history with them through their use and rendering of Iroquois governance and treaty. The Kaianere'kó:wa, "the Great Law of Peace" is brought to life through invocation; the normative limits to their relationships to outside communities imagined through references to the Kaswentha, "the Two Row Wampum"; and their passage into other nations and states rendered possible by the Jay Treaty of 1794, signed between Britain and the United States. In emphasizing these historical, mnemonic, and legal rights in the present day, they carry the historical and *intended* meanings of these forms of recognition with them in their day-to-day lives. For example:

> The parties to the Silver Covenant Chain agreed to come together regularly to polish the chain so as to restore their original friendship. They also promised to pass the treaty down from generation to generation so that its intent would never be forgotten. The Mohawks of Kahnawà:ke have carried the idea of the Two Row and the Covenant Chain through history and use it to guide them in their contemporary relationships. Most Canadians however, are unaware of the nature, intent and purpose of the peaceful and co-operative relationship that was originally formed and agreed to by their predecessors.
>
> The Mohawks of Kahnawà:ke honor the legacy left by their ancestors and will continue to advocate renewing the historic relationship with Canada based on the respect and recognition of the principles embodied within the Two Row Wampum.[46]

The diplomatic history that the people of Kahnawà:ke share with other Iroquois nations and the residue of these encounters are material that rendered them recognizable and important in moments of encounter with other Iroquois nations, with settler peoples, with other Indian communities and nations, and then with the political regimes of the United States and Canada. This historical consciousness is, as the above quote attests, very alive in the present and forms much of, for example, Louis Hall's discourse. However, the historical recognition that the Iroquois enjoyed in the past now shifts through the legal, disciplining registers of political discourse and categorization within colonial regimes. In this respect, the people of Kahnawà:ke are status Indians and thus "wards of the state," or what some may view as partial citizens, or "citizens plus."[47] They have the legal status only, it seems, of protected peoples, but it is this status that they use to protect and entrench their semiotic and material resources in light of state encroachment and then refuse forms of recognition if they so choose. It is at this point that this book begins.

Cartography of Refusal

Mohawk Interruptus, then, is a cartography of refusal, one that takes shape in the invocation of the prior experience of sovereignty and nationhood, and their labor in the present. In this first chapter we have seen the constraints to the phenomenon at hand, of people thinking and acting as nationals in a scene of dispossession. The book now moves through the empirical case of Kahnawa'kehró:non, or Kahnawà:ke (the place, but more the people of that place, wherever they may be), to demonstrate the fundamentally interrupted *and* interruptive capacity of that life within settler society. Their political consciousness and actions upend the perception that colonization, elimination, and settlement are situations of the past. Kahnawa'kehró:non are not settled; they are not done; they are not gone. They have not let go of themselves or their traditions, and they subvert this requirement at every turn with their actions. Their struggles with and against a membership policy, their own regime of recognition, is a symptom of the continued colonial requirement that they disappear and a symptom, I would say, of colonialism's ongoing life and simultaneous failure.

An important part of understanding Kahnawà:ke's contemporary struggles is acknowledging how it has been constructed in the ethnological and anthropological literature on the Iroquois. This may seem an odd route to go; for those readers invested in questions and literatures of contemporary politics, ethnology would not be the go-to domain for an analysis of the political in settler states. However, as one will read in subsequent chapters, anthropology has very much been the domain of defining the political for Indigenous peoples historically, and in fact was the mode for constructing and defining Indigeneity itself. In the case of Kahnawà:ke, this mode of apprehension has mapped out in ways that have been particularly judgmental, authenticating, or disauthenticating—ultimately, *adjudicating*—all with the intent of upholding the law and the filter of comprehension: hierarchically arranged ethnological categories. In chapter 2, I specifically lay out the course of modern history for Kahnawa'kehró:non with attention to territory so that their struggles with and against contemporary settler states are clear and they can move out of the ethnographic frame of failure. As the politics of this community are still entangled in some ways with these conceptual filters of linguistics, ethnology, ritual—as anything they do is read against these adjudicating, authenticating frames of analysis—the territorial and experiential history that produces them in particular ways has to be laid out so that the filters that misapprehended them can be revealed and narrated as well. Chapter 3 moves from that territorial history to an anthropological history of writing that contains and constrains Iroquois politics into certain geographic spaces and versions of tradition, explaining how the desire for fetishized cultural purity could not be met at Kahnawà:ke. In chapter 4, I move from that atrophied scene of a purist "canon" of knowledge into the space of what it necessarily excludes: the community and the people in question and the centrality of ethics when researching and writing in this historical, conceptual, and political context. I refuse to practice the type of ethnography that claims to tell the whole story and have all the answers. This is not an even playing ground for interpretation, and I do not pretend otherwise. I call this heightened awareness my "ethnographic refusal." In chapter 5 we see contemporary ethnographic engagements with the United States–Canada border contextualized in the legal history, particularly the Jay Treaty of 1794 that Mohawks work from when they cross. As such the chapter moves us to contemporary representations of Iroquois politics, how those politics and the people they impact move across the border, and the subsequent vilification and criminalization of them by the Canadian press. Chapter 6 analyzes the so-called Oka Crisis of 1990, when Mohawks took up arms against the expansion of a nine-hole golf course into their territory, and how this crisis links to the membership debate in Kahnawà:ke. I argue that these are both symptoms of the ongoing, gendered violence against land and Indian women perpetrated by and as a result of settler colonialism. As such these supposed "events" and "crises" are of a piece with each other. Ethnographic vignettes and interviews on membership and citizenship entwine through this chapter to demonstrate the different ways in which people think about and push back on the expectations that they disappear—as women, as Indians, as people tied to land. Through these ethnographic engagements we also see that citizenship, instantiated in different ways, is a living form of claiming, of being claimed, and of feeling within the polity, rather than an act of government conferral.

Kahnawà:ke and its people are unique within the landscape not only of anthropology, Native and Indigenous studies, and the specificity of Iroquois studies, but also of most political studies. This unique positioning owes to the history of anthropology, the particular culture base of the community, and the settler history of Canada (and the United States), all of which contribute to the reading of Kahnawà:ke as improperly Iroquois or impossibly nationalist (since they are Indigenous and thus non-Western). This oversight has much to do with the conventional foci of both anthropology (the traditional domain of Native American studies) and political science (the traditional domain of nationalism studies), and there are theoretical and methodological reasons for these occlusions. Neither discipline has harnessed the conceptual tools to engage the possibility of Indigenous nationhood; nor could they do it in ways that were consistent with the words and actions of the subjects. Neither has seemed to take seriously either the claims that settler colonialism places on subjectivities, or the politics of peoples in these geopolitical spaces.[48] The attention that has been paid to colonialism as a situation of "elsewhere" and "before" has left the politics of "the nations within" North America largely unexamined and undertheorized. This book will attempt to reverse that trend.

TWO

A Brief History of Land, Meaning, and Membership in Iroquoia and Kahnawà:ke

Time out of Place

BROOKLYN—October 2001

"My father's father had to be from Kahnawà:ke, that is the dialect of Mohawk he spoke."

"Oh yeah," I say agreeably and smilingly, "who is your father?" He tells me his father's name and then his grandfather's name. I have no idea who they are. I ask him to explain them to me: who are they related to? He cannot seem to tell me this.

"How is he from Kahnawà:ke?" I ask.

He answers, "He can't be from Kahnawà:ke, this is my great-grandfather."

This is puzzling for me, and I am pretty sure I am not hiding it well. This person—I will call him "Richard"—has been identified in a book as being from the community. That is how I find him. I ask people, "Have you ever heard this name?" (his last name, a generic-sounding English one), and they have not. This is odd, but his membership is still within the realm of the possible. Maybe his grandmother is the one from Kahnawà:ke and she married out and got a different last name, and maybe his mother married out too and that is how he has this name that no one knows. So I still look forward to interviewing him. We have e-mailed for a year prior to the interview, and he consents to be interviewed. Talking with him seems especially promising, since he is identified in the book as someone who was involved in cultural revival in the seventies.[1]

Yet, the answers he is giving me are simply not "right." They make it impossible for me to place him. None of the usual questions of family or place yield an answer that would situate him in the social, historical, or cartographic universe of the community other than as a friend or guest. The most critical question, the question of family, the sure-fast, surefire means of placing someone within the tendrils of membership, keep slipping from this conversation. I cannot grab on to what he is saying. He seems so thoroughly anchored in Brooklyn and the 1970s that I cannot get a handle on him as a Kahnawa'kehró:non.

[Did I make a mistake with this one?] "Then how is *he* from Kahnawà:ke?"

"Don't forget, I am [late 1960s]—we are talking about someone who fought in the Civil War. He was from the original Kahnawà:ke, the one in upstate New York."

"Oh."

I realize that we are not even in the 1970s, wrong century even. That settles it for me. I realize that these questions are useless, that I have to cool it. This is confusing but perhaps good. Once I let go of the compass that guides most of these interviews, we spend the next two hours talking about people from town in the early 1970s. We talk about where they lived, what they were up to, when they moved back up from Brooklyn. We talk about the first Longhouse, about Ganienkeh and the potbellied stove that he drove from Kahnawà:ke to Plattsburgh to buy.[2] We also talk about Handsome Lake. He wonders if the potbellied stove is still in the Longhouse. I wonder, too.

Why was this exchange so puzzling? Perhaps because a very complicated story has been simplified through history, and this man's complicated claim does not "line up" with that simple history as easily as we are used to.

KAHNAWÀ:KE

In addition to the social and territorial past described above, Kahnawà:ke's history includes the larger matrix of Iroquois history in the northeastern United States as well as its experience as a reserve ("reservation") community in what is now southern Quebec. Kahnawà:ke's history also includes the particular constraints that the Indian Act placed on Indigenous action in Canada. As a reserve community, Kahnawà:ke embodies the intersecting processes of colonialism, traditionalism, and nationalism that shape colonial and postcolonial societies around the world. The "Oka Crisis" of 1990 forcefully brought to public attention the fact that the Mohawks of Kahnawà:ke, with the Mohawks of neighboring Kanehsatà:ke, understand themselves as a nation and deign to act as a sovereign entity. Yet this sovereignty often exists more in consciousness than in practice, as the community confronts the competing claims to sovereignty of materially dominant state(s) that sit atop their land and administer their populations.

The founders of Kahnawà:ke left the traditional territory of the Six Nations Confederacy in the late seventeenth century, moving from the Mohawk Valley in what is now upstate New York to the south shore near Montreal, in search of trade, temperance, and freedom from political troubles within the Confederacy. The historical and political experiences of this Mohawk community share an Iroquois past that is well documented for New York State (Trigger 1985; Richter 1992; Snow 1994) but less so in southwestern Quebec (Voget 1951, 1953; Ghobashy 1961).

For some anthropologists and historians, Kahnawà:ke and Kahnawa'kehró:non occupy a position of nominal importance in the larger picture of anthropological and, in particular, Iroquois studies. Much literature from the time by Lewis Henry Morgan, the foundational ethnologist in Iroquois studies, and American anthropology for that matter, was occupied with recording what was perceived to be a "vanishing aboriginal past," resulting in an almost exclusive scholarly focus on those Iroquois communities where traditional political and religious practices were in evidence (Morgan [1851]1996; Fenton 1940; Shimony [1961] 1994). As Kahnawa'kehró:non moved from the Mohawk Valley, seeking salvation and respite from conflicts there, they were consigned in the literature to a marginal analytical space offered to "praying Indians." This approach persisted in spite of a past that was marked by religious syncretism, countercolonial practice, traditional revitalization, and nationalist consciousness.[3]

This chapter starts with a quote from an interlocutor from Brooklyn to illustrate how space and place are clearly connected to history and to shifting notions of membership. When my own research had moved away from the reserve, from its surrounding areas, and from Canada, I was immediately presented with the challenges posed by this interlocutor, which in a way is the challenge of membership itself. How was I to process this person, who speaks of Kahnawà:ke in fairly intimate and specific terms but does so within an unintelligible timeframe? Or, rather, how do I recognize this person as a Mohawk from Kahnawà:ke, or a Mohawk at all? What are the terms of recognition? Is it memory; is it blood; is it participation within the space most of us recognize as "home" (the reserve)? What if someone seems to have these things but in strange, unfamiliar, or unrecognizable ways? The connection of this interlocutor to the community is transhistoric and translocal, moving him (and this conversation) from the Mohawk Valley south to Brooklyn, New York. This is a migration through time that has long passed, but is clearly alive in his consciousness; how then, was or is this person part of the membership? How does the structure of settler colonialism inflect this conversation and give weight to these questions, making them moral and ethical impasses as I write? How do *I* write about this man?[4] What matters in this matrix of reckoning and recognition: is it a metaphor of blood, is it knowledge, or is it the historic place of this articulation? What are the terms of recognition that shall be afforded to him, and what terms of recognition matter for him?

I raise this issue because it was one of the moments during fieldwork that challenged an emerging paradigm in my research on the primacy of kinship and family, and family as a political form of relatedness (and social legitimacy, with or without legal recognition), a paradigm offering the comfort of relative clarity and lack of ambiguity. At the same time, this moment clearly brought to light the territorial history of the community, one that people recall in vernacular ways, but rarely (or never) in such an immediate and bodily manner. I had somehow, in all of my thirty-one years, never met anyone who "claimed" membership or belonging to Kahnawà:ke without being unambiguously *somehow* from there, and by "somehow" I mean with family: cousins, aunties, uncles, grandparents, and deep social connections, with a storied life that was embedded within the narratives of others who were themselves *from* there. I remember sitting in his office in Brooklyn and thinking "This is really different." And it seemed, at the time, extremely bizarre for me. I also thought, "I don't know if people from home would go for this." But he knew a lot of people from home, so clearly they "went for this." Or, something like this. I wondered if to triangulate him, to ask about him, do we claim him? The moment agitated even my notion of "we," as I thought, "I am not sure I claim him, I can't figure out his family, he has no family." He was fine—friendly, knew people, had experiences that were very specific, very storied, in themselves, that accorded with things I had heard of and liked hearing more of—but he seemed incredibly foreign.

He was pleasant, and helpful. Here was someone before me who may (or may not, I thought at points) be of the Valley rather than of the temporally present Kahnawà:ke. Although all Kahnawa'kehró:non and "northern Mohawks" (all, at this point, are "northern") are descended from the Valley, the connection and *claim* to identity and legal personhood today is not predicated so directly *back* to this temporal location. Or is it? *Should* it be? It was as if this interlocutor took an "ancestry" model of identifying himself and made it a legal claim—"my grandfather's father was from the Valley." This is descent derived from ancestry, and (as one is wont to hear with Americans, "I am 'Italian' because my great-grandmother or grandmother emigrated from Italy") does not seem to have wings with people I was talking to, who defined someone by his or her immediate relations, his or her family in situ, not en passé. What to do with this contemporary embodiment of territorial history? What to do also with the possible untruth of this assertion? I wondered if I was asking the right questions.

TERRITORIAL REDUX

In Kahnawà:ke, historical events and political processes dovetail into a political sensibility that is self-consciously sovereigntist and bent at this historical juncture on defining the legal basis of recognition of personhood within the community, away from the constraints of the settler states that enframe them. As such, in the following section of this chapter, "Kahnawà:ke's Beginnings: 'Christian Dogs' and the Genesis of Difference," I will present a territorial and event-driven social history of the community in order to argue two points: one, that the territorial history of the Mohawk nation, and Kahnawà:ke in particular, shapes the central question of membership; and two, that those factors also shape the methods that are then used to examine membership and nationhood. To this end I will lay out some of the historic moments in Kahnawà:ke history that structure the problem of membership—moments that precipitate anxiety over material and semiotic resources (claims to land, claims to personhood)—and elaborate the situation of mistrust that characterizes the Kahnawà:ke-Canada-Quebec relation as well, perhaps, as mistrust between Kahnawa'kehró:non themselves. Moments of recognition, or misrecognition, through time are critical in this event-driven chronology of the community. It is imperative to state now, in advance of the history that follows, that this history is directed toward the enunciation of the problem of membership and the historical consciousness of the community, rather than a preconceived notion of their tribalism or ethnicization.

Consider these historical moments taken from literature belonging to the community, each articulating a fear or an immanent sense of disappearance. The first reconstructs the perspective of a Mohawk woman by O. M. Spencer, a white captive taken by Kahnawà:ke Mohawks in the early nineteenth century. The second is from Arthur Parker's version of the Great Law of Peace, in which the Peacemaker predicts the imminent death, or perhaps loss of reason, of the Iroquois people.

> She then enlayed on the anger of the Great Spirit against the red man, and especially those of her own nation, nearly all of whom had perished: and, melting into tenderness, she concluded that herself and children, the remnant of her race, would soon sleep in the ground: that there would be none to gather them at the feast of the dead, or celebrate their obsequies. (Spencer 1836, 194)

> Then Dekanahwideh continued and said: "It will be hard and your grandchildren will suffer hardship. And if it may so occur that the heads of the people of the confederacy shall roll and wander away westward, if such thing should come to pass, other nations shall see your heads rolling and wandering away and they shall say to you, "you belong to the Confederacy, you were a proud and haughty people once," and they shall kick the heads with scorn, and they shall go on their way. (Parker [1916] 1991, 104)

Here we have nineteenth- and twentieth-century fragments from two different sorts of literature—a captivity narrative and a version of the Great Law of Peace, or Kaianere'kó:wa. The latter is a narrative of a deeper history than the first, but was recorded at a later time, evidencing the sense of "remnant status," or immanent loss, for Mohawk nationhood that is based on bodily and, perhaps, cultural death. Here we find laments for the physical loss of bodies to warfare and disease, with "heads rolling" as a metaphor for loss of reason, a loss of Confederacy protocol.[5] And with that position we see "tradition" articulated as an invocation to stay alive: "if you do not do this, then this will happen"; "keep your heads"; and "fight."

This history of death and anxiety about disappearance has a clear impact on the way Kahnawa'kehró:non deal with the problem of membership and how they invoke their past relationships, both within the reserve and with the outside world. John and Jean Comaroff discuss the broader process of historical reckoning as "active . . . sometimes implicit, sometimes explicit—in which human actors deploy historically salient cultural categories to construct their self-awareness" (Comaroff and Comaroff 1992, 176). "History" in this respect is produced through discussion, debate, and enactment, through social interactions that perpetuate and create the past, through the living of the present, even if in this case, that living is preoccupied with avoiding political and social death. Such social interaction is structured by "the everyday historical memory that informs a subject's sense of what is normal, appropriate or possible" (Foster 1991, 241).

In Kahnawà:ke that memory structures day-to-day relationships, and in doing so feeds into the politics of the reserve. Historical memory determines social acknowledgment, recognition of social life in the construction of the present. It is not uncommon, in the small community of 6,154 members, for individuals to completely ignore each other, to confer on each other a social death owing to events in the past that can no longer be recalled, thus entrenching existing social cleavages or creating new ones. As well, everyday historical memory is wedded to the constant critique of all things perceived as illegitimate or foreign: The Mohawk Council of Kahnawà:ke, the "band councilors/chiefs," neighbors, the Longhouse, the Longhouse people, "Brooklyn Bums." For example, at a Meet the Candidates Night with community members (June 1996), candidates running for the MCK each spoke about their vision for Kahnawà:ke's future and what they would do for the community once elected. One candidate based his entire platform on critiquing the existing council and decisions made by social and community service leaders. He at one point asked the community: "Who made the decision to put the curbs up the way they did? [roads were repaved, sidewalks and curbs were constructed on one part of the reserve in the Summer of 1995] Was it Council?! Council shouldn't do that—they should talk to The People [the community] before they go and do that. The curbs are no good, and who put that white woman in charge of the bank? [Kahnawà:ke has a 'Caisse Populaire,'[6] branch on reserve] There should be an Indian in charge over there! It's no good the way this town is run right now!"

This discourse evidences the critical, seemingly tireless discourse of engagement with things considered foreign, obtrusive, and impinging, and may be directed at other individuals as well as the Mohawk Council, taxis, or bank management. Structurally the constant critique may express the ideals of Confederacy politics and function at the same time as a mechanism through which all people actively engage in the affairs of the community, no matter "where they sit" in the spectrum of political possibilities in Kahnawà:ke, or where they may have sat in the Longhouse of precontact Iroquois history. It is a (sometimes really exhausting) style of political participation and representation. It also keeps leaders, friends, and neighbors highly accountable to "The People."

This critical imperative is one of the key elements of traditional political culture that almost *aggresses* the present. Politics in Kahnawà:ke rest upon two related principles: accountability to the people and leadership (Alfred 1995, 89). These principles flow from the main features of what Gerald (Taiaiake) Alfred calls "Iroquois democracy": consensual decision making and a participatory political process (ibid., 78). In Kahnawà:ke's life as a community, the achievement of consensual decision making and participation in all levels of political processes have been cleaved by influences from and interactions with the outside, namely, with Canada and the United States, as I will detail in this and later chapters. However, the commitment to the ideals of consensus and participation remain. In Kahnawà:ke, questions concerning self, peoplehood, and nationhood are clustered around the issue of membership in the community. At present, the criteria necessary for determining Indian status are being discussed and reconsidered on social and political levels. The result of this discussion was the Kahnawà:ke Membership Law (2003), which supplanted the Mohawk Law on Membership. Passed into effect in 1984, the Mohawk Law on Membership—with its requirement of a measurable quantum of Mohawk blood for determining citizenship—is a lightning rod for controversy in the community.

This controversy concerning the Mohawk Law on Membership has been institutionalized into the formal political bodies in the community. Of these, both Longhouses establish that citizenship should flow from one's clan rather than blood. Therefore a Mohawk is one whose mother is a member of a Mohawk clan. The MCK, on the other hand, offers citizenship or membership to those who have four Mohawk great-grandparents. Hence the membership debate can be understood as a struggle between discourses in the political geography of Kahnawà:ke, one employing "culturalist" definitions of Mohawk identity and the other employing genealogic-cum-"racialist" definitions (as each great-grandparent is assumed to have 100 percent Indian blood—a reckoning process that Kim Tallbear has in a different context also flagged as similarly reified).[7] United only in their rejection of Canadian control over membership, these alternatives at once oppose and embrace each other, creating fissures of discord.

On a collective level, the Mohawk Law on Membership is at once a response to and an interaction with a changing world that is pushing Mohawks inward to themselves for instruction on how to manage the present. In this respect the law is a product of processes and events that have forced a seemingly radical reconsideration of Mohawk identity, community, and nationhood, events and processes initiated by the formation of a new, settler society that required Indian lands, that hemmed people into fixed grids, and then worked to modify those spaces culturally and politically through law and through force. All this occurred with the goal of an endgame of integration and assimilation, the disappearance of what was different. What follows is context for this fractious problem of membership.

Kahnawà:ke's Beginnings: "Christian Dogs" and the Genesis of Difference

They had arrayed themselves in their finest dresses as for a day of triumph—they were armed with knives and hatchets and clubs, and anything on which they could lay their hands, while fury was painted on their countenances. As soon as they joined the captives, one of the Indians came up to Etienne. "My brother," said he, "your end has come. It is not we who put you to death, but you sealed your own fate when you went to live amongst the Christian dogs [early Kahnawa'kehró:non]." "It is true," answered Etienne, "that I am a Christian, but it is no less true that I glory in being one. Inflict on me what you please, for I fear neither your outrages nor torments. I willingly give up my life for that God who has shed all his blood for me." (Kip 1846, 121)

Contemporary Kahnawà:ke requires an accounting that stretches back to its inception as an emergent community in the political geography of the eastern woodlands of what is now understood to be the United States (and parts of Canada). To understand the historical events and processes that culminate in the consciousness and political behavior of the present, we have to look to its start—at its first interactions as a refuge for Indian converts to Christianity. In this respect there are three formative underpinnings that measure into the politics of Kahnawà:ke today: an ideological difference from other Iroquois peoples; internal forms of difference that are ideological and experiential; and the concomitant importance placed on territory after movement, encroachment, and loss. In concert, these underpinnings inform the historical account of Kahnawà:ke's particular style of politics and concern over membership and rights to resources.

Kahnawà:ke was formed from Mohawk migrations out of the Mohawk Valley of upstate New York to a French Jesuit settlement called Kentaké (La Prairie) just south of Montreal.[8] Kanienke, "the land" or the territory of the Mohawk people, was a vast area covering much of what is now southern New York State up into the St. Lawrence lowlands. After shifting alliances between the French, the Dutch, and then the British during the early period of New France, some Mohawks of the Valley relocated to the village of Kentaké, on the south shore facing what is now Montreal.

From 1668 onward, the borders of the white settlement of Kentaké had become a refuge for Christian Indians of the region (Alfred 1995, 39), and by 1669 the community had gone from five "cabins" (longhouse living structures) to a settlement of eighteen to twenty families (Parmenter 2010, 141). When the Jesuits recognized the popularity of the settlement, they established a permanent mission there on a seigniorial land grant from the king of France, Louis IX, to serve the influx of other Christian Indians. Here it must be noted that the Mohawks who migrated from the Valley did so for a variety of reasons: to avoid disputes in the Iroquois Confederacy as well as the British presence in the Valley, to participate in the fur trade, to pursue Christianity, and to find temperance from alcohol (Havard 2001, 37). Jon Parmenter's seventeenth-century history emphasizes the many motivations that drove Haudenosaunee north, which, he argues—by reading in between the lines of mission accounts—can be discerned "as an effort to expand League homelands" (ibid., 142).

Early Kahnawà:ke therefore must be conceptualized as a refugee community that was constituted by different kinds of Iroquois people as well as other Christian Indians from Quebec, but, per Parmenter's study, they were moving north not only to be "good Christians," but to expand Confederacy territory. Although these were in some ways a "different" sort of

Iroquois, they were still much of the same kin and political matrix as their brethren down south. The cultural composition of the community was initially heterogeneous, as Abenaki, Huron, Oneida, Onondaga, and Mohawk people also settled there. By the 1670s, however, the community became more "Mohawk" due to large influxes from the Valley, so that "by 1677, Mohawks dominated the community. . . . Still allied to their southern kin and seeking more than religion at Kentake, [they] came into political conflict with the other peoples represented in the community. . . . The character of the community changed from strict religious devotion to a mélange of Mohawk culture, religion and the atmosphere of a trading and diplomatic center" (Alfred 1995, 40). The "Mohawkization" of the community continued through the next fifty years, while the settlement was moved four times upriver to where it now stands in relation to Montreal. Although material and salient expressions of Mohawk culture were evident—language, longhouses, and style of clothing—one can assume that other influences were being interwoven into the fabric of the community. In addition to the Jesuit presence there (and the prima facie commitment to Christianity), early Kahnawa'kehró:non were also involved in a fur trade that brought other elements to bear on the consciousness of the people and their expressive culture.

The Mohawks of Kahnawà:ke as an Iroquoian people had among their numbers assimilated outsiders—whites and other Indians who had been taken captive prior to the move to the North and who continued to impact Kahnawà:ke's politics.[9] Like others assimilated into Mohawk culture and society, descendants of the captives taken from the Mohawk raid on Deerfield, Massachusetts, in 1704 figured into the politics of the community, as they still had ties to their white families in the southern British colonies and affected the political decisions of the Mohawk community. To honor the kinship ties of the descendants of the Deerfield captives, the Mohawks at Kahnawà:ke adopted an official position of neutrality during the Revolutionary War (Alfred 1995, 49).

Thus early Kahnawà:ke was founded on a willful departure from the Mohawk Valley and a heterogeneous composition. However, that departure should not be understood as a complete rupture from the larger matrix of Iroquois political culture. Iroquois politics and governance were intricately bound up with kinship. Deborah Doxtator's research at Six Nations, Tyendinaga, and Tonawanda demonstrates with meticulous detail that it was through the adaptive structure of clan (one's kin) that one achieved a place in the order of things, but it also *ordered* relations between others and adapted or dealt with the onslaught and demands of settler colonialism (1996).

Although the early Mohawks of Kahnawà:ke may have appeared to some to eschew the metaphysical aspects of Iroquois culture in favor of Catholicism, they were still operationalizing the tenets of a clan system of descent. They were still incorporating outsiders through captivity and adoption long after their migration to Kentaké from the Valley. Ascribed differences, such as race, did not figure into the Mohawk's potential equation for a captive; what mattered were situational factors: their nation in relation to current Iroquois foreign policy of the time, their fortitude, their usefulness, and their commitment to Mohawk ideals (Simpson 2009).

The heterogeneous composition of the historical community may be viewed as the setup for the conditions of the contemporary crisis over membership. "Premodern" (and later modern) Mohawks were open to those who at this time might be considered outsiders, to people of different nations and races. The clan structure that was in place made it possible for all those people to become Mohawk (Simpson 2009). Thus identity was not a problematic, an ethical issue, a matter to be confused by. It was not confused with political membership; it was political membership. And this was so because the governmental authority within the community could choose to recognize (or not) those who had rights to residency and life in the community, who had clans and thus families and responsibilities to something much larger than themselves. However, that historic structure of admission and the resultant "racial mixing" of early Kahnawa'kehró:non is today perceived to be a problem that Mohawks have inherited from the past and must guard against for the future, as it appears to some to have portended a current "cultural loss." However, anthropologists and Mohawks remark on this sense of cultural loss only because the critical context of land loss and sovereign diminution is not centered in their assessment of the membership problem.

This land loss was, to say the least, profound. Anxieties about a diminished land base were reasonable at *any* Iroquois community in the nineteenth century. Tyendinaga was reduced from 92,700 acres in 1784 to

17,000 acres in 1900, and Six Nations was reduced from 674,910 acres in 1784 to 43,696 in 1900. Tonawanda was reduced from 46,209 acres in 1797 to 7,549 in 1900 (Doxtator 1996, 129). Laurence Hauptman argues that the Iroquois lost 95 percent of their land base in New York State because of white pressures on their land (1988, 5). Kahnawà:ke's history is very much a part of this story of devastating land loss. Discounting Kahnawà:ke's inherent territory—the Mohawk acreage in New York State—the numbers that are used by the Mohawk Council of Kahnawà:ke in relation to the land claims related to the original seigniorial grant are the original 1680 (seventeenth century) sixty thousand acres of land, plus about three thousand acres deeded in the eighteenth century on the western boundary (Chateauguay).[10] This signifies that fifty thousand acres of Kahnawà:ke territory have been "lost"; most specifically, it was deeded away by the Catholic Church, which accepted rents from white settlers and "sold" land that it neither had the authority nor the sanction to sell. This happened throughout the entire eighteenth and nineteenth centuries.

With these processes accounted for, we now must ask what events have seized the consciousness of the community throughout the course of their lived history and have shaped their formulations of membership today. What are the salient categories of collective experience that Kahnawa'kehró:non call upon when they are confronted with a need to define themselves—when confronted with the settler state? And perhaps, what category do they invoke to defend themselves to each other? The groundwork has been laid for this community to be perceived as ideologically different and yet attached to other Iroquois (through a clan system), as racially and culturally (to use concepts that are available for our use today) complex and as territorial. We have a picture of a community that had ideological entries and exits, that allowed its assimilated outsiders to leave their stamp on Kahnawà:ke's politics and culture, and that in turn did the same to those who became Mohawk. This key feature of incipient openness has been transformed through Kahnawà:ke's existence into a sensibility and policy of closure. We now must take account of the events and interactions that have forced Kahnawa'kehró:non into their historically inverted position on membership.

These Indians though of such mixed descent, as scarcely to reckon a single full blooded individual among their number . . . still cling to their roving habits, and many of them are Voyageurs and Canoemen in the employment of the Hudson's Bay Company. A considerable number are occupied during the Summer in rafting timber and as pilots through the rapids of the St. Lawrence. (Canada 1858, 20)

He remembered now, the 1870s when, with the aid of his sons and friends, he built a thirty foot boat, sturdily made from the finest woods our lands could offer. He had taken as much sass from the rapids as he could stand. So many times they had frustrated him when his fishing took him too close to the rushing waters. He was going to beat those rapids by using his brains, his woodworking skills . . . his talents . . . and his friends. He was really infatuated with that white water, admiring its spirit and the way it intimidated trespassers. But all these qualities didn't alter that Sawatis had to be the boss. (Beauvais 1985, 40)

From its inception, Kahnawà:ke did not exist in a vacuum, independent of the surrounding society or the workings of "the state" (or multiple states, or emergent states). Kahnawa'kehró:non were integrated into the larger market community throughout the early modern period as fur traders, soldiers, crafts people, and river guides. Along with material resources, this integration carried with it a migration of new ideas and practices into the community. The society within Kahnawà:ke adapted to and integrated elements from the larger, settler society outside of the reserve. These experiences and relations continued unthreatened when Kahnawà:ke acquired "reserve" status as a settlement on Crown land subject to the law and protection of Canada in 1850 (Alfred 1995, 153). In 1890 the re-serve status of the community was cemented when the Indian Act was accepted by male vote, and inaugurated a lot of dissension, within in the community (Reid 2004). At that time, the Indian Act eclipsed the tradi-tional government that was in place and set up a band council of locally elected men. Just prior to the acceptance of the Indian Act and the new institutions that accompanied it, the Canadian government initiated a land survey to implement a land-tenure system based on individual allot-ments rather than communal ownership. At the same time, Kahnawà:ke received its first membership list of those eligible to be band members (Alfred 1995, 56).

The material and symbolic extension of Canada into the reserve is a critical moment in Kahnawà:ke's history. Canada's presence—perceived in cycles as sometimes foreign, imposing, and undesirable and at other times as useful and tolerable—would serve as a point of contention to which Kahnawa'kehró:non return. However, the positive or negative reception of Canada's presence in the community depended on whether Kahnawa'kehró:non thought they were being encroached upon. These perceptions have been framed by Canada's appropriation of the land, appropriations that dovetail with the Indian Act's presence in the community and thus with the imposition of heteropatriarchal, patrilineal, and electoral governance.

The modern political consciousness in Kahnawà:ke has its impetus in the construction of the St. Lawrence Seaway canal in 1957, an event that figures heavily in the historical memory of Kahnawa'kehró:non and has been identified by Alfred as the impetus for nationalist assertion (1995). This event embodies the experience of the intrusion of Canada into the territory and minds of Kahnawa'kehró:non. The construction of the seaway is the first interaction perceived to jeopardize Mohawk identity and culture as it tore through the site of Mohawk economic and cultural activity: the riverfront (Phillips 2000).

Having provided Kahnawa'kehró:non with the food that it offered, in the late 1800s the St. Lawrence River became a site of further economic activity for Kahnawa'kehró:non. Mohawks continued to fish the river, but they also took to the river as guides and deliverymen. There was great pride in the lives of Kahnawà:ke boatmen (Beauvais 1985). Those that navigated boats up and down the St. Lawrence River were perceived as brave, strong, and tenacious. They were experts at navigating the river and this expertise translated into fame for the entire community, as Kahnawà:ke boatmen acquired a reputation for their heroic exploits (Beauvais 1985, 101–3). Through the cultivation of bravery, the river was a training ground for other heroic activities abroad, such as the Nile River expedition, where the experience of Kahnawa'kehró:non in the rapids served them well during the British expedition (Jackson 1885), as well as for showmanship (Beauvais 1985) and later for ironwork (Katzer 1988). When taken together, Kahnawà:ke's activity on the river and the formative experiences of the community constitute crucial ecological factors in the formation of Mohawk selfhood in the modern period. Expertise and bravery on the river was something that Mohawks identified with and that was also affirmed by outside society. When the St. Lawrence Seaway Authority, with the assistance of Canada, removed the riverfront from Kahnawa'kehró:non, they confiscated Mohawk experience—an appropriation that was outside the established parameters of the Kahnawà:ke-Canada relationship.

The construction of a seaway canal was unacceptable to Kahnawa'kehró:non. When the St. Lawrence Seaway Authority sought community approval for their plan to expropriate 1,260 acres of land from the riverfront of Kahnawà:ke, the community held a referendum and voted against it. Canada then passed the St. Lawrence Seaway Act in 1955 giving Canada the right to expropriate land in Canada's interest. Kahnawà:ke resisted, and the consequential dispute over the seaway took Kahnawà:ke into the Canadian judicial system. The band council appealed to the courts and then to international authorities on the grounds that the expropriation of reserve land was in violation of the British North America Act and the Indian Act (Ghobashy 1961, 50–66; Alfred 1995, 158–61). All appeals were lost, and the band council as well as individuals affected by the seaway began the arduous process of negotiating compensation for the lands that would be lost to construction. In the end, the seaway uprooted families from their homes and removed the vital riverfront of the reserve.[11]

What happened, then, when the Seaway Authority appropriated the riverfront from Kahnawà:ke? On the level of Kahnawà:ke lived experience, summer swimming spots and boat launchings were lost. New, huge, loud ships passed along the new shoreline of the community. The historic "village" on the riverfront was lost, as well as homes that housed families. More significantly in terms of a nationalist or sovereigntist consciousness, Kahnawa'kehró:non lost all trust or faith in Canada, its judiciary, and the international community. Kahnawà:ke appealed to the courts of Canada and the United Nations. Neither recognized the unjust seizure of Mohawk land, leaving Kahnawa'kehró:non to fend for themselves to the bitter end. In a letter to the Human Rights Commission on September 27, 1960, the elected grand chief Matthew Lazare wrote: "The decision to confiscate Indian Reserve Land in connection with the St. Lawrence Seaway project is part and parcel of the plan to evict the Indians from their Reserve and force them to abandon their way of life, culture and traditions. The Canadian Government continues to infringe on our rights and to force their way into our midst" (in Ghobashy 1961, 60).

The strong language of Matthew Lazare's final point—"The Canadian Government continues to infringe on our rights and to force their way into our midst"—summarizes Kahnawà:ke's grievance with the Canadian state. If there ever was the illusion of an equal nation-to-nation relationship between Canada and Kahnawà:ke prior to the construction of the seaway, it was now over. The seaway land seizures represented a disregard for Mohawk political will and disrespect for Mohawk territory. This included the riverfront, the land, and the lives lived in and around these significant sites of meaning.[12] The meanings attached to these places were constructed from swimming, fishing, and living on the river, but they came as well from the Mohawk past, the migration to this far-off place in Kanienke, the settlement in the North that this branch of the Mohawk Nation made their own. As such, the seizure was a violation of Mohawk experience, and it created a reservoir of territorial outrage that Kahnawa'kehró:non still draw from today.

With the seaway debacle, Kahnawa'kehró:non realized that their self-perception as brave, heroic, river-riding people—as a people who historically had their own constitution with which to govern themselves—conflicted with their legally defined perception by the state. They were "status Indians" under the jurisdiction of Ottawa and therefore subject to discretionary "intrusions" by Canada. Hence their years as a relatively independent people were over. Canadian and American indifference to Mohawk self-perception, as well as the appropriation of the sites and symbols of Mohawk identity, fed into a new formulation of who they were: a group of people with a shared past and present interests, who were radically different from those around them, and who could now be intruded upon, in what were perceived to be terrible ways, without consent, with indifference, and with the law.

How did the postseaway historical and political consciousness differ from the consciousness of Kahnawa'kehró:non of the previous decade? What was happening in the 1940s and 1950s that may have shifted the people of Kahnawà:ke into looking at themselves and their relationships with the world outside in a different way? This was impossible to gauge during fieldwork undertaken in the near present. However, Fred Voget, examining political cleavages in Caughnawaga of the 1950s, writes of the "native modified group" ("those that clearly recognized the separation of Indian and white") (1951, 230) within Kahnawà:ke of the time, that "no attempt is made to identify themselves with the Canadian and American societies established upon their former lands. On the contrary, they emphasize that their Indianness raises them above national governments and allows them to pass readily from one country to another. Moreover the important historic role of the Iroquois has awakened a national consciousness based on their original autonomy and structured according to the traditional organization of the League of the Five (or Six) nations" (Voget 1951, 223).

Kahnawa'kehró:non of the time were divided in their political orientation. Voget estimates that three hundred members, or 10 percent, of the population, were Longhouse or "traditional" in their rejection of Canadian and American authority. Longhouse people of the 1950s and Longhouse people today refuse the legitimacy and institutional apparatus of the Canadian state and do not participate in any level of government that is not Iroquois. They do not vote in either band council elections nor in Canadian or American elections, because these are viewed as foreign political bodies that should have no authority or influence over Mohawk decision making. The Longhouse people of Voget's study referred rather to the Kaianere'kó:wa, or The Great Law of Peace, as interpreted by Handsome Lake, a Seneca prophet of the nineteenth century. Nonetheless, Kahnawa'kehró:non of the late 1940s were attempting to unite over proposed revisions to the Indian Act (Bill 267) that would enfranchise as Canadian all persons possessing one-quarter Indian blood or less (ibid., 223). This legal specter of loss presents to Kahnawa'kehró:non the quantitative value of "blood" to the Canadian state and the presumed danger of racial mixing. Voget informs us that "members of the politically active segment have endeavored repeatedly to induce electoral participation by the Long-House membership but to date all attempts have been refused, since such activity does not conform to the Confederate Constitution [Kaianere'kó:wa]" (ibid., 222).[13] When I asked an interlocutor about this moment in Kahnawà:ke's history, he said he did not recall its specificity, but that "there has always," for as long as he could remember, "been racial tension." Yet the seaway debacle orients sentiment squarely to the state and away from the mess of state-generated internal strife. David Blanchard, doing his research in Kahnawà:ke during the late 1970s, glossed pre-seaway consciousness in the following sweeping manner:

Life in the community was good. The majority of the populace was uninvolved politically. Longhouse membership remained low, and few people opted to participate as electors or candidates in the council elections. This is not to say that the community was unaffected. Children growing up in the 1940s and 1950s developed the attitude that the longhouse, and all that it symbolized, was something separate from themselves. The alienation experienced by this generation was one that worked on them from without. "We are real Indians, so you are not." Many children believed this message, and in the words of one informant, "I grew up cheering for the cowboys. When I found out that I was an Indian I cried." (1982, 304)

It is unclear how Blanchard can make claims regarding the 1940s and the 1950s with such scant evidence (and without suppositional disclaimers), but he does offer insight into the pathos of identity that merges in one interlocutor. What we might take away more from Voget and Blanchard is the range of political options available to people and the specter of blood in Canadian forms of recognition that would, if they could, incorporate Kahnawa'kehró:non into the Canadian state as citizens and disappear them both as Mohawks and as recognizable and recognized Indians.

Further along these lines, Voget does not state in his article whether those in the community were lobbying others to vote in band council elections or municipal elections, but we can hazard a guess that it had to have been band council, since Indians in Quebec were only granted the right to vote federally in 1969. Older Kahnawa'kehró:non to this day still admonish younger community members against even thinking about participating in external elections with this warning: "You vote and you will lose your rights [status]!" We can gauge from both Voget and Blanchard that Kahnawa'kehró:non had a clear consciousness of themselves as Indian, whether this consciousness was formed by vilified representations of Indians in Westerns in the 1950s or in response to Ottawa's definition (over one-quarter blood), and that this consciousness moved them politically.

Thirty years after the seaway was constructed, Kahnawà:ke was faced with another threat to its territorial boundaries. This threat was perceived to come simultaneously from within the community and from the outside. Aimed at redressing the patrilineal bias in the Indian Act, Bill C-31 was passed into effect in 1985 (see discussion in next section). With this legislation, Indian women who lost their status upon marriage to non-Indian men (or nonstatus Indian men) were put back on the federal registration list of Indians in Canada (Cassidy and Bish 1989). It was now up to each band to put these women and their children back on their local band list as well.

Histories of Being Refused: The Indian Act in Canada

In part, this is where the ethnographic story begins, with confusion and exasperation over gender bias, if not domination, and a frustration with history. I was stimulated to initiate this project on Mohawk nationhood and citizenship by the complete disjuncture between what was written about Kahnawà:ke and the things that mattered the most to them. I was interested in the unambiguous, sometimes virulent and violent boundaries that were being drawn within the reservation community over the question of "membership." At the time I started to think about my research, the elected government of the community had already devised, with some participation from the membership, a code from 1984 that would require a 50 percent (Mohawk) blood quantum for membership in the community. This membership code itself was stimulated by several factors, most recently an international human rights decision that made Canada amend its Indian Act and reinstate onto a federal registry previously disenfranchised Indian women and children (Bill C-31). Aimed at redressing the patrilineal bias in the Indian Act, Bill C-31 was passed into effect in 1985. With this legislation, Indian women who lost their status upon marriage to non-Indian men (or nonstatus Indian men) were put back on the federal registration list of Indians in Canada.[14] It was then up to each reserve to devise its own membership codes, and to then admit (or deny) membership to these women and their children in its own local registries (Green 2001, 723).

Bill C-31 followed on the heels of a decade-long battle that saw nonstatus Indian women go head to head with their reserve or band council governments, the state, and, finally, international authorities. The women had unsuccessfully petitioned their band council governments to let them return, to raise their children, and exercise their rights as Indians. The band council governments upheld the Indian Act and challenged the women to bring their case to court. The women then organized into political action groups, Equal Rights for Indian Women and the Native Women's

Association of Canada, which then brought the Canadian government to court for the inherent gender bias in the Indian Act. They lost their case. It was only when they brought the case to the United Nations Human Rights Commission in 1982 that Canada was found to be in violation of the Covenant on Civil and Political Rights. Canada then amended the Indian Act and removed the bias of determining membership in Indian bands along the father's line. Perceived as a victory for Indian women (and perhaps for all women, as there was coalition building between women's organizations at the time), Bill C-31 was intended to mend the fabric of Indian societies torn apart by unjust legislation. In practice, however, matters were much different.

Kahnawà:ke had already assimilated some tenets of the Indian Act into the social fabric of the community. The means for defining kinship and determining community belonging, the traditional means for determining descent through the mother's clan, was supplanted by the Indian Act and its European model of patrilineal descent. Kahnawà:ke had formally accepted the Indian Act in the community in 1890; however, as a reserve on Crown land, the community had been subject to elements of earlier versions of the act since 1850. That year, however, Indian status was transferable to both male and female non-Indian spouses of Indians. Therefore non-Indian men or women could hold land, operate businesses, and claim tax exemption on the reserve. Unwilling to accept the possibility of white men holding land in the community, Kahnawà:ke contested this aspect of the act and brought it to the courts so that it would be changed in 1851.

The Indian Act had transferred matrilineal descent and property holding to the father's line—an unambiguously raced and gendered injustice fought against by Indian women, disenfranchised from their Indian status across Canada. But the complex of factors—Canada's bestowal of the right to determine membership after a hundred years of living under the Indian Act, and Canada's reinstatement of the women on a federal registry—led, in part, to the development of a blood-quantum code in Kahnawà:ke.[15] This code was in defiance of Canadian norms for political recognition but appeared to be "objective" and gender neutral. The membership code was contested and defended by, it seemed, everyone within the community and sometimes all at once. Bill C-31 seemed to be just the most recent imposition (read by some as being told who was an Indian, *again*), and this iteration of the code reflected a century of colonial impositions, along with a desire for scientific rigor and objectivity. No one was completely happy with the code, but everyone agreed that "something had to be done" and that membership was the number one issue facing the community. In such a context, not only were boundaries being constructed and deconstructed daily; there were a heightened awareness and a deep and generalized concern over how to determine who rightfully belonged.

As discussed earlier, Kahnawà:ke had already assimilated some tenets of the Indian Act. The means for defining kinship and determining community belonging, the traditional means for determining descent—through the mother's clan—was supplanted by the Indian Act and its European model of patrilineal descent.

The 1851 change to the Indian Act is still recalled in Kahnawà:ke and is recounted in the context of maintaining local control over membership. "The beginnings of the argument are here," an elected councilor on the MCK stated during a band council meeting in November 1994. During that 1994 meeting, he brought up Kahnawà:ke's role in changing the Indian Act in the context of the impending Twinn Case, concerning membership in a western band community (and the implications, he said, that this case would have for all Indian communities deciding their membership).[16] The elected chief stated that the Twinn case "took documentation from Kahnawà:ke" because, as he put it, "we made every effort to take control of our land." In narrative he spoke of the anxiety in 1850 over white men owning land, noting retrospectively that "women were the possessors of the land" (traditional descent and governance). Thus, in 1850 the community approached the Department of Indian Affairs and said that women should not be able to confer Indian status to their husbands, because white men could then own the land on the reserve. He narrated this history in the public meeting in 1994 as the origin story of the amendment to the act. What is significant to this discussion is not the historical veracity of his claim. Rather, it is that this elected leader, and thus the MCK, would perpetuate this as historical truth. In stating that the "beginnings of the argument [on membership] are here," Kahnawà:ke is injected into the historical imagination (and record) as the progenitor of this form of membership. As well, the position is made harder to contest on the grounds of its being "un-Mohawk." We will see in chapter 6, however, that there are clear alternative forms to the history of membership that are at play in Kahnawà:ke and Iroquoia. Still, the elected chief concluded his statement by saying that the "C-31s" (see discussion below) who have been reinstated by Ottawa and theoretically can come into Kahnawà:ke as members would never "fit" socially. He said, "There is no way that they could fit into our community" (they would be strangers). Of the Twinn case he said, "It is meant to scare you—it scares me." He warned those at the meeting, "Should you disappear as Mohawks, the land goes back to the Crown" (author field notes, November 28, 1994).

As discussed above, from its formation, Kahnawà:ke was, by contemporary standards, or optics, a racially and culturally heterogeneous community. Even the use of "race" and "culture" seem inappropriate here, shockingly out of time, as I try to narrate a past. As sovereign political orders, these First Nations took, bartered, naturalized, killed, and loved according to their philosophical and political charters, before biopolitics and race became unambiguous techniques of settler-state sovereignty and governance.[17] Yet, when channeling backward, we can see that outsiders from other communities and polities (what some now would understand also as "races") were integrated into the community. This "difference" was not problematic until the construct of race became important to Kahnawa'kehró:non. Race became an issue at the time when being Mohawk became being Indian and being Indian carried rights. Yet even more than this coupling of concepts that are layering one atop the other in this historical moment, these modes of identifying native people are occurring at a time when white governance is hardening into a bureaucratized state that needs land for its own growing populations. The band councilor or elected chief above is articulating this fear of "elimination."

Nineteenth-Century Race and Sex

Patriarchy and bureaucratic control converged in the consciousness of Kahnawa'kehró:non when the 1850 proto–Indian Act legislation was contested for making white men into de jure Indians.[18] There and then we see the ascendancy of race consciousness hinging on the sex (and the perceived threat and power) of other people. From this we can deduce that white men were perceived as threatening but white women were not. We can hypothesize, then, that within a colonial scene where land, identity, and place were enframed in juridical and rights-based language and legislation, this imperative to keep white men away from institutional power and property was maintained through the technique of status. White women, under the provisions of the Indian Act, were permitted to marry and settle on the reserve, whereas white men, after 1851, were not. Although white women could acquire Indian status through marriage to an Indian man, and in doing so reside on the reserve and transmit status to their children unproblematically, they could not vote, run for council, or sell or transfer land to others besides their children—and only then if they were widowed or divorced. White men, on the other hand, as status Indians were far more threatening because they could be landowners, band councilors, and voters.[19] Although the presence of white women (as de jure Indians) may have been profoundly aggravating to Indian women, who had to leave upon out-marriage, it probably was not *threatening* to the stability of the broader community in terms of property or land ownership. I deal with these issues in light of contemporary Kahnawà:ke at length in chapter 6. But here I want to ask what this tells us about Kahnawa'kehró:non of the mid-nineteenth century. And what will this tell us about Bill C-31 and the Mohawk Law on Membership?

Race and sex became meaningful categories for determining membership in the consciousness of Kahnawa'kehró:non when resources were threatened and Mohawks became "Indians." From the perspective of Kahnawa'kehró:non in 1850, white men outside the reserve had power and influence that could supersede the power and influence of a Mohawk outside of his community. Beyond the boundaries of the reserve was white society, and, with this social fact in mind we might infer that Kahnawa'kehró:non might not have wanted white men to affect the distribution of power within the society in Kahnawà:ke. Extinguishing the rights of Mohawk women may have been less of an attempt at discriminating against their own people than at protecting the community from a possible takeover by non-Indian men.

If these inferences are correct, it was Mohawk women who paid the legal price for some sort of broader political protection through their disenfranchisement and legal exile from their natal homes, which must have been an enormous cost to the traditional structure of the community given the clan-bearing, clan-transmitting, and property-owning status of women.[20] Iroquois women were the primary caregivers in the community; they raised the children, taught them their language, and ran the households when their men were away working. They also advised men on what to do in terms of the formal politics of the community.

The powerful role of women had been forgotten for some. After 140 years, the Indian Act had become woven tightly into the consciousness of many Kahnawa'kehró:non. Kahnawà:ke enforced Canada's rules with respect to the women who married non-Indians, because the rules had become useful to some, men in particular, and perhaps because the power of white men—represented through the seaway debacle, the person of the Indian agent, and other media—was still threatening.[21] These rules served their purposes in resource allocation and in the fomentation of a patri- lineally based, heteropatriarchal property regime on the reserve. This legal order also served the ascent of a sovereigntist state apparatus within the reserve, one that formed in response to a settler-colonial political order that was becoming more broad sweeping, governmentalized, and racializ- ing (Backhouse 1999). The effects of this sovereign influence might be that women who married non-Native men were still viewed as relatives, but as relatives who were "polluted"—who had gone outside the conceptual and legal borders of the reserve and, in doing so, had acquired the stigma of betrayal. The stigma was imprinted on them by Kahnawà:ke's fears of the world outside, the fears of the power white men may carry, and fears of the further dissolution of territory.

Abstracted to the contemporary era, women were now held responsible for their own predicament of disenfranchisement, rather than the system of ideas that governed race and gender-based exclusions by the state. After 1985, these women were reconceptualized and reduced in the imagination of Kahnawa'kehró:non to the legislation restoring their enfranchisement; they were called "C-31s," as were their children. The bill that legislated their return to Indian status has become their categorical identity within the community. Prominent among these women was the late Mary Two- Axe Early. In the 1950s Mary Two Axe married an Irish man and moved to Brooklyn, New York—living there throughout her married life. When her husband passed away, she attempted to move back to Kahnawà:ke and was blocked by the provisions of the Indian Act. Because she was no longer considered (legally) Indian, she was denied rights accorded to Indians: property ownership and residency on the reserve. Two Axe-Early quickly joined Verna Lovelace, a Maliseet from Tobique reserve in New Brunswick, in her battle against her band and then against the federal government (Barker 2008).

At the same time, Kahnawà:ke readied itself for the conflict over membership represented by nonstatus women. As early as 1972, community members were voicing their concerns over intermarriage. By that time, intermarriage with whites was associated with culture loss (Alfred 1995, 164). Therefore, marrying non-Indians was viewed as contributing to the erosion of Mohawk society and culture, a major concern of the community after a hundred years of aggressive assimilative efforts by the Canadian government (Milloy 2008).[22] By 1978 Kahnawà:ke had formed a committee to examine the problem of intermarriage and to look into the question of a membership policy. In 1981 the band council came up with three recommendations for the creation of a membership policy: "1. The eviction of non-Indians on the reserve; 2. A moratorium on mixed marriages; 3. Establishment of a biological measurement" (Alfred 1995, 165).

Evicting non-Indians from the reserve was the only recommendation that was not put into policy in 1981. Those in the community who did vote consented to the Moratorium on Mixed Marriages.[23] Effective May 22, 1981, any Mohawk who married a non-Indian lost his or her rights to residency, land ownership, voting, and office holding on the reserve (Alfred 1995, 165). Moreover, in 1984 the third recommendation was operationalized through the Mohawk Law on Membership, which came into effect that year. With this law, all people born to Mohawk parents after 1984 were to possess at least 50 percent blood quantum to be put on Kahnawà:ke's band list. This law clearly conflicted with the upcoming provisions of Bill C-31, which reinstated, on the federal register, the children of women who had lost their status in marriage. These children may have blood quantum below 50 percent if their mother was herself 50 percent. Therefore, the Mohawk Law on Membership was designed to exclude some who might return to the community as social outsiders, strangers who might then have rights to residency.

Bill C-31 was perceived from both inside and outside the community as jeopardizing jurisdiction and territory. It was from the socially and historically embedded nature of this threat that the issue of membership received its potency and its urgency. Today many believe that no matter what the personal circumstances of each person may be (and whether that person is your mother, brother, or cousin), the collective will of Kahnawa'kehró:non will decide which people in the future will have a right to live on the land and partake of the history that flows from it. This collectivist stance is clear in the abstracted text from the revised Kahnawà:ke Membership Law that appears in chapter 1. The community's history with Canada—perceived in cycles as foreign, imposing, and sometimes tolerable—is collapsed into disdain with the passage of Bill C-31. Canada was overstepping the boundaries of its relationship with Kahnawà:ke *again*. How could Canada tell Kahnawà:ke who should live in the community and who should not? How could Canada tell Kahnawà:ke who was Indian and who was not? The absurdity of this presumption from Canada propelled Kahnawa'kehró:non with dissension and discord that remain in the present, into their own moment of sovereign exception. And refusal.

Conclusion

I have presented this admittedly partial territorial and event-driven social history of the community in order to argue that the territorial history of the Mohawk nation shapes the central question of membership. Consequently, those factors also shape the methods that are then used to examine membership and nationhood. The voices within this book evidence the concern over the loss of territory and the loss of jurisdictional authority that motivate much of the membership debate. Much of this anxiety stems from the events of the past: of the historical injustice that Kahnawa'kehró:non have experienced as they watched their seigniorial land grant get smaller and smaller and as they engaged the state in opposition to the construction to the St. Lawrence Seaway. But these anxieties and politics also speak from the ethical and methodological problem of this history as it aligns or misaligns with issues and questions of recognition. How does one recognize the different factors of the problem, or recognize someone who speaks from this complicated past? The interlocutor "Richard" who opened up this chapter, we might say, speaks from this past, *is* of this past, and remains to me, so many years later, an indecipherable cipher of this complicated history. Others might say he is just not of the place that is being examined; he is of a temporality, of a past place. He simply cannot be known in a genealogical way by people who now sort these things out. Can you claim an identity or a membership within a political grouping if it does not claim you? This seems a thin composition of a much deeper question, and is often the way in which these questions get constructed in debates over Indigenous identity these days—identity actually gets conflated with one's sense of self, with one's "ancestral" recall of things (sometimes based on very strange and dubious evidence, family photos, cheekbones, etc.) without care for or commitment to the political reckoning system of the polity in question. My point is not to challenge this interlocutor's truth claim but to point out the way in which the narrative he provides highlights the very problem of settler colonialism, of fragmentation, of doubt. He did not seem to doubt himself one bit, and that is interesting, as there are people with deeply entrenched, genealogical connections who are under scrutiny, who are debated, who are disenfranchised.

He appears still to be out of the way, anomalous, and very compelling, but not for these reasons. Now, so many years after my interview with him, I think back to him as I continue to meet people who claim Indian identities in similar, very abstract, culturalist, or behaviorist ways, in ways that are actually not about political recognition or refusal but individualist self-fashioning. These claims of Indian identity do not rely on those political matrices of reckoning, the reckoning where people (more than one), know you before you know you. One might think most immediately to the controversy and confusion regarding claims to Cherokee heritage or descent on the part of Harvard law professor and Democratic U.S. Senator Elizabeth Warren. Further, regarding Harvard's purported "use" of her to evidence diversity: did she knowingly allow herself to be identified by them as a minority when she was a junior professor, regardless of what the Cherokee Nation or her family, her extended family, thought of this?[24] Was hers a proper mode of self-designation in light of Cherokee sovereignty and jurisdictional authority over membership? This question of origins, of self-identification, provided terrific fodder for conservative Republicans to malign her as disingenuous, fake, a false beneficiary of benefits that should accord to the "certifiable" or "truly" minoritized and, in this, statistically scarce. Again, this was all unfolding during her campaign for Senate. It all seems very American—invoking ancestry rather than Indian citizenship or membership, investing centrality in settler citizenship and political identity in one sovereignty (that of the United States) and then leaving that sovereignty intact, through her thin recourse to a family photo documenting the "cheekbones" of an ancestor as evidence of Cherokee specificity.[25] This fetishism of body parts serves as a paltry claiming tactic and substitution for Indigenous governance systems—charters, philosophical orders, normativities, and clans, living people of those places who would or would not know Warren. The mode of self-identification on the part of the Brooklyn interlocutor Richard seemed very American and thus vulnerable to a similar sort of scrutiny. My point is not to perform such a scrutinizing autopsy on his claim, rather to highlight it again as anomalous but also culturalist in its act of claiming ("this is the dialect my father spoke") in light of the place that he invokes and then questions that obtain to the claim.

Kahnawà:ke and many Kahnawa'kehró:non refuse these modes of self-fashioning, and part of this is because of its status as a place and a people both subjected to and yet distanced from the corpus of various forms of recognition, as a place of ongoing implicit and explicit refusals to even see themselves this way. More specifically, the community is "an out of the way place" in the context of the territorial history of the Iroquois, and, as we will see in the following chapter, more so in light of the written, very canonical, and anthropologically driven history about the Iroquois. Conceived as a village of "praying Indians"—as travelers, showmen (and women), and now ironworkers—Kahnawà:ke has *not* seized the ethnographic imagination the way that other Indigenous communities that are *more perfect, more culturally "intact,"* such as Six Nations or Tonawanda, have. In the following chapter, I will illustrate the ways in which early ethnology and later ethnography further constructed Kahnawà:ke as an "out-of-the-way place," and most specifically a place of impure "culture," rather than a site of vigorous political assertion and sovereignty.

THREE

Constructing Kahnawà:ke as an "Out-of-the-Way" Place

Ely S. Parker, Lewis Henry Morgan, and the
Writing of the Iroquois Confederacy

Kahnawà:ke and the Perversion of Tradition

What makes Kahnawà:ke knowable in a territory of ideas, in a
disciplinary form? What drives these representations, and what is
it about this body of knowledge that may see this community (and
thus people from it, their politics, their claims, their bodily form)
in particular ways? That knowledge has informed the understanding of "culture" rather than the scene of object formation—
ongoing land dispossession—and the very focused attention
(which results in an omission) that Kahnawà:ke receives as a distant place, as a place of impurity, and finally as cultural pathology.[1]
Here I want to move the understanding of settler colonialism into
the ambit of specific area studies so that we can see how Indigenous elimination holds hands with disciplinary formation, which
is evident in the way anthropology does or does not study particular "cultural" groups and why. The intent here is to understand
how we come to know or not know forms of difference, in the
geopolitical place of the present. How do we know these people?
How do we imagine them as insignificant; or as significant; or
significant in particular ways; or simply "different"? What moti-
vates these modes of knowledge construction? And how does this
construction *operate*, how does it function?

So far in this story, the politics of Kahnawa'kehró:non have
been embedded in a local and national Mohawk history whose

external politics are motivated by land expropriation and the formation of the settler regimes of New France, Quebec, and Canada. Issues relating to land expropriation and to jurisdiction and questions of political authority and autonomy are not unique to Kahnawà:ke or other Iroquois reservation communities. Yet the discussions within the community relating to issues of membership, jurisdiction, and autonomy *appear* unique (and we could argue, if we chose to, *anomalous*) when one tries to situate that history in the literature on the Iroquois. When we attempt to place, or even find Kahnawà:ke, within that literature, we find instead that the "data" on the community suggest contrivance, cultural invention, anomaly, and even pathology. Consider here an excerpt from a field report by the Tuscarora linguist and ethnologist J. N. B. Hewitt on his visit to Kahnawà:ke in 1928,

> At Caughnawaga [Kahnawà:ke] . . . I renewed my quest for any *definite knowledge* of the institutions of the League of the Iroquois on the part of the 17th Century emigrants from the Mohawk and other Iroquois tribes of the Colony of New York now living there. It was found that the Caughnawaga Indians have practically no *trustworthy* knowledge of the *structure* and the *institutions* of the ancient League. They have forgotten this *knowledge* so completely that, probably unwittingly, they have confused the ethical principles of civil government propounded by the founders of the League with the religious teachings of the Seneca prophet, Handsome Lake. This confusion of two distinct forms of *discipline,* in such ways that they have come to be regarded as essentially one and the same, has unfortunately resulted in a singular religious antagonism to them in the minds of these Christian converts. . . . These *perverted* views of the institutions of the League are most tenaciously held, the tenacity varying usually in inverse ratio to the probability of their truth. (Hewitt 1929, 179–80, emphasis mine)

There are several adjectives implied to cling tenaciously to Hewitt's nouns, and should be singled out for what they tell us about his views of Kahnawà:ke and of the tradition—or culture—under discussion, and then for what these views tell us about anthropology when he drafted his report. First, "trustworthy," as used to describe "knowledge," leads us to conclude that the Kahnawa'kehró:non that Hewitt spoke with were either unreliable or unable to concur in their accounts with the knowledge he already had. Hewitt would have collected this knowledge as a linguist among the Iroquois and most likely among Seneca informants at Tonawanda (his foundational account of the Iroquois creation story was published in the *American Anthropologist* in 1892). Second, their knowledge did not concur with the *particular* knowledge of *structure* and *institutions* that held sway at this time within anthropology. Third, that the Caughnawaga Indians had *forgotten* or *confused* the message of the Peacemaker with the Message of Handsome Lake and thus did not know the differences within their tradition as articulated by anthropologists. Fourth, this confusion made them *hostile* to the traditional beliefs of the Iroquois. Thus, people at Caughnawaga were somehow unreliable, forgetful, confused, hostile, and culturally *perverse* Indians. It is not my point here to lament the ways in which the anthropological gaze may have overlooked a culturally worthy community, or even to entertain the notion that this form of recognition is required for cultural integrity, or to suggest even that these early fieldwork reports are in fact, "history," or the only rendering of cultural history that matters. It is enough to flag Hewitt's discourse as one that is meaningful to anthropology but perhaps not very meaningful to the people of Kahnawà:ke (and in this, not very important at all to those who are interested in local and subaltern histories). Nevertheless, some questions very worth taking up are how Hewitt could have arrived at such a conclusion, what the anthropology was behind that conclusion, and what that then tells us—not necessarily about Kahnawà:ke, but about people who thought about Indians (some of whom were Indian themselves), and what that meant for the writing of history, ethnography, and the space between what is conceptualized and written and what is lived and experienced. It might be more politically salient to ask how those representations then effect political-life trajectories, perceptions, and political intelligibility for Kahnawa'kehró:non, and for Indigenous people more broadly, if anthropology is the primary way in which they are known. Although chapter 4 will demonstrate in broad strokes the manner in which the "Iroquois" have been constructed in particular ways (and how this has prompted a mode of writing in the present), here I will detail very precisely the history of how and why.

Anthropology is a practice of documentation, of theorization, of desire.[2] This chapter is concerned with those processes as they manifest in anthropological writing on the Iroquois. The intent here is not to rehearse the literature but to account for a scene of apprehension, to offer an account of the literature and a subsequent analysis that demonstrates the interruptive capacity of ethnography. I begin by identifying and discussing the philosophical and theoretical underpinnings of historical and anthropological writing on the Iroquois. I then consider those theories as they were put into practice, in the moments when ethnology itself and the Iroquois came into disciplinary being—what I call scenes of apprehension—that were predicated on social and political relationships. The relationship between Ely S. Parker and Lewis Henry Morgan and their project of writing on the Iroquois, *The League of the Iroquois* (Morgan [1851] 1996), is critical to this moment of arrival. This seminal text introduces us to the dominant themes and trends that will assemble into a canon of writing on the Iroquois.

What this story demonstrates is that the literature on the Iroquois is a realization of early anthropological desire—a desire for order, for purity, for fixity, and for cultural perfection that at once imagined an imminent disappearance immediately after or just within actual land dispossession. This realization is found in the *authenticating discourse* on culture and history that permeates the literature. I am interested here in investigating the ways in which the literature on the Iroquois, from the work of Lewis Henry Morgan to the present, has labored to authenticate early ethnographic assertions and place the Iroquois within Western epistemes. This research loop seeks to confirm an early Iroquois "cultural pattern" and has been assembled into a regulatory body of literature, a rigid *canon* of literature whose shape and content is defined according to the disciplinary taste and practice of its early, key contributors. We will find that in their project to confirm the veracity of early reports on the Iroquois, scholars have taken an unproblematized and narrow model of "tradition" as their unit of analysis. The product is this canonical body of literature that, in its narrowness, is removed from the bulk of the people that it purports to represent.

The chapter seeks to reveal the historical and anthropological processes that placed the Iroquois within a frame of desire and continues, tirelessly, to write of them as if they were still at the first scenes of their arrival in the anthropological imagination. "The Iroquois" of the literature have been as much about their anthropologists as they have been about "culture." Thus, in its conclusion, this chapter points toward a different tradition in Iroquois study, one that is respectful of the value of things that precede the present, but endeavors to move the Iroquois to a future that is not bound so inextricably to the desires of others. Thus, in this chapter I will map out a history of ideas about the Iroquois in order to revisit *in a different register* and in a focused manner the very specific ways in which *desire* operates in the production of anthropological knowledge and weds elegantly, effortlessly, and very cleanly with the imperatives of settler colonial projects predicated upon a desire for territory.

From "Pattern to Process and Back Again": Backstreaming and the Troubled Language of Tradition in Anthropology

> The area [Northeast] is still rich in problems despite the fact that its aboriginal peoples have either long since disappeared or retain only a tantalizingly small part of their old culture. (Fenton 1940, 165)

One of the dominant themes on writing about the Iroquois has been the search for stability and coherence as anthropological subjects, subjects that exist within the anthropological world in a patterned and orderly way (Sapir 1927; Fenton 1940; Voget 1984, 348–53).[3] This search for stability has led analysts from the very dawn of Iroquois literature to fixate on tradition as their unit of analysis. Tradition suited the theoretical approach of early "annalists,"[4] because it appeared to be an instance of cultural stability and cultural difference, two preconditions for anthropological inquiry of the time. The tradition that "Iroquoian" analysts have seized upon, however, is one that grew as a result of acculturative and colonial forces (Linton 1936, 1940; Voget 1951; Freilich 1958), rather than one that was implicit, unassumed, and "authentic."[5]

Depending on the theoretical approach of the analyst, the distance of tradition from its precontact base may either render it a construct (when generous) (Hobsbawm and Ranger 1983) or a deviation (when disappointed) (Hanson 1989). If situated into a theory of culture that is processual, that takes meaning and the workings of power into account, then it is neither; it is a symptom of a moment of conjuncture, a response to expectation, a form of inward redress. Culture in this context has been rendered a fetish and not treated with attention to the context of its origin, as with any form of knowledge or practice. Nadia Abu El-Haj analyzes the salience and staying power of these reified traditions through the notion of "resonance," a form of authority that allowed for the working and reworking of the Orientalist canon over long periods of time, specifically "the (discursive) context within which both innovations occur" (2005, 544–45). This is a close reading of Said's work, in particular, Abu El-Haj's disaggregation of Edward Said's form of historicism and critique from the central tenets of this literature on tradition in anthropology—a literature that took some inspiration from him.[6]

Tradition has been the central occupation of the Iroquois literature, but this is not limited to the objects of inquiry, their culture; it is also the preoccupation and practice of ethnological subjects, self-consciously "traditional people." But this literature has not taken up the fields of that traditions articulation, the self-consciousness and necessity of performing particular forms of knowledge for particular people—the context of its articulation, as Abu el-Haj has argued. There has been a vibrant "tradition" of having a tradition among Iroquois people since they first became a subject of historical and anthropological reflection. This form of "backstreaming"[7]—of viewing the present through periods and points of the past that are deemed relevant or especially meaningful—has been at work in communities for at least as long as there has been a need to index the past to deal with the present (and is therefore not limited to the Iroquois, as the following discussion will illustrate). The Iroquois' own backstreaming is evident in the Code of Handsome Lake, or the Karihwí:io,[8] the "new religion" that altered previous culture codes to deal with the changing political and economic landscape caused by white settlement (Wallace 1978, 442–48).

A question that arises from the practice of backstreaming is whether this was a strategic cultural innovation or was representative of Iroquois notions of time. Horatio Hale's translation of Mohawk and Onondaga condolence texts in his nineteenth-century work *The Iroquois Book of Rites* (1883) suggests that Iroquois government may offer some insight into their sense of time. The process of mourning the death of a chief and installing a new one in his place regenerated the Confederacy with every passing, and created an appearance of seamlessness and continuity in the political system, without the stops and starts of charismatic or elected leadership systems. Hale translated this system of title holding for his readers as "the chief dies but the office survives" (1883, 68), allowing the chiefs to occupy stable structural positions in spite of the different personalities and histories of titleholders.

William Fenton's later discussion of Iroquois time hinges on ritual, calendric, and ecological imperatives; ecology shaped the Iroquois sense of time (1978b, 300). After reconstructing the annual lunar and agricultural cycle of the Iroquois, Fenton concluded that the festivals that mark the time to plant, harvest, and hunt owe their life to the "Handsome Lake Religion" (ibid., 301). The adoption of the "new religion" invigorated Iroquois relationships with their landscape and their past. These notions of time put forth by Hale and Fenton are not in any way inconsistent with the notion of backstreaming. This strategy preserved the ideas, structures, and practices that amalgamate into "tradition" in ways that appear to invigorate and conserve culture and identities deemed necessary in the political present. Thus backstreaming and the elements of time that it chose to preserve rendered the Iroquois ideal subjects of anthropological analysis (and, at times, very unruly subjects of the state). However, most important to the discussion at hand was that the Iroquois "tradition of having a tradition" was the very thing that anthropologists desired. It was the very thing they lacked, or seemed to lack—a culture unambiguously connected to the places they lived upon. The Iroquois culture that appeared to them had a wholeness and stability, patterned into ritualized practices that were both intelligible to outsiders and appeared to be in jeopardy of being lost (Morgan [1851] 1996, 444–61; Deloria 1998).

Anthropological work on the Iroquois has fixed upon intelligibility, cultural pattern, and persistence, that which is clearly discernible to outsiders. This tendency has led to an agenda of research that has rendered meaningless any elements of culture that appeared familiar to the Western eye, or culturally anomalous to outsiders, ignoring those processes that might be meaningful to insiders but unintelligible to outsiders. As a result, the Iroquois canon—the textual atrophy of anthropological desires of the nineteenth century and early twentieth for wholeness, purity, pattern, and preservation—is constructed from what is discernible to an outside eye: procedure, hierarchy, and structure.

The process of evaluating topics and texts in the Iroquois project would not be a troubling one if the Iroquois canon dealt in the currency of fictional practice, if it comprised literary works that lay outside the realm of actual people and events. In such a case, the elevation of a body of texts by agreed-upon standards of taste and refinement is somewhat understandable. It is troubling, however, that such a process of evaluation has occurred in the context of Iroquois research and that similar values have been assigned to accounts of "culture." Culture is a theory and a set of meanings, processes, and practices that are both shared and contested; it is not a matter to be assigned a value nor is it to be adjudicated. Asserting that the Iroquois literature has been assembled into a canon is not to argue that tradition (reified or not) is not valued by contemporary Iroquois people, or devalued by their historical antecedents.[9] Rather, what I am arguing is that there is a disjuncture between the "tradition" and "culture" of Iroquois people and the "tradition" at work in the canon of Iroquois studies. However flexible and meaningful (and vexed, no doubt) tradition is in Iroquois day-to-day experience, the tradition of the literature is narrow and procedural.

The literature on the Iroquois operates according to tight, discursively controlled, theoretically delimited, and canonical imperatives. In other words, the theory of culture is one of an ultimately discernible cultural pattern, the unit of analysis is tradition, and the rest (according to this logic) is epistemologically unrecognizable. Research topics, papers, and books, *versions of history* and event, are admitted to or rejected from the ethnological body based on an epistemological logic of rendering matter, appearance, and data that are assimilable or unassimilable to the ethnologic eye, and the kind of difference that matters. Fredric Jameson's "political unconscious" (1981) is helpful here as it points to something besides a conscious point of accumulation for what can appear as data to the conscious mind.[10] With Jameson's recourse to the psychoanalytics of narrative and apprehension,[11] we can see why something will come to appear to gain salience, why, in this example, a version of tradition becomes so desirable, so fetishized. We must, however, account for this reasoning in relation to settlement, an ongoing structure of dispossession that targets Indigenous peoples for elimination, a structure that shapes discernibility and the desire for discernibility.

Things, people, and matters that could not be assimilated to the ethnologic eye and mind at certain times could not be apprehended, or were simply discounted because the eyes and ears that apprehended them were narrowed and tuned to see and hear certain things.[12] The narrowness of these approaches has strained the relationship between the Iroquois and academics well beyond the ethnographic and into interpretations of the Iroquois past.[13] Such "strains"[14] arise in the literature because the historical paradigms of anthropology and archaeology demand "an objectivist history" (Landsman and Ciborski 1992, 445). There are politics and sensibilities that shape these demands: settler populations that now sit on these territories without any sense of their historicity, without any sense of a prior ownership, of forced relocation; the conditions of reservationization; and in the case of General Sullivan's campaign through Seneca territory in the eighteenth century, terrible bloodshed.

Yet in the afterword to James Axtell's book *After Columbus* (1988), the historian's reflection upon Indigenous and settler pasts and explicit exposition on the writing of history contains all of this, even where it is supposed to narrate it, and it does so by defining what counts and who will count it. Axtell defines and defends "objectivist history" as the task of the historian, as the service that he performs for Indians and for knowledge production. Here he argues, "The historian's first and most important duty, therefore, is to ascertain the full and complicated truth about his subjects and to present it as clearly, forcefully, and impartially as he can" (ibid., 244). Axtell's exposition of the job of the historian cements our understanding of the dominant paradigm of knowing and writing the past in Iroquois studies. It is interesting and instructive for what it says about this objectivist position in the relational process of knowing that past and the people who inherit it. Axtell assigns Indians a very limited space in the production of knowledge. Their role in the research, writing, and knowing enterprise is one of suggestion box, as "people who can suggest important questions that non-Indians might never raise because of ethnic, temporal, professional, or other brands of myopia" (ibid., 246). Whether this "suggestion" can actually set a research agenda is never discussed. Further, since "native people can seldom provide answers, they are uniquely qualified to raise questions that the historian may wish to pursue in the ethnohistorical record" (ibid.). Aside from the staggering racism and ahistoricity of Axtell's supporting point,[15] there is a commitment to facts that appear to lie outside Indian purview and beyond Indian access. The critical point in this exposition and definition of an objectivist history is its necessarily "narrowing" field of vision that lies within the late twentieth century, where he argues, "In the end, only this record—written and archeological, oral and artistic—can give us reliable answers about the past, native or European" (ibid.).[16]

These are frameworks that have shaped the methodology of research into an authenticating loop that seeks only to confirm early accounts of Iroquois cultural practice and history. Thus the methods of history, linguistics, ethnography, and archaeology are enlisted to confirm and affirm earlier accounts of Iroquois life. This industry of fact checking has created a body of ethnological knowledge that has circumscribed the Iroquois past (and present) to the domain of white prescience. As well, it has created a limited semantic and ideological space for contemporary Iroquois people to inherit. It has ignored social history, ignored (for the most part) mainstream political process, and, in so doing, ignored the bulk of Iroquois experience. When desire and fetishized authenticity set the research agenda, as it has in the case of the Iroquois literature, it places the analyst in a position of cultural appraisal (and ownership) rather than analysis.[17]

This Island, This History on the Iroquois' Back: Early Ethnology and Writing on the Iroquois

The Iroquois surely had a history before Lewis Henry Morgan. But it is with him that their ethnological life had its start, so their history appears to begin with him.[18] Yet it is to Ely S. Parker that Lewis Henry Morgan owed this ethnographic life, so this discussion of the literature he sparked will begin with the two of *them*. When Lewis Henry Morgan wrote *The League of the Iroquois* in 1851, he dedicated the book to Ely S. Parker, "a Seneca Indian," and inscribed the book for posterity as a product of their "joint researches." The joint researches to which he referred had their start in a chance encounter between the Indian student and the white lawyer in 1844. This bookshop meeting in Albany, New York, resulted in an anthropological classic that changed the practice and face of anthropology as well as the Iroquois for years to come.

Although the Parker-Morgan dialogues took place long ago, they are interesting to us for reasons that belong very much in the present. Their dialogues excite questions regarding the construction and maintenance of scholarly knowledge, the construction of an anthropological and an Iroquois canon, and the construction of tradition (both scholarly and Iroquois) through such a process. The dialogues tell us much as well about the relational basis of knowledge in early ethnology. Before discussing this "canon," however, we have to understand Morgan and Parker within their respective times. We have to put them in their place.

Morgan and Parker were both from places of dispossession and possession, and it is for that reason, perhaps, that they were drawn to each other. They were each within societies that were undergoing rapid change, but this change was hinged completely on the processes of land loss. These economic, ideological, and political changes provided fertile ground for both to value that which they regarded as unchanging and instructive: "tradition." The tradition that Parker would turn to was that of the Karihwí:io, the Code of Handsome Lake, a revitalization and reinterpretation of the "Old Religion" of his own people. Morgan's tradition was law, precedent, and legal order, as well as something that he at first could not find, something elusive—the question of origins. How was it that he was there, where he was, in Aurora, New York? He arrived at his own tradition, one of rational and scientific inquiry (ethnology), through the Iroquois, through his study of their ways, and through his relationship with Ely S. Parker. Their relationship—negotiated through the idioms of inquiry, science, and sport—created the beginnings of the American anthropology of today.

American anthropology was born, in part, from mimetic play. The science that captivated Morgan was ethnology, but he had to make it. And this making was born from the literally inventive activities of "playing Indian," of approximating Indianness. Of donning the garb, writing speeches, doing as one thinks Indians do (or, rather, did) in that particular time. Morgan's excitement with meeting Ely Parker was prompted by his activities with a hobbyist club in Aurora, New York, called the Gordian Knot. In its earliest stages the Gordian Knot was modeled upon quasi-Iroquoian principles and practices that were removed from the experiences and structure of the living Iroquois in the surrounding areas. Nonetheless, the Gordian Knot (with its realist and representational deficiencies), served as a structural and temporal link between the past and present for its members.

In order to situate Morgan properly, we must ask questions about these playgroups. Why did they choose Indians to imitate, and what was the function of their mimetic play? In his history of Indian playgroups in the United States, Philip Deloria traces their genesis to a broader cusp of American modernity. Here Deloria argues that the hobbyists were articulating ambivalences and fears about industrialization and the loss of a raced, white manliness associated with the taming of the frontier (1998, 95–127). After the Revolutionary War, the new "Americans" sought to create an identity, a home, and a history for themselves in the states. However, their "roots" clearly lay elsewhere, and this was deeply problematic for them as they saw "evidence" of others where they were—arrowheads and pottery shards that suggested very strongly that they were not the first to be there. This was not their place. The problematic of how they were to make themselves at home in their new place was reflected in their struggle to create for themselves a literature and art that reflected an "American" style that was produced by Americans (C. Walker 1997, 6–7; Deloria 1998, 75). It was to satisfy their need to be at home, to have a historical link with the past of the new place, rather than to be "immigrants" or "settlers." It was *against* their notion of "the Indian" that they constructed their new identity and nationhood as Americans (Pearce 1953; Berkhofer 1978), but it was with the adornment and then the capturing study of the Iroquois that they created ethnology, the early study of "cultural" difference.

The Gordian Knot, a protoscientific society of propertied white men in upstate New York, attempted to make a history and a literature for themselves. In its earliest stages, the Knot served as an occasion to recite poetry and provided members with a forum to develop their new national history and literature. In order for this project to take off, Morgan had to embed the new history within a context, one that was very much like the structural dilemma within which he found himself. Thus the mythic charter of the Knot was temporally and geographically divided into an "old world" and a "new world." Morgan translated this into an "Old World Gordius" of the distant past and placed his participants within the New World, as Iroquois. Divided into these two epochs, Morgan's group now had what they needed, "to establish the historical framework for [the creation of] an epic national history" (Deloria 1998, 77). This history was broken into perceived epochs of Iroquois history—a past occupied by deceased Iroquois that was then linked to the New World history of living settlers. Creating a place for the settlers-as-Indians, Morgan's scheme was premised entirely on the notion of the Iroquois as a vanishing people.

More than mere playgroups, these fraternities and clubs were crucial factors in the indigenization of the "New World" peoples, of Euro-Americans, through the selective deployment of signs and symbols of Indians.[19] This incorporative process offered a psychic resolution for the settlers, a solution to the problematic of how they were to make sense of the space that they inhabited and of their relationships to those people who had preceded them in this space. Through the incorporation of Indian signs and symbols, the hobby group created the mythic connection with a place and past in what was previously, unambiguously Indian territory.

Morgan and his forefathers were a part of the symbolic and physical settlement of New York State. However, the mysticism of the Gordian Knot was fast supplanted by the rigor of science, when the actual, bodily Iroquois appeared to him in the form of Ely S. Parker. With the processing of an actual Indian, Morgan transformed himself from lawyer/hobbyist to ethnologist/scientist, and the Gordian Knot went from playgroup to Indian support group/amateur ethnological society. Upon meeting the actual Iroquois, Parker, and his family at Tonawanda, the reconstruction of them as real people, with very real issues, began. In dealing with corporeal, sentient, very real Iroquois, Morgan traded one belief system, that of romanticism, for another, science. The Seneca then pivoted between the categories of "informants," "collaborators," and perhaps even "friends." More than anything, they became talking testaments of the Iroquois past, of a purer, better time. They were the keys to Morgan's first ethnological study, *The League of the Iroquois,* as well as to the ethnological, linguistic, and anthropological studies that followed in his footsteps. "The society did much to place Ely's Brother Nick and his sister Carrie in the State Normal school in Albany and *finally led Morgan with Parker* to write the *League of the Iroquois,* a book that has become classic wherever Indian books are known. This book was the first detailed description of an Indian tribe ever written and has made the name of Lewis H. Morgan imperishable" (A. Parker 1919, 81, emphasis added).[20]

One can only imagine how Ely Parker processed the white man who walked over to him in the Albany bookshop and immediately asked him if he was an Indian. Parker was sixteen at the time and in Albany to represent and interpret for the Tonawanda chiefs. The chiefs wanted a repeal of the Buffalo Creek Treaty signed between the Seneca and US federal government in 1838. Although some Seneca signed the treaty, dubious circumstances had attended this event; there was talk of alcohol and accusations of misrepresentation. Confederacy procedures for making such agreements with foreign nations were not honored, and the treaty was declared illegal by the Seneca, who faced further dissolution of their land base and removal to Kansas if the treaty were upheld.[21] Other young, educated Seneca before Parker had been critical in negotiations between the state and the Seneca, during both the signing (and resistance to the signing) of the treaty and the tumultuous years that followed (Littlefield 1996, 83–84; Vernon 1985). In their struggle to persuade their people to adopt one position or another in relation to removal, they wrote polemical tracts and speeches that have been identified as the dawn of Seneca literature (Littlefield 84, 99).

Ely Parker is a foundational writer in the body of Iroquois literature (by Iroquois); yet much of that writing is embedded in the texts of others or is addressed to others in the form of correspondence. It is because of this that we will never know what Parker thought to himself when Morgan approached him and asked if he was an Indian. What remains of his writing takes the form of letters to Morgan, to friends, and to family. The precious fragment of his own manuscript on the Iroquois totals seven pages. Much of his writing, perhaps the most important part, remains embedded within Morgan's text.[22]

Parker remains as much enframed in the lives of important white men as his own writing does. There are two book-length studies of his life (Parker 1919; Armstrong 1978), a biographical chapter on him in Liberty's *American Indian Intellectuals* (Tooker 1978c, 15–32), a chapter on his career in the civil war in Laurence Hauptman's *The Iroquois in the Civil War* (1993), and an analysis of his League writings in Michaelsen's article in the *American Literary History* (1996). Joseph Genetin-Pilawa has done recent and important work on his life and policy vision as the head of the Bureau of Indian Affairs (BIA), within the broader period of "Reconstruction" in American history and close analysis of the Buffalo Creek Treaty and of Parker's post-Morgan work as the commissioner of Indian affairs (2012). With the exception of Michaelsen's piece, most of the work details and discusses the important events in Parker's life, without considering his own reflections and correspondence and its significance to anthropological thought. The question of his role in the writing of the *League* and the dynamics of his life contained in the biographies tell us more, of course, about his accomplishments than we will find in the works on Morgan. From the biographies we learn of his own position in Seneca society, as well as about the unfolding of his careers in law, engineering, and war. Yet except for Michaelsen's, none of these works takes up his authorial role in the production of the *League*.

These textual traces are important for anthropologists because they lead back to the Confederacy itself, to the textual and historical imperatives for constructing and recording tradition, and to the Iroquois of ethnologic and ethnographic imagination. Armstrong tells us that, upon meeting Parker, Morgan returned to his hotel room and asked questions of the Seneca delegation for "as long as propriety would admit" (Fenton [1962] 1996, x). The timing and circumstances of their meeting could not have been better for either, since each represented the desires and lacks of the other. From his mother, Parker belonged to the "chiefly" line of the Seneca. Ely Parker was the grandnephew of Handsome Lake,[23] the prophet of the "new religion" and would eventually hold the chiefly title and name of Donehogawa, or Keeper of the Western Door. As well, he was the nephew of Red Jacket, an orator and pine tree chief,[24] who resisted the teachings of the Prophet (Parker 1919, 216; 1998, 54; Armstrong 1978, 8). Both Handsome Lake and Red Jacket were matrilineal ancestors of Parker, and both were important figures in Iroquois society of their time, as well as in the history that has since been written about the Iroquois.[25]

Although Parker was only sixteen when he met Morgan, he was in a unique position within his own society to mediate and negotiate Morgan's demands for knowledge as well as the demands for reparation that his own people placed upon him vis-à-vis white society, demands that we can take also to be desires (Tooker 1978c, 19–23). He was an interpreter and negotiator for his people; a "cultural broker" who mediated the interchange of peoples and cultures (Hagedorn 1988, 61). But in his relations with very important white men, first Lewis Henry Morgan and then Ulysses S. Grant, he represented, in many ways, the model of a "good Indian" who would not only interpret and mediate the larger question of culture but also serve as a baseline for their knowledge and identity construction. Here a "good Indian" is an Indian that does not threaten white people, is knowledgeable about his/her culture and history, and is forthcoming about that knowledge with white people. This notion of a good Indian has been put to work in popular history (Francis 1991), but has not been refined further as a trope or as a term that migrates through time, shifts meanings, and affects materiality in any way. This notion has not been tied to analysis of actual political and military processes. Nonetheless, it may be argued that Parker appeared as a good Indian, unlike other individual Native people of the time—such as Crazy Horse, Big Bear, or Chief Joseph—who would embark on military campaigns to defend their territories against white settlement. Parker and the Seneca took legal and political channels to deal with their dissipating land base. Their position in relation to settlers was clearly one of subjugation.

Space does not permit me to detail the historical factors that positioned the Seneca as a subjugated people within the imaginary of American statehood prior to this important meeting between Morgan and Parker in 1844;[26] however, it is clear that these factors are the very ones that positioned Parker as a mediator who would not threaten or topple the ongoing project of settler statehood, but would in fact argue, within the laws laid down by that state, for justice. This is not the case with Geronimo. Suffice it to say that the Seneca were profoundly weakened after Sullivan's army burned their villages, destroyed their crops, and felled their orchards in 1779 (Fenton 1998, 104). The Congress at Fort Stanwix was signed in 1784 and then at Canandaigua in 1794; the first represented a punitive settlement and the second an agreement of peace and friendship (Fenton 1998, 15). Nonetheless, the Seneca lost most of their territory after the American Revolution, a total that Hauptman places at 95 percent of their original land base (ibid., 5). The following period in Seneca history is understood by Fenton as "a scene of social disorder, loss of political power, and personal despair" (ibid., 104).[27] This was a time that was ripe for Handsome Lake's message of reform and rejuvenation in 1799. The Seneca were militarily denuded, and the "Confederacy" underwent its reformulation from a spiritual and political governing structure to a social and symbolic one. In this context, the Iroquois appeared markedly different from the settlers, who subjugated and dispossessed the Iroquois. They were ideal candidates for ethnographic contemplation.[28] They would then meet Morgan in the safe social space cleared by hobbyist curiosity, scientific inquiry, and land expropriation. In this respect, the timing was perfect for American anthropology and the Parker-Morgan relationship. The Seneca he met appeared to Morgan to be remnants of a vanishing people, and Parker was an exceptional representative of the lost possibility for which the Seneca stood. He was a knowledgeable and useful repository of (and key to) cultural knowledge. As well, he was an Indian, someone who would be ranked in Morgan's ethnological scale of order as "barbarian,"[29] whose humanity could then be recognized and affirmed by the trappings of Western civilization: education and then employment.

Building a Literary Canon with Science: The *League* and Its Successors

"The idea of Indian social grades with titles is all a vain and foolish fancy of the early imaginative writers, who were educated to believe in such things; and the idea is retained, used and still disseminated by our modern susceptibles that love and adore rank and quality and that give and place them where none is claimed" (Ely S. Parker in A. Parker 1919, 216). The collaboration between Parker and Morgan for the purposes of research (as well as their friendship) links power to the production of texts in early ethnographic encounters. Such encounters are of special interest to us for what they say about the registers and circuits of knowledge that accompany European colonialism and settlement. Intercultural interactions and their texts also tell us something about the history of Indigenous peoples and their unique place within settler societies.[30] Literary analysts argue that we must take these texts very seriously for reasons that are extremely compelling but somewhat shortsighted. Nonetheless, in following this line of argument, in order to "recover unheard voices" and appreciate what the archives often neglect, intercultural interactions such as that between Morgan and Parker (and "minority discourses" in general) offer us a voice and a story that represents a "Native perspective" regarding processes of colonialism and settlement in the New World.[31]

In taking the lives and stories of individuals such as Parker seriously, more is to be gained than merely "hearing-a-formally-unheard-voice." If we take from literary analysts the notion of "recovery" and make it a part of the process of knowing the past, or "recovering the past," the project of history is expanded. At that point of expansion, we can enfold within "history" its many producers and many texts: slavery narratives, creation stories, that which was assumed to be unscientific or spurious.[32] This expansion, I will argue later, is the matter of a history that can stand in the present. The stories of the Parkers are alternatives, of a sort, to the dominant discourses of literature and history *only* in that they are Indian stories, and Indian stories for the most part have not really mattered much. They may also be regarded as alternatives only if they are viewed as a matter to be teased from dominant discourses, a "hidden transcript" within a story of society (J. Scott 1990). But the stories and the lives of the Parkers are also part of an elite discourse, and as such are a dominant history within a history. Their *particular* Indian story has mattered greatly, as it adhered to what Indian stories were supposed to be within the settler imagination: stories of structure and stories of tradition. In adhering to what they should be, their story forms the metanarrative of Iroquois people; it is key in the production of a canonical way of knowing and transcribing the Iroquois past. The knowledge that Parker possessed is articulated to other pasts, such as European settlement, that are also charged by distributions and relationships of power and, in this, to the project of settlement. Before continuing with the Parkers and the history that they created with the help of anthropology, I want to examine briefly the notion of Native narrativity and tradition. Robert Allen Warrior describes the examination of Native texts and discourses as a "way of privileging neglected voices and strategies." In this, the consideration of these texts is for him and for others, part of a larger project of identifying literary, intellectual, and political traditions that can help Native people and other subaltern peoples to deal with contemporary challenges (Warrior 1995, xxi; see also Michaelsen 1996; Littlefield 1996; Alfred 1999). Similar to Warrior's very contemporary project, Ely S. Parker's was also part of the search for a tradition to cope with the present while preserving the past—a form of the backstreaming mentioned earlier.[33] However, unlike Warrior, his voice is, on a certain baseline level of representation—that of the *Western* canon and the formal Iroquois record—clearly unheard. Although he and his family were the progenitors of a dominant discourse on tradition and history, his "voice" remains contained within the offices of translation and subsumed in the discourses of science. It is obviously understudied, possibly uncredited, and then strangely muted by the formal history that surrounds his relationship with Lewis Henry Morgan and *The League of the Iroquois*.[34] However, rather than relegate him to the limited space of resurrection in the name of "recovering a lost voice" or "recentering the margin," he must be situated within the traditions that he clearly created or transmitted: writing on the Iroquois and of the Karihwí:io, or Good Message of Handsome Lake. When resituated into his familial and cultural context, Parker emerges as a designer and author of culture, rather than a subaltern whose discourse must be disentangled and teased from a metanarrative of domination.

The Parker of the chiefly line of the Seneca, but of a new sort that exercised power with pen and paper in hand, was on a mission in Albany to get the Buffalo Creek Treaty repealed. It is in this context that his response to Morgan's queries makes sense. Morgan immediately set about asking the Tonawanda chiefs in Albany with Parker about the structure of the League, the number of chiefs that the Seneca sent to Confederacy meetings, and the names of the clans, which he called "tribes," in the *League* (Morgan [1851] 1996, 79–82). So impressed was Morgan with the new information that Parker and his family offered that he immediately made changes in the mythostructure of his other life. He changed the name of the Gordian Knot to reflect that the knowledge he had gathered and his society became more specified, the "Cayuga" branch of the "Grand Order of the Iroquois." Morgan then made Parker an honorary member of his group (Resek 1960, 30) and published his findings as the "Vision of Kar-is-ta-gi-a, a sachem of Cayuga" (Tooker 1983, 144; Trautmann 1987, 47). Of the key meeting in the Morgan-Parker relationship, William Fenton would later write in his introduction to the 1962 edition of the *League* that "American ethnology was born in a hotel room" (1996, x).

I would argue rather that American ethnology was born from the desires of each protagonist in the writing of the Iroquois past: Morgan grapples with American modernity and Parker with land losses. Each protagonist in the writing of the ethnological Iroquois saw his nation undergo terrific changes, and each himself underwent a transformative process. As a result of these processes, Morgan and Parker had to manage the wants and needs of not only their own people but themselves. So on a certain level, American anthropology (and Iroquois studies) showed its face in a hotel room, but much more was at work in getting that face in there. The literature that follows on the meeting between Morgan and Parker was shaped by their intercultural dialogue. And as we will see shortly, subsequent literature bears the traces of those historical and political agendas and their interests. Such critical context for the *League* has been ignored or elided by the scholarship that it prompted. Nonetheless, the initial interaction allows for a consideration of the Confederacy tradition by scholars interested in Iroquois culture, society, and history and, quite ironically, by the living Iroquois of today.

Patterns in the Literature on the Iroquois: Defining the Canon

At this point, we are ready to turn our attention to the literary heritage that both is and is not Parker's: the "canon" of Iroquois studies. *The League of the Iroquois* ([1851] 1996) is the first ethnological record of the history, structure, and procedure of the Iroquois and, as such, set the standard for works to come. There are many other studies that elaborate on the work of Morgan, but the most important and influential works in Iroquois studies may be narrowed to seven texts that followed on Morgan's trail. These works cemented the ethnological approach, while carrying Iroquois studies to new levels and into other disciplines. Here we find Horatio Hale's edition of *The Iroquois Book of Rites* (1883); Arthur C. Parker's *The Code of Handsome Lake, The Seneca Prophet* (1913) and *The Constitution of the Five Nations or The Iroquois Book of the Great Law* ([1916] 1967); William N. Fenton's program for research "Problems Arising from the Historic Northeastern Position of the Iroquois" (1940); Annemarie Anrod Shimony's ethnography *Conservatism among the Iroquois at the Six Nations Reserve* ([1961] 1994); Anthony F. C. Wallace's history *The Death and Rebirth of the Seneca* ([1969] 1972); and, finally, William N. Fenton's history *The Great Law and the Longhouse: A Political History of the Iroquois* (1998).

Before discussing how these particular works are canonical, let us first take up the question of "canon." What are the forces that attach value to certain works and devalue others? Or, what makes for a canon? In particular, what makes these works canonical in such a large ethnological body of literature? John Guillory offers some illuminating lessons on the origin of "canon" from literary history. In his essay "Canon" (1995) Guillory tells us that the contemporary meaning of "canon" is derived from the Greek word *kanon,* meaning reed, rod, or instrument of measurement. The meaning of canon evolved through time from an instrument of measurement to mean those texts that were deemed valuable or worthy of preserving.

The above-mentioned works are canonical because they are highly influential and can be found in most bibliographies within Iroquois studies. However, this does not answer the question of how the canon was formed—the process of valuation and devaluation that follows a published work. We will find that each canonical work elaborates Morgan's approach in a way that cements and then amplifies the original, ethnological project. Kuper defines ethnology as the "comparative study and classification of peoples, based on conditions of material culture, language, and religious and social institutions and ideas, as distinguished from physical characters. The influence of environment upon culture" (Kuper 1996, 3). In the canon of Iroquois literature, the commitment to ethnology, and to documentation, authentication,[35] has remained constant to the present day. The emphasis has been on isolating historical, material, and linguistic variables for the twin purposes of documenting forms of "vanishing" cultures and then comparing them to earlier versions of themselves (via Morgan) and others.[36] This approach persisted into the 1970s even though Iroquois people and culture did not vanish and there is little to no cross-cultural comparison in the field.

As anthropology was a discipline premised upon cultural difference, we find that those scholarly factors that shape the canonical works are underpinned by very important relations between Iroquois and white. With the exception of Fenton's 1940 program, each canonical work rests upon Iroquois people who shifted between the registers of "collaborator," "friend," and "informant" in relation to their white, and sometimes Iroquois, ethnographers. The question of whether those relationships were acknowledged, celebrated, or suppressed factors into the value that is attached to each work.

We may now ask how an underpinning relationship with an Iroquois person (or persons) factors into the influence and authority of a work. Are there not other factors that elevate or diminish the power and influence of a text than this underlying business of relations? Yes and no. In typical anthropological fashion, value is attached to texts by the factors of *distance* and *difference.* In this, the space that the researcher placed between himself/herself and the culture and people that s/he studied was critical. Iroquois ethnological texts enjoy greater influence as they appear *closer* to Iroquois culture. Yet, as anthropology fancied itself a science of man—one governed by notions of objectivity, one that aimed to produce replicable results—that difference was closed by closeness and mediated by something, or someone. Hence the important role played by the (Iroquois) interlocutor (informant, collaborator, friend), while the writer (either Iroquois or non-Iroquois) remains *distant* or *different* from that culture. The text is thus most valuable when it is mediated and its interlocution performed by the purest representative of what science was after: an instructive symbol of precontact history.

How do these factors of value and devalue then shape the "canon" of Iroquois studies? The *League* owes itself to the cultural mediation and translation of Morgan's Seneca collaborator and friend, Ely S. Parker, a condoled chief. From this point we see a shift in the Native-anthropologist relationship and in the conditions that shape "value." The register of identification and gratitude offered to the Iroquois mediators moves from "collaborator" to "author-informant" with the second book in the canon, Hale's *The Iroquois Book of Rites* (1883). In this book Hale is the editor, rather than the discoverer and author, of Iroquois texts that were used by chiefs at Six Nations and Onondaga for the condolence ceremony. Because Hale positions himself as an editor, he is indebted to and acknowledges the contribution of the work of J. S. Buck (at Six Nations), John Johnson (at Six Nations) and his son George Johnson (at Six Nations), and Daniel La Fort (at Onondaga). Hale offers us historical context for the texts along with his notion of their authorship (1883, 39–47).

The register of acknowledgments and value is then shifted by the work of two Iroquois researchers: Arthur Parker (Seneca) and J. N. B. Hewitt (Tuscarora). Both acknowledge their informants, rely on their own sources of knowledge (Parker more than Hewitt), and then disagree with each other over matters of method, interpretation, and the reliability of those that shared knowledge with them. Their intellectual differences settled, it seems, around the translations and interpretations of the Great Law of Peace,[37] but spilled into their involvement in pan-Indian issues of the day (Hertzberg 1971, 133–34). It is difficult to assess the value of each researcher's contribution to the canon, as each offered works crucial to the history and culture of the Iroquois. Parker published more than Hewitt, but this is probably because Hewitt was a meticulous and very careful researcher (Swanton 1938). Nonetheless, Parker's "The Code of Handsome Lake" and "The Constitution of the Five Nations" encode the Karihwí:io and the story of the Peacemaker in ways that were foundational for later studies of revitalization and the Confederacy itself (Fenton 1968, 46–47).

Morgan, William Beauchamp, Hale, and Parker gathered the ethnological core of Iroquois literature. Voget characterizes this as the "salvage" phase in the literature, a period that is dominated by the approach of "Culture Historicism" (1984, 344). From there the literature shifts in method, but not approach. Memory studies and oral history are supplanted by historical, anthropological, archaeological, and linguistic modes of inquiry. With this shift, the core of memories, reconstructions, and texts, such as the aforementioned *The Iroquois Book of Rites,* became the basis for what Voget characterizes as "the historical upstreaming phase" (ibid., 347). At the start of this phase, the research agenda was that of "culture history," a period that marks the advent of William N. Fenton in Iroquois studies as well as the widespread institutionalization of anthropology in American universities.

William Fenton's first contribution to the canon, the lengthy article "Problems Arising from the Historic Northeastern Position of the Iroquois" (1940), marks the shift away from oral history and memory studies to a very narrow historical project and a return to the question of Iroquois history and origins. With this article, Fenton defines the Iroquois according to their linguistic origins, maps out their cultural linkages, and calls for "studies of cultural adaptations" (ibid., 348). He argued for a program of research that was focused on the "authentication of facts about Iroquois culture and history" (ibid.). In this article, Fenton synthesizes the existing historical research on the Iroquois, positions them temporally according to colonial documentation, and inaugurates the authentication phase of research. Here he concludes, "Despite the large amount of historical and anthropological attention that the Iroquois have received, they remain improperly understood" (Fenton 1940, 243). In order to "properly understand" the Iroquois, he argues, it is the job of anthropologists to understand the Iroquois' "intrusive cultural and linguistic position in the Northeast" (ibid., 243). His method for executing this project was "upstreaming." This analytical tool enabled a view of the past through the lens of the present, by "reading history backward" (Fenton 1998, 19). Voget elaborates that this "method in effect was a kind of ethnographic historiography, which explains his unswerving determination to establish the true nature of recorded facts and events" (1984, 348–49). Anthropologists and ethnohistorians such as Elisabeth Tooker would spend their careers authenticating those earlier facts and executing the Fentonian program in Iroquois studies, an approach that persists today (see Tooker 1998).

With the advent of Fenton and the period of historical upstreaming, we find the work generally concerned with the verification and interpretation of earlier Iroquois memories and the texts that they produced (Shimony [1961] 1994; A. Wallace [1969] 1972, 1978; Tooker 1978a; Fenton 1998). The post-Fenton Iroquois project represented a return to the textual and material origins of knowledge on the Iroquois, but the actual Iroquois interlocutors do not appear within the texts as they did during the salvage phase. Shimony's ethnography, *Conservatism among the Iroquois at the Six Nations Reserve* ([1961] 1994), is the first work of its kind since Morgan's and is rich in ethnographic detail. In *Conservatism* she maps out the structure of the Longhouse at Six Nations, the medicinal practices of herbalists, and the roles and responsibilities of officers of the Longhouse. Her work is *remarkably* procedural and, because of this, it is a much more elaborate and detailed study than Morgan's. Consider here her description of roles, functions, and times in the Longhouse: "The duties are apportioned between male and female deacons, but the Longhouses follow slightly differing patterns. Date setting, for example, falls to the women at Sour Springs much of the time, while at Onondaga and Seneca Longhouses the men are usually in charge. At Sour Springs the two head deaconesses together set the time for the following ceremonies: Bush Dance after Midwinter, Maple (when held, for it is not usual now at Sour Springs), Seed Planting Festival" (1994, 74). This careful attention to detail harkens us back to Ely S. Parker's characterization of early ethnographers and their craft: "those that love and adore rank and quality and that give and place them where none is claimed," which presses into play the earlier question that was asked of knowledge, of knowing the unknown (Ely Parker in Parker 1919, 216). How does Shimony know what she knows? This is an ethnography that she has written, and we can be certain that Shimony was not born knowing which "deaconess" set the date for a festival. She had to learn this from someone, or some people. How would the earlier canonical writers have dealt with the question of knowledge? Morgan might have inscribed the book to whoever kept him abreast of these activities; Hale might have offered authorship to his informants; Parker and Hewitt would have placed them within their footnotes (and then offered negative reviews of the each other's work); and Fenton would have called for a return to the archives for authentication of the present through the past. But Shimony leaves us guessing. We can assume that the older Iroquois people that appear on the cover of the Syracuse edition of the study (1994) are close to her, but there are no indications within the text that they are her collaborators. She offers thanks in her introduction to her "informants," but never identifies them by name. She does, however, identify and express gratitude to William Fenton and William Sturtevant for reading the thesis.

Shimony's work is a masterful study of a cultural whole, one that appears to integrate all parts of traditional practice.[38] She marshals temporality, ritual ideology, and materiality into one integrated text. A. Wallace's history of the Seneca *The Death and Rebirth of the Seneca* is another well-integrated study. Using a macropsychological theory of drives and repression, Wallace's history documents and accounts for the collective history of the Seneca. His working of cultural "revitalization" enjoyed influence beyond the realm of the Iroquois project. Much like Fenton's second contribution to the canon, Wallace's history is a traditional "history" and relies on textual archives rather than informants or friends. In this way, Iroquois voices and knowledge are not directly present at all within his text.

Fenton's *The Great Law and the Longhouse: A Political History of the Iroquois Confederacy* is the synthesis of the Iroquois project and the final canonical work in Iroquois studies. The book is organized chronologically and spans the formation of the League in legend as well as its practice through to the signing of the Canandaigua Treaty in 1794. There the history, already spanning over seven hundred pages, ends. The political history of the Iroquois Confederacy continues well into the present, and in this respect there is much that Fenton's seemingly exhaustive history omits. The canonical cutoff point and scope of his book are understandable, however, in light of his focus. Fenton always concentrated on cultural patterns that are understood as "traditional," which for him (and others, including contemporary Iroquois) are the "Old Religion" and "the League" of prehistory, the structures that were in place before the white man came. This he labors to understand and situate in Western epistemes.[39] Yet, the culture and people that he worked with were, by the ethnographic standards of his day, derivative and impure. They were negotiating and managing the experience of contact and colonization with only "traces" of what was presumed to be their original ethnological, cultural core intact. Rather than deal with the processes of colonization and cultural construction, he limits his units of analysis to what was "traditional," or as Shimony termed it at Six Nations, "conservative" ([1961] 1994). He focuses on the "traces" of cultural knowledge and practice that appeared pure and unchanged from the past. The people he worked with were knowledgeable about tradition and Iroquois lore, but that knowledge and lore was of "the New Religion" of Handsome Lake, the preacher/prophet who revitalized and reinterpreted the Great Law of Peace to adjust Iroquois people structurally and ritually to the demands of a settler landscape.

Through his vision Handsome Lake reinterpreted "tradition"—understood as the "Old Religion" by anthropologists and understood in radical shorthand as the "Longhouse" by contemporary Iroquois.[40] The resulting "New Religion," or Karihwí:io, has been recorded and reinterpreted by Hewitt, Parker, A. A. Goldenweiser, Fenton, and many other ethnologists and anthropologists thereafter. The point here is not that the culture that Morgan, the Parkers, Shimony, or Fenton were dealing with was derivative, or invented, or a less pure form of culture. The point is rather that their life's work has been focused on defining and refining tradition (through methodological and analytic tools such as upstreaming) to find what is purer—to locate what lay before the prophet/preacher and the polluting presence of white settlers. The point here as well is that culture is not a matter of degree, or of factual or temporal relationship to a past. And in part, what is being coded as culture is in fact a theory of jurisdictional authority and legitimacy that is being rendered into matters of memorizable form, procedure, and function. Fenton tells us with candor in his concluding chapter, "Beauchamp, Hewitt, Parker, Goldenweiser, Speck, Shimony, and I have all, in our concerted effort to recover the nature of the original league by salvaging its surviving legends, rituals, and political structure, contributed to the invention of tradition" (1998, 713).[41] Their own desires and inventive process have been the textual inheritance of the Iroquois, and the dominant space for perceiving their actions and, most important for this book at hand, Iroquois engagements with each other and with the state.

Repatriating the Rafters

Unfortunately for us, Fenton does not examine the epistemological and historical basis of his own "inventive" processes. Such reflection would have shed light on the very questions that inspired this chapter: the question of desire in ethnological practice; the construction and power of tradition in anthropology and other disciplines; the fundamental *relations* that motivated the writing of the Iroquois past (Parker-Morgan); and the ethnological body, or canon, of the Iroquois and the way this operates in current practice. Edward Said's *Orientalism* ([1978] 1994) accounted for and analyzed a body of ideas and texts that moved through ancient Greece into the (then-contemporary) near present with close attention to the way in which an entire geographic region, people, and "culture" but also philosophical systems were rendered textual matter to be made discernible, and also intellectually and politically presided over. More than figuring the matter of "othering" or rendering exotic and external to the self (an imagined Western self), this was a deep intellectual history of the textual, philological, and philosophical practice of evacuating history, specificity, complexity, and sentience from the space of the living. The living did not matter. Their own historians (Ibn Khaldun, among many, many others) did not matter; they were constructed as matter to be made knowable in certain terms, terms that were produced in the Western mind and then found in the Eastern archive (or territory). In this way, Napoleon knows what he will find before he gets to Egypt. Similarly, Morgan has a preconception of who an Indian is, what an Indian looks like, and knows to ask Ely Parker, a stranger to him, "Are you an Indian?" And then he knows to ask for certain things ("your traditions"), as if they were properties to be shared, to be codified, to be entrapped and learned by others.

Moreover, the question that many ask in cultural analysis today—the question of power, of effect—is ignored by Fenton and many others in Iroquois studies. It may seem programmatic and, on a certain level, puerile to state that the Iroquois are more than the sum of their patterns, that they are more than what is discernible to analysts trained to conceptualize and then treat culture as a matter of ritual and procedure removed from the time and space within which they occur. As well, it may seem doctrinaire to state that people should not be expected to inherit and then live within the analytical frameworks of another.

What then is tradition, and who makes it? Whose tradition matters? What does culture stand in for? Can the sovereignty of people in scenes of rapid, sometimes violent dispossession be rendered ethnologically? I cannot offer definite answers to these questions, but this chapter has mapped out the ways in which a very sturdy body of historical and anthropological literature has worked to record and analyze what was tradition and to represent and in this particular context *adjudicate* versions of kin, descent, history, and spatial order that made "The Iroquois." This was done by very particular, mostly Euro-American men, and sometimes women, who, for the past 150 years have produced a version of ethnology (in the case of Morgan) and then culture-histories (for most of those who followed) that created a regulatory body of knowledge. This body of work has a deep resonance today, in a settler-colonial nation-state that uses anthropological and historical archives to determine legal presence, to adjudicate claims to land. Much was elided or overlooked in this process, and might include Morgan's not-so-Indian playmates—Parker's own writing and those who are still missing: Parker's sister, Parker's brother, the Iroquois who were not Seneca, the Iroquois who were not traditional, the so-called mission Iroquois. This was the designation for Kahnawà:ke, "mission Indians" or "praying Indians," those who were, according to Hewitt, "confused about their culture." With this genealogy and discursive formation accounted for, we can now go to the ethnography itself and to the simultaneous question of how to write what was formerly incomprehensible, what could not be apprehended, and perhaps interrupt, if not refuse, these earlier forms of adjudication and apprehension.

FOUR

Ethnographic Refusal

Anthropological Need

To speak of Indigeneity is to speak of colonialism and anthropology, as these are means through which Indigenous people have been known and sometimes are still known (Pagden 1982).[1] In different moments, anthropology has imagined itself to be a voice, and in some disciplinary iterations, *the* voice of the colonized (Said 1989; Paine 1990). This modern interlocutionary role had a serious material and ideational context; it accorded with the imperatives of Empire and in this, specific technologies of rule that sought to obtain space and resources, to define and know the difference that it constructed in those spaces, and to then govern those within (Asad 1979; Said [1978] 1994, 1989). Knowing and representing people within those places required more than military might; it required the methods and modalities of knowing—in particular, categorization, ethnological comparison, linguistic translation, and ethnography.

These techniques of knowing were predicated upon a profound need, as the distributions in power and possibility that made Empire also made for the heuristic and documentary requirements of an ecclesiastical, metropolitan, and administrative readership. This readership derived its interest in "new worlds" or "discovered" or "settling spaces" explicitly for interests of conversion, a "harvest of souls" in the language of French Jesuits to New France in the sixteenth century (Mealing 1963; Blackburn 2000). The Jesuits' letters to France gave accounts of their mission, on the progress of learning Indigenous languages, on mapping, and on their need for provisions, but, most important, they provided accounts of Indigenous "culture" and "belief," on geography, on the mechanics of conversion that were of such a protoethnological discourse that they have been used to reconstruct (with archaeology) authoritative accounts of, for example, Huron and Iroquois history (Trigger 1988, 1991). Linda Colley's unique history of Empire moves through genders and locations to demonstrate that Empire indeed required these stories of captivity and regaled them but also that Empire was very much an uneven process and was work. Here she argues that during the Seven Years' War, "the British learnt first hand the sheer physical extent and complexity of the lands they and their settlers had so casually accumulated. It was now that they were made to realize how varied the people of North America were, and the degree to which their own white settlers were more than simply mirrors of themselves. And it was now that they came to understand far more vividly than before that, for all their dwindling numbers, Native Americans could still be highly dangerous as well as potentially useful, and necessarily had to be taken seriously" (2002, 172).

Thus English and French readers enjoyed "the captivity narrative" of ensnared settlers within an emergent New England and New France (along with Algeria and Australia) that regaled readers with stories of Indigenous brutality, sexuality, paganism, and at times kindness, while also learning about the politics, governance, and gender configurations of these places and peoples in the seventeenth and eighteenth centuries.[2] These protoethnographies and ethnologies had not only an administrative, missionizing, and governmental use; they also serve as an important (albeit explicitly positioned) archive for regional, cultural, and broader senses of history, anthropology, and literature in the present.[3] These sometimes very popular accounts made their way to governments as stories of the difference that "culture" stood in for in these "new" places.[4]

These accounts were required for governance, but also so that those in the metropole might know themselves in a way that fit with the global processes under way. Like "race" in other contexts, "culture" was (and still is in some quarters) the conceptual and necessarily essentialized space standing in for complicated bodily and exchange-based relationships that enabled and marked colonial situations in Empire: warfare, commerce, sex, trade, missionization. Culture described the difference that was found in these places and marked the ontological endgame of each exchange: a difference that had been contained into neat, ethnically defined territorial spaces that now needed to be made sense of, ordered, ranked, governed, and possessed.[5] This is a form of politics that is more than representational, as this was a governmental and disciplinary possession of bodies *and* territories, and included existent forms of philosophy, history, and social life that Empire sought to speak of and for.

In this chapter I will argue that if we take this historical form of ethnological representation into account, we might then be able to come up with techniques of representation that move away from "difference" and its containment, from the ethnological formalism and fetishism that I mapped out in the previous chapter. I am interested in the way that cultural analysis may look when difference is *not* the unit of analysis; when culture is disaggregated into a variety of narratives rather than one comprehensive, official story; when proximity to the territory that one is engaging in is as immediate as the self. What, then, does this do to ethnographic form? I will argue that when we do this type of anthropological accounting, "voice" goes hand in hand with sovereignty at the level of enunciation, at the level of method, and at the level of textualization. Within Indigenous contexts, when the people we speak of speak for themselves, their sovereignty interrupts anthropological portraits of timelessness, procedure, and function that dominate representations of their past and, sometimes, their present.

When I first started this research as a graduate student, I found portraits of Indigenous peoples, in particular Haudenosaunee peoples, to be strange in light of the deeply resistant, self-governing, and relentlessly critical people I was working with. When I started to do my work on a topic that simply matters to the Mohawks of Kahnawà:ke—the question of who we are, and who we shall be for the future—I found the anthropological histories on the Iroquois and methods used for cultural analysis to be exceedingly narrow, ritualistic, and procedural, so much so that they could only see certain peoples and practices, that they privileged particular communities and peoples in ways that stressed harmony and timelessness even where there was utter opposition to and struggle against the state. These "patterns" were evident in the canon just delineated in the previous chapter. Again, this is more than a representational problem or a superficially representational problem. The people that I worked with care deeply about ceremony and tradition, but hinged those concerns to the language and practices of nationhood, citizenship, rights, justice, proper ways of being in the world, the best way to be in relation to one another, political recognition, and invigorating the Mohawk language. They did not talk about the usual anthropological fare that dominated the prodigious amount of research done on "the Iroquois" and, sometimes, on them. They clearly had and have critiques of state power, hegemony, history, and even one another that made them appear anomalous, if not aberrant, to the literature written about them. Recall J. N. B. Hewitt's quote that Kahnawa'kehró:non had "forgotten," "confused," and "perverted" what they knew of tradition.

This was, and is, an assessment of knowledge and a simultaneous statement of judgment and value—and one that is ignorant or dismissive of the scene of dispossession and the complicated history of this place and, as such, is unfair. And so it was that I sought to figure out why this was and reveal it. I asked questions about the questions that mattered to the community and I had to write in certain ways, as these matters belonged to Kahnawà:ke and yet were being used to vilify the community and to vilify sovereignty in the mainstream press.[6] Their discussions had import for much larger questions concerning *just* forms of dominion, sovereignty, or citizenship. I want to reflect upon the dissonance between the representations that were produced and what people say about themselves (imperfectly glossed here as "voice"), and I want to do this now in order to ask what knowledge and representation might look like in disciplinary form and analysis when we account for histories such as the one sketched out above. To further that goal, I consider what analysis will look like, or sound like, when the goals and aspirations of those we talk to inform the methods and the shape of our theorizing and analysis.

What we saw from the Morgan and Parker history in the previous chapter is the not-so-subtle relationship between territorial dispossession and science—the way in which Iroquois dispossession provided the occasion for the initial dialogue between Ely Parker and Lewis Henry Morgan. More than merely an occasion to chat, the process of elimination that marks the settler-colonial project shapes these dialogues, as it was the inevitability of the decline, of the death of Indigeneity that shaped the form that Morgan's inquiry would take. The sturdy, the salient, the apparent, the lively sense of an imminent *cultural* death that made for certain things that mattered in the ethnological and ethnographic eye—the calendrical rituals, the songs that accompanied these rituals, the precise translation of wampum, the affixing and then dating of wampum—all of these forms of authentication in fact adjudicated a sense of deep skepticism that accompanied the difference that presented itself to Morgan's successors (such as the Tuscarora J. N. B. Hewitt), when things did not appear as they should have. Part of this fetishized, deeply controlled canonical approach to "culture as the pure," "culture as tradition," "culture as what is prior to settlement" disavows or pushes away its context of articulation: the political project of dispossession and containment, as it actually works to contain, to fetishize and entrap and distill Indigenous discourses into memorizable, repeatable rituals for preservation against a social and political death that was foretold but did not happen.

Particular Ways of Knowing

Thus, context is key for getting at what you can't get at until you account for all this. More specifically, unlike anthropologies of the past, accounting for Empire and colonialism and doing so in the context of "settler societies" (code for proximal-to, or once "Indigenous") is now a sturdy subfield within anthropology and informs most if not all contemporary analysis within those geopolitical spaces. This is owing to political currents, critiques, and philosophical trends outside of and within anthropology that have embedded the discipline within the history of colonialism, have highlighted ethics and form, and pluralized the places and peoples that are now considered viable for ethnographic analysis. Although more critically inflected than in the past, anthropological analyses of Indigeneity may still occupy the "salvage" and "documentary" slot and rely on enduring categories that emerged in moments of colonial contact, and that still reign supreme in some quarters. In those moments, people left their own spaces of self-definition and "became." But this category did not explicitly *state* or theorize the shared experience of having their lands alienated from them or that they would be understood in particular ways. This shared condition might be an innocent tale of differential access to power, of differing translations of events, were there a level field of interpretation within which to assert those different translations, as well as an agreed-upon vocabulary for comparison. No situation is "innocent" of a violence of form, if not content, in narrating a history or a present for ourselves. But like the law and its political formations that took things from Indigenous peoples, academic disciplinary forms had to be contended with too. Anthropology and the "law" (both, necessarily, reified here) mark two such spaces of knowledge and contention that have serious implications for Indigenous peoples in the present (L. Baker 1998, 2010).

As an example, Aileen Moreton-Robinson cites Captain Cook's 1770 account of the people he first encountered in what is now Australia. It was "stated that the Indigenous people of Australia had no form of land tenure because they were uncivilized, which meant the land belonged to no-one and was available for possession under the doctrine of *terra nullius*" (2004, 75–88). This legal doctrine of "empty land" held sway in Australia until the High Court overturned it in 1992 with the Mabo decision, and it offers stark testimony to the distinct power of one account over another in defining not only difference but establishing *presence,* by establishing the terms of even being seen: a historical perceptibility that empowered possibilities of self- and territorial possession in the present (Russell 2005). We see in this example how historical perceptibility was used, and is still used, to *claim,* to define capacities for self-rule, to apportion social and political possibilities, to, in effect, empower and disempower Indigenous peoples in the present. Such categorical forms of recognition and misrecognition are indebted to deep philosophical histories of seeing and knowing; tied to legal fiat, they may enable disproportionately empowered political forms (such as "Empire" or particular nation-states, such as the United States, Canada, and Australia) to come into being in a very short time. Without that category of knowing and its concomitant force, land could not be wrested from those who belong to it and to whom it rightfully belongs.

Thus concepts have teeth, and teeth that bite through time. By legally acknowledging the presence of Indigenous peoples in Australia, Mabo enabled Indigenous peoples there to finally claim legal title to their ancestral territories. Yet they could only do so after 215 years of settler occupation that coincided with 215 years of their continued presence on their own lands.[7] These historical and legal effacements of Indigeneity are predicated upon accounts such as Cook's, accounts that became histories that dialectically informed theories, which then emboldened the laws of nation-states. The traffic between theory and event moved colonies into nation-states. This trafficking disabled future claims of Indigenous occupation and ownership of territory because, in part, their own voices were imperceptible, or unknowable, or unimportant, or were sieved through analytics or narrative forms that interpreted their aspirations in ways that were not their own and/or were unrecognizable (Andersen and Hokowhitu 2007).

These effective effacements rested upon ways of knowing that imbricated the ethnological, ethnographic, and cartographic with social and political theory (Ryan 1994; Brealey 1995; Harris 2002) and enabled the justification of dispossession (Pagden 1982; Turner 2006). Cook's thinking was very much of a piece with that of political theorists such as John Locke, who argued in *Of Property* ([1797] 2003) that the origins of property reside in that which is mixed with labor. Thus, that which does not *appear* to have been mixed with labor is alienable. But only certain forms of labor, those which are perceptible to certain viewers, matter. However, of equal import for Indigenous peoples is the conflation of property with a larger economy of social and political rank and value. According to Locke, "Amongst those who are *counted the civilized part of mankind*, who have made and multiplied positive laws to determine property . . . is by the labour that removes it out of that common state nature left it in, made his property, who takes pains about it" ([1797] 2003, emphasis mine).[8] This fragment from *Of Property* enunciates the hierarchies of social value and their accordant rights, which were tied to the understanding of people and a social ranking as defined within an agrarian-based, panoptic view of humanity: people laboring specifically in scenarios defined by a behavioral performance of extraction or mixing, (a labor) that was sedentary, fixed, observable. This would be labor in the fields, labor in gardens—labor in a manner that moved these spaces out of "the commons" and into the realm of the private. His foil for this argumentation was "the wild Indian" of then-"America," who "knew no enclosure" (and thus, had no private property) (111). This foil helped to define property as only that which was mixed with labor and belonged to those who perceived it, in contradistinction to the living histories of Indigenous peoples in those places who labored, but in different ways (Moreton-Robinson 2000).

The visual intelligibility of cultural form, and specifically of labor, is critical here to recognizing and apportioning rights, and it is broken down and sieved into different hierarchies of value and accordant analytics—in their contemporary forms, those of "structure," "practice," and "meaning." We must be mindful however, that in its theoretical and analytic guises "culture" is defined in anthropological terms most consistently by its proximity to difference, not its sovereignty, its right to govern, to own, or to

. And that difference was to be defined against the sameness and om-
:nce of a stable ontological core, an unquestioned "self" that defined
ifference (and thus "culture") for a readership, one that corresponded
to a metropole and to a colony, a self, and an other (Cooper and Stoler
1997, 1–56).

Territories of the Familiar

It is in this brief context of anthropological need and political history that
I will now talk about forms of analysis after such an accounting—an accounting that we have to think of in terms of scenes of apprehension—
materially and symbolically shaped spaces of discernment that distill
into "representations" or renderings of difference that govern the way
that we know things. The thing I seek to uncover here is the possibility
of an improved ethnographic form within Indigenous North America, of
work that does this sort of historical and discursive accounting in order
to move carefully and gingerly into the remains—not of culture—but the
remains of what has been produced by these delineated processes. Here
occurs the conflict, the consternation, and the struggle against state en-
trapment, subjugation, demobilization, "savagization"—all of which have
afflicted Iroquois people, Kahnawà:ke Mohawks especially. In particular,
I am interested now in moving to the idea of a restrained familiarity and
in this, ethnographies of refusal, and the making of claims and the staking
of limits. The discursive appeal to the language of territory is deliberate,
although the territory that I wish to talk about is the space of method,
critique, and construction in *contemporary* ethnographies of Native North
America and, in particular, this ethnography of Mohawk nationhood and
citizenship across the borders of the United States and Canada. In a sharp
move away from the ethnohistorical/salvage paradigm that evacuates theory from the space of "native North American anthropology," evacuates
the very conditions of ethnography itself and specifically the prodigious
anthropology "of" the Iroquois, I will return to refusal.

The early American anthropologist and now-familiar Indian advocate
Lewis Henry Morgan theorized that the Iroquois, a once-significant military power in what is now the northeastern United States, were (in his
moments of reckoning) of such a "civilized" state that they were, in fact,
ceasing to be different from Euro-Americans and thus most worthy of the
trappings of civilization: education and agriculture. This was of a piece

with his political advocacy, itself an outgrowth of his "play" as an Indian, and later with his scientific observations and analysis of Indian culture, also an outgrowth of earlier play (Deloria 1998). We are already familiar with his foundational ethnological status within American anthropology, but it is also important to understand that Morgan was an advocate of sorts, and he was highly critical of the government of his time. As such, he wrote at least two well-intentioned and bold articles that some have argued were an unusual and early form of advocacy in anthropology (Sanjek 2004). However, his explicit writings on Indian "advancement" were tied to a racialized social hierarchy that placed African Americans at the bottom of the social order (L. Baker 1998) and expressed the belief—as we know from our discussion of the early, crucial research of Phil Deloria (1998)—in the inevitability of Iroquois decline and eventual and inevitable "absorption" into white civilization and, thus, citizenship. Morgan then advocated for Iroquois citizenship because he believed Iroquois to be "ready" for and "worthy" of such a change in their legal and political status, but also because their absorption, so to speak, into the white race was inevitable and most virtuous. Perhaps this was owing to his particular friendship with Ely Parker and his family, a friendship that resulted in part in jobs for Parker, in education for his sister Carrie, and, of course, an ethnological archive for Morgan. He grew intellectually intimate with Indians who could translate more than the terms of difference, those who could seriously shape knowledge to their liking, and I would say to their advantage. Recall that the Parkers are descendants of Handsome Lake, and it was his vision that was "tradition" in parts of Iroquoia, but it became a version of tradition that now has the sanctity of cultural and anthropological purity in some Iroquois territories—the Karihwí:io.[9] Their translatability evidenced perhaps this deadly readiness for political absorption into the settler state, readiness that was owing to their "civilized state" (contra the Aboriginal example cited by Moreton-Robinson above). Civilizational aptitude was perceived to be tantamount to the death of Iroquois culture— the death, really, of difference—so the remnants needed to be recorded and documented in *The League of the Haudenosaunee* (1851) at the same time that Morgan advocated for a more citizenship-worthy social status for them (Bieder 1986).

The *League* prompted many studies in its wake, and prompted as well a subfield of specialization in North American anthropology called Iroquois studies. Focusing almost exclusively upon the history of the Five and then Six Nations, Iroquois studies quite literally took off where Morgan left off, and as such is a documentary form. Although generated within a North American anthropology informed by international currents and translations in social and cultural theory, there is scant theory evident in the key, heavily cited texts of this subfield beyond those of Edward Sapir (1927), the linguistic and psychological anthropologist who influenced William N. Fenton and many others. As we saw from the previous chapter, the anthropological and historical project it embodies may be characterized as one that seeks to authenticate (and then adjudicate) cultural forms rather than analyze them. This is interesting, for many reasons, but perhaps most important for the discussion at hand is the largely agreed-upon fact that the Six Nations were and are among the most strident and vociferous critics of British and French settlement and also among the most insistently and stridently sovereign Indians in North America (Johnston 1986; Woo 2003). Kahnawà:ke Mohawks, as we will see in the chapter on Oka (chapter 6), are themselves among the most strident of the strident in defending territory—whether that be internal to the reserve or beyond.

These sovereign articulations do not match up with the anthropologies of timeless, procedural "tradition" that form the bulk of knowledge on the Iroquois. And so it is within this particular tradition, embedded in the structures of anthropological need discussed above, that I now want to turn to a very simple thing and the collective subjects of this book: those currently living within presumably settled places. I also want to turn to questions of ethics and the normative work of representing and analyzing their nationhood within those spaces. If we are to do analyses of such political forms, we must consider not whether sovereignty matters—that should be evident enough (bracketing the salvage/ethnohistorical blind spot of some) and central enough—but ask, "Does sovereignty matter at the level of method and representation?" I argue that it does matter, as these studies are knowledge formations that not only "correspond" to a reality and theorize it, and perform analysis for others to think with and to learn from; they also enact certain possibilities for the people they purport to represent, as well as for those who read and engage with these representations as students, as the curious, as subjects, as those who might or might not govern.

Sovereignty matters, as a methodological issue in and of itself, because it speaks from jurisdictional authority: the right to speak and, in this case, to not speak. Gerald (Taiaiake) Alfred has argued that in fact, sovereignty is simply an "inappropriate concept" because of its roots in singular authority, Western domination, and imperialism; because of its utter foreignness from Haudenosaunee and in fact all Indigenous philosophical traditions (2002). I agree with his characterization of the history of the concept and the hell that it has wrought upon people who were "made" sovereign or whose lives were lost for the jurisdictional aspirations and techniques of others. But I think it is a critical language game in the conditions of settlement—this structural condition of ongoing Indigenous dispossession and disavowal of that dispossession and structure. It is critical as it can signal different processes and intents to others in ways that are understandable. As such I want to think about the juridic and the textual at once and link the notion of jurisdiction over texts to writing. Or, perhaps, the imperative to write in particular ways. So, I too think sovereignty matters, and such mattering also engenders other ethnographic forms; in this case, one of refusal. This form of refusal does not operationalize or genuflect to recent formulations of alternative methodology such as "radical Indigenism"—something that is neither radical nor Indigenous but rather, in the name of "tradition," structuring yet another expectation of a culturally "pure" Indigenous subject (Simpson 2007). Rather, it is an argument that to think and write about sovereignty is to think very seriously about needs and that, basically, it involves an ethnographic calculus of what you need to know and what I refuse to write. This is not because of the centrality of esoteric and sacred knowledge. Rather, the deep context of dispossession, of containment, of a skewed authoritative axis and the ongoing structure of both settler colonialism and its disavowal make writing and analysis a careful, complex instantiation of jurisdiction and authority, what Robert Warrior has called "literary sovereignty" (Warrior 1995).[10] My notion of refusal articulates a mode of sovereign authority over the presentation of ethnographic data, and so does not present "everything." This is for the express purpose of protecting the concerns of the community. It acknowledges the asymmetrical power relations that inform the research and writing about native lives and politics, and it does not *presume* that they are on equal footing with anyone. This presumption of equal footing is false. Thus, this refusal and recognition of sovereignty should, I think, move us away from previous practices of discursive containment and pathology that have marked work on the particular Iroquois that concerns this book.

Research in Dangerous Times

In such a context of ethnographic and textual domination and indifference, as well as heightened sensitivity and outsider attention to the community because of the membership debate, I knew that there were limits to what I could ask—and then what I could say—within the scope of this research, and those limits extended beyond any statement on ethical forms of research that either the American Anthropological Association or the Social Sciences and Humanities Research Council of Canada (two professional and research-regulating bodies for anthropologists in Canada and the United States) required.[11] These conditions have led to this book as an ethnography that pivots upon refusal(s). I am interested in the larger picture, in the discursive, material, and moral territory that was simultaneously historical and contemporary (this "national" space) and the ways in which Kahnawa'kehró:non had *refused* the authority of the state at almost every turn and in so doing reinstantiated a different political authority. This practice of refusal includes the ways in which the formation of Kahnawà:ke's initial membership code (now replaced by a lineage code and board of elders to implement the code and determine cases) was refused; the ways in which their interactions with border guards at the international boundary line were predicated upon a refusal; how refusal worked in everyday encounters to enunciate repeatedly to themselves and to outsiders: "This is who we are; this is who you are; these are my rights."

There was no place in the existing literature for these articulations; nor is there now a neat placement for them within postcolonial studies or analysis. Kahnawa'kehró:non were not free from occupation, which is naturalized as immigration, as multiculturalism, and was and is a legalized, settler occupation of the territory that they claim. Thus there was no doubleness to their political consciousness, a still-colonial but striving-to-be "postcolonial consciousness," that denied the modern self, which Frantz Fanon, Homi Bhabha, and Anthony Giddens speak of and from (Fanon 1967; Giddens 1991; Bhabha 1994). That self would need to be constructed within and against others, even as the self "turns away" as we see in Glen Coulthard's reading of Fanon's experience of the child saying "look, a Negro" (2007). Here I want to push "turning away" into the ambit of refusal—of simply refusing the gaze, of disengagement—and to the possibilities that this structures: subject formation, but also politics and resurgent histories. In my ethnographic work I was deeply mindful of the range of possibilities available for political life, for identification and identity within and against recognition, all instantiated in refusals. There seemed, rather, to be a "tripleness," a "quadrupleness," to consciousness and an endless play, and it went something like this: "I am me, I am what you think I am, and I am who this person to the right of me thinks I am, and you are all full of shit, and then maybe I will tell you to your face" and "Let me tell you who you are." There was an enjoyment in this, as we will see below and in subsequent chapters, occasioned by border crossing, engagements with officials that deigned to ask and then tell Mohawks who they were, who they *are*, and what their rights are. The struggles in these moments form part of the quotidian life of self-consciousness and political assertion. There was something that seemed to reveal itself at the point of refusal—a stance, a principle, a historical narrative, and an *enjoyment in the reveal.*

"No One Seems to Know": Doing History and Ethnography in the Familiar

This question of recognition has surfaced repeatedly through time and, although completely originating in Canadian settlement and the Indian Act, its contemporary guises are mostly local. In the beginning of my own research on this subject, the Mohawk Council of Kahnawà:ke placed a notice in the weekly newspaper, *The Eastern Door.* It read: "The following members of the community are housing non-natives," with the name of the community member, their band number (number on the local Indian registry), and the name of their non-Indian guest. We have seen a concern over non-Indians in Kahnawà:ke from the signpost on expulsions in chapter 1, but I learned through archival research that this concern extended back to the earliest correspondence between the Indian agent and Ottawa. Readable now in Record Group 10 (RG10) of the National Archives of Canada, late nineteenth-century letters from an "Indian Agent" documented Kahnawà:ke's "sensitivity" to outsiders: "To the half breed Canadians of the village. We wish to have a final decision to know if DeLormier, Giasson, Deblois, Meloche and others are masters in our Reserve. There are eight of us who write (Indians) and if you do not leave the village look out for your heads, your buildings, your cattle and take warning of what we now tell you" (in Reid 2004, 30). This was a warning to "half breeds" and whites living within Kahnawà:ke in 1878, a time of great scarcity (of firewood and land). This warning, publicly posted to the "half breeds" and "whites"—who all owned disproportionate amounts of property on the reserve—enunciated a still earlier anxiety over the distribution of resources and power and the state's wrongful recognition of certain whites as Indians.

Thus the notice in *The Eastern Door* was not without context, and the context is the material and semiotic history from which Mohawks speak and by which they are simultaneously informed: profound land loss, scarcity of firewood, the one year that white men could legally obtain Indian status (1850–51) and buy and sell land, more encroachment, the earlier "settling" of New York State and loss of the Mohawk Valley, the end of the Indian Wars, the Riel Rebellion in Canada, and the ascendancy and decline of the British in North America. I do not wish to say that managing these historical vicissitudes ethnographically and in the present is unusual for those who wish to understand the intersecting matrices of colonialism/ dispossession and sovereignty as central to the people with whom we work. But in my brief discussion of the loss of land, the push back on white presence, you can see also the ways in which I came to understand this project as structured a very sensible anxiety over a corporeal and political disappearance tied to that land loss. And this is less loss, really, than lawful theft at the hands of a (white) settler state. This state brought Anglo-Victorian law into the community and used "race" to define Indigeneity, then instilled heteronormative marriage with the power to define legal personhood and thus to *remove* Mohawk women from their territories, their homes, and their families upon marriage to non-Native men (Cannon 1998, 2005; Lawrence 2003; Barker 2008; Palmater 2011). This law expelled them.

The Indian Act, a specific body of law that recognizes Indians in a wardship status in Canada—not a nation-to-nation arrangement by any stretch—created the categories of personhood and rights that severed Indian women from their communities when they married white men. It did the reverse to Indian men; white women *gained* Indian status upon their marriage into an Indian community. This created the conditions for the adoption of blood quantum in this community and for the contestation (and accordance) of it that prompted my initial research.[12] How does one, on the one hand, write about this or analyze what is so clearly offensive to the anthropological sensibilities of access, replicable results, and liberal norms of "fairness," and reconcile it, on the other hand, with the plight of those who are struggling every day to maintain what little they have left? And, how does one do this when they are struggling so clearly with the languages and analytics of a foreign culture that occupies their semantic and material space, and naturalizes this occupation through history writing and the very analytics that are used to know them?

The work of understanding these issues of membership, sovereignty, and autonomy within communities requires a historical sensibility (and reckoning) that is deeply horizontal as well as vertical. Although there was a hearty oral archive of the structuring logics of exclusion—of how people got to get "here," how they married each other when they did—there was also the logic of the present that I saw and lived and suffered through and enjoyed (and still do). This is the enfolding fulcrum of belonging—ensnaring, pushing, tussling, stretching, and living "genealogics" of the present that have cradled me my entire life, as my own person, as a "Simpson," as a cousin, sister, daughter, friend, and perhaps a character in an unfolding narrative that is of and not of my making. Kahnawà:ke and other spaces like it comprise tolerance, exceptions, snubs, social lacerations and affections—what I call in the final chapter of this book "feeling citizenships." These are alternative citizenships to the state that are structured in the present space of intracommunity recognition, affection, and care, outside of the logics of colonial and imperial rule (i.e., the Indian Act or blood quantum). Here is an example of these alternative logics from "C." Yet here there is also a refusal, or a denial, within the space of ethnography:

> **Q:** Tell me what you think our ideal form of citizenship is. . . . Are citizenship and membership the same thing?
>
> **A:** From my understanding, and whomever I ask, I get these gray, cloudy answers in return, so I am not quite sure. I am a citizen of Kahnawà:ke, but I am not a member of Kahnawà:ke. I am not on this mysterious list that no one seems to have any information about. So although I dearly love Kahnawà:ke, there are many positions I will never be able to hold until this membership issue is cleared up, so I don't know much about it, other than, I don't think it to be fair. There are those who leave the community, as I said—we all come back to Kahnawà:ke, but there are those who leave for twenty-five years and they come back and they're a member, and they will have all these opportunities that

I won't, even though I've never left. I don't think that's fair. But I think there's a distinction—one could be a citizen without being a member.

Q: Interesting, and that citizenship is based on . . . Let me push you on that then—how is that different; explain it to me.

A: Citizenship is—as I said—you live there; you grew up there; that is the life that you know. That is who you are. Membership is more of a legislative enactment designed to keep people from obtaining the various benefits that Aboriginals can receive. So I am a citizen—I live there; that is who I am; yet I cannot be a member because of these laws, which I feel is unfair. If I had been there my whole life, I should have the same opportunity to run for Council that anyone else can. Yet I cannot.

Q: Do you think that's because of public sentiment, the Indian Act, is that because of—

A: I don't know what you know, or what others know—this is an area that I can't get straight answers from; no one seems to know. . . .

Q: What do you think the legacy of C-31 is in Kahnawà:ke?

A: I think I really don't know much about this. There's this generation of people, myself included, who were young during that time, and we had no recollection of that time or even of these laws. As I said, I inquire, but nobody seems to know; I don't seem to get answers from anybody. . . .

Q: But you ask people?

A: I ask people. The same thing with this traditional government movement that is happening in Kahnawà:ke—people speak of traditional government; they speak of Bill C-31; and no one seems to know anything about it.

Q: In your personal experience, how did you come to understand C-31?

A: With what I do understand with it, I think from my mother. From what I understand, she tends to avoid speaking of this; I believe she was one of the C-31 people, but I don't know for sure.

Q: To get it [her status] back?

A: To get back on, she married my father, who was a Canadian; she was taken off this list; she got back on with C-31—and all the details I do not know.

Q: 'Cause it's unpleasant?

A: She doesn't speak of it and, as I say, I inquire, but I receive no answers; people seem to sidestep it or give these very vague summaries. It's almost like it is a taboo subject.

Q: Would you like to see it discussed more openly, or to find stuff out or be able to . . .

A: I would like to, out of curiosity, know a bit more about it. But if I don't, I will live my life, and for the most part I don't think it will really bother me other than not being able to be on this list, I guess.

"No one seems to know" was laced through much of C's discussion of C-31 and of his own predicament. I knew he was speaking indirectly, because I knew his predicament. And I also knew everyone knew, because everyone knows everyone's "predicament." This was the collective "limit" of knowledge and of who could or would not be claimed. So it was very interesting to me that he would tell me that "he did not know" and "no one seems to know." To me these utterances were quite the opposite of "Richard's"—which were spoken from a confounding placelessness of the past, irretrievable to me. C's predicament meant "I know you know, and you know that I know I know . . . so let's just not get into this" or "let's just not say." So I did not say, and so I did not "get into it" with him, and I will not get into it with my readers. What I am quiet about is his predicament and my predicament and the actual stuff (the math, the clans, the mess, the misrecognitions, the confusion, and the clarity)—the calculus of predicaments. And although I pushed him, hoping that there might be something explicit said from the space of his legal exclusion—or more explicit than he gave me—it was enough that he said what he said. Enough is certainly enough. Enough, I realized, was when I reached the limit of my own return and a collective arrival. "Can I do this and still come home; what am I revealing here and why? Where will this get us? Who benefits from this and why?" And "enough" was when my interviewees shut down (or told me to turn off the recorder), or told me outright funny things like, "nobody seems to know," when everybody *does* know and talks about it *all the time.* Dominion was exercised over these representations when it was determined that enough was said. The ethnographic limit, then, was reached not just when it would cause harm (or extreme discomfort). The limit was arrived at when the representation would bite all of us and compromise the *representational* territory that has been gained in the past hundred years, in small but deeply influential ways, with the kind of politics that are outlined throughout this book, both inward and outward, communicated by a cadre of scholars and artists from Kahnawà:ke, and then from all of Iroquoia, whose work has reached beyond the boundaries of the community.[13] It is very difficult *now*, in 2012, to write as if Haudenosaunee peoples are disappeared, as if they are outside of time, as if they are governed solely by protocol, as if they cannot or will not speak for themselves or engage with a modern and contemporary world order of nation-states and global capital that presumes and is predicated, in part, upon Indigenous disappearance.

At the start of this chapter, I discussed the anthropological relationship to Empire, one that was encouraged by a need to describe the difference that was found in new places. This need precipitated certain cultural forms and modes of analysis. In this process, people became differentiated, their spaces and places possessed. "Culture" served a purpose of describing the difference (always against a norm of a presumed sameness) that was encountered in those places. Describing difference also involved the analysis of difference, one that had (and still has) serious implications for Indigenous peoples, especially in their attempts to write their own histories, to claim their own intellectual and material space, and to exercise dominion over it.

The work of Indigenous studies scholars rests upon Empire as well, and through the vocabularies and analytics it put into play. This study certainly joins others that presume a political life for Indigenous people, of inherent and unceded sovereignty; of robustly acknowledging the centuries of warfare, exchange, alliance making, diplomacy, petitioning, letter writing, and resistance. And this is not only *historic* resistance to settler encroachment, but recent and armed resistance to the settler societies that have claimed and now claim North America. These nation-states have the gall, the mendacity, and the hyperbolic influence to call and then imagine themselves as something other than dispossessing, occupying, and juridically dubious. The political life of Indigenous people demonstrates these inconsistencies, these structural flights from morality, and the complicity of capital accumulation with dispossession and raced, dominating culturalism. This chapter has argued and shown, as will the chapters that follow, that by acknowledging this *historical* process we might be able to produce forms of analysis that move away from cultural fetishization and timeless tradition into the ambit of politics and critique that Indigenous peoples are articulating. It is in robustly acknowledging these complicated histories of agency, imposition, pushback, acquiescence, aspiration, and sovereignty that anthropological limits are produced. These are complicated things; not everything can be conveyed; this is so *not* a kinship pattern. Rather than stops, or impediments to knowing, those limits may be expansive in their ethnographic nonrendering *and in what they do not tell us.*

I reached my own limit when the data would not contribute to Iroquois sovereignty or complicate the deeply simplified, atrophied representations that Iroquois and other Indigenous peoples have been mired in anthropologically. The people I interviewed do *know* the different forms of recognition that are at play, the simultaneities of consciousness that are at work in any colonial encounter (including those with me) in the exercising of rights. Their knowledge translates into the "feeling side" of recognition, one that is not juridical; it is homegrown and dignified by local history and knowledge. What is theoretically generative about these refusals? They *account* for the history detailed above; they tell us something about the way we cradle or embed our representations and notions of sovereignty and nationhood; and they critique and move us away from statist forms of recognition. In listening and shutting off the tape recorder, in situating each subject within her or his own shifting historical context of the present, these refusals speak volumes because they tell us when to stop. Whether or not we wish to share that is a matter of ethnography that can both *refuse* and also take up *refusal* in generative ways.

Refusal courses through this chapter as an a posteriori method and mode of writing that made eminent sense after doing my fieldwork. There was no name for what I was engaging with then, for the very careful way I approached my writing. I had yet to account for the weight of the literature, the complete pathologization of Kahnawa'kehró:non and our politics by Iroquoianists. I just read their work and assembled a "canon." I hadn't stood fully in front of its effects; I just knew people in Kahnawà:ke generally did not think much for Handsome Lake, but even that was not a total social fact. When doing formal fieldwork, I did not yet have the language for the calculus of refusals everywhere I went, by everyone I talked to—this labor-intensive process of assertion: around membership, which registered then to me as a kind of stubbornness, an excess of will. I did not understand the ways my endless aggravation at the border, at any place I used my status card to get my tax exemption honored, the ways in which people treated me when they saw that card and sometimes in the bordertown, regarded me, how this was tied to long, terrible legacies of racial and, I now understand, political hatred. I simply tried to understand over and over again, How could our women be willingly disenfranchised by this community when they were the clan holders? How could we bring in blood? (Why aren't we being as we are supposed to be, as we *used* to be?) When the women used to appoint chiefs, not elect them, or vote for them? I, too, had not accounted for the scenes of apprehension that were structuring my own questions, scenes that constrained fundamentally the ways in which I asked questions, simply made the cuts on the body, the discursive snubs, the sneering border guard, the objects of ire, of analytical energy. That was all interesting then, but there were larger fields of articulation that these things were moving through: the ongoing conjunctures of historical and political conflict, the structural life of settler colonialism that authorized every conflict over interpretation that I now call a refusal.

FIVE

Borders, Cigarettes, and Sovereignty

The White Man put that there, not us. I don't know why we have to put up with this bullshit.

—One Mohawk man speaking to another about border issues over dinner at a Red Lobster in Lachine, Quebec, during the late 1990s

The Iroquois interrupt the portraits of timeless, procedural tradition that have framed scholarly understandings of them, but also state and legal interpretations of their actions, which are also often based on anthropological and ethnological understandings. Nowhere is this made clearer than in Iroquois interpretations of the Jay Treaty of 1794 and Iroquois movement across the United States–Canada border, an international border that cuts through their historical and contemporary territory and is, simply, in their space and in their way. It is through their actions and, in particular, their mobility that Indigenous border crossers enact their understandings of history and law, understandings that are then received in particular ways. Like the Kahnawa'kehró:non who were seen by the Tuscarora linguist J. N. B. Hewitt to have "confused and perverted tradition," the border crossers in this chapter are viewed as aberrant because they interpret and deploy their own sovereignty in ways that refuse the absolute sovereignty of at least two settler states, and in doing so they reveal the fragility and moral turpitude of those states.

To be *within* a state is to some extent to be *of* a state, since one must come up against its image, its history, and its law as one moves through and upon it. It is in relation to this process of coming up against the state and the actual cost and labor of the conditions of "nested sovereignty" that I now want to analyze how an Iroquois location within political regimes (the United States, Quebec, and Canada) agitates notions of separateness and difference that cause us to ask several questions of citizenship and the exigencies that are posed by border crossing. Does an affiliation with the state or lack thereof translate into citizenship? Does geographic positioning translate into a form of citizenship? In other words, if you are born in a place, does that mean that you are of that place? What if you refuse this tacit form of citizenship? And, *how* do you refuse it? *Can* you refuse it and still move? What is the role of *the border* in articulating grounded forms of citizenship outside the space of the state? I work through these questions with contemporary and historical accounts of the legal life of the international boundary line that cuts through Iroquois territory and that all Iroquois communities moved through, and still move through, to enact their ceremonial cycle, to work, to shop, to visit each other. This mobility is sometimes a daily condition of life in the reservation community of Ahkwesáhsne. Ahkwesáhsne means "where the partridge drums" (Morgan ([1851] 1996, 474) and is a Mohawk reservation that is bifurcated by the international boundary line between Canada and the United States and is also surrounded by, or lies within, New York State, Ontario, and Quebec. The community is bound up with the very beginning of settlement, but also the precontact understanding of territory.

Borders

The study of borders within North America is dominated by and imagined almost exclusively within the Chicano studies literature.[1] In that literature the act of crossing borders is an occasion for transgression, a means of decentering the national narrative of a culturally homogeneous and monolithic nation-state.[2] Unlike Chicanos, who move through juridical identities and designations as they cross the border (from Mexican, Mayan, or otherwise, into "Chicano" status within the United States), for Iroquois peoples the border acts as a site not of transgression but for the activation and articulation of their *rights* as members of reserve nations, or Haudenosaunee, or Iroquois Confederacy peoples. Thus the people who are crossing borders are reserve members or Iroquois before they cross, they are especially Iroquois *as* they cross, and they are Iroquois when they arrive at the place where they want to be. However, the maintenance of this arc through the day-to-day arenas of recognition (crossing the border and exercising rights may be a daily exercise for someone from St. Regis or a weekly exercise for an ironworker from Kahnawà:ke) can be difficult. Although crossers may perceive of themselves as members of a sovereign nation, the state may not. The criteria for recognition laid out by the state may render the right to exercise the Haudenosaunee right a *claim*, and a claim that is difficult to prove or to maintain without the proper *identification* and *proof*, but still, they *try*.

Consider here what it sounds like to try. The following stories account for this effort—the conversation, where it takes place, and the political labor of the explanation—the moment of articulation between law, history, and the body that constitutes Iroquois peoples' experiences of "crossing."

ON NOT PASSING AT THE BORDER

We had disembarked the late bus from Montreal to New York City and were waiting in line to see an agent. People around me looked blanched and tired. While in line, I surveyed the passports around me and tried to guess who was going to get pulled over based on the color of his or her passport. In my years of riding buses across this border, I have noticed that the red passports seem to slow the line down.

I finally got to my agent. She was a white woman, and I heard her speaking French to the person before me. I remember thinking that it was curious for an American border guard, and then I handed her my status card. I was making lists in my head of things I had to do the next day, and I stopped when she asked me where I was going. When I started to answer her, I noticed that she was flipping my card over and over in her hand. I said, "I am going to Brooklyn." She asked why; I said for research. She was staring at my eyes when I spoke and I thought *immediately*, "This is rude." I realized in that moment as well that she was the perfect amalgamation of every person who had aggravated me on a profound level in my life. This was weird, but then I found out why I was struck by this impression—it was anticipatory. She asked me, directly, jarringly, "Are you 100 percent Indian?"

Floored, I said, and without any hesitation, "Yeah." (I lied.) The feeling of "uh, oh" settled in my stomach shortly after I said it. I figured, now this is what *trying to pass* must feel like for those who explore this option daily.

But I also figured that the question was so rude and invasive that I was justified in saying whatever I could to end this encounter, fast.

Then she asked me another question, I am not sure what it was: How long will you be in New York, why are you going there? . . . something like that. I responded, "to do research." She asked, "Where will you stay?" "With my parents," I told her. And then she asked, "Are both your parents Indian?"

"My father is." (I told the truth.)

She now had the truth of my lie, and just like a lie that is unacknowledged and public and forced, it propped itself up and sat between us like an indolent and demanding child. We then talked *around* the lie. I was so annoyed with her and with myself and I remember starting to silently and simultaneously demand answers of myself and of her:

Why did I say "yeah" before?

What is my problem?

What is up with this lady?

Why do I, why do *we*, have to answer these questions from strangers and strangers with attitudes!?

Why is she treating me like this?

I had no answers at the time.

She was watching my eyes *again* when I said instead, "Look, I am a status Indian; I belong to a community; this is my card."

She left the lie and my card alone for a moment and then asked me, "Have you thought about applying for a green card while you are in the States?"

She pushed me over the edge of civility and patience. I was having trouble keeping cool because this was taking way too long and she was treating me like *I* had a red passport and was suggesting that I needed a *green* card. So I replied: "I don't need to apply for a green card, I am an Indian!"

At that moment I wanted to say so many things to her, such as "How did she get *her* green card; what is her white quantum; do you have to have a rudeness quantum of over 50 percent to do this job?" But she surely would have detained me if I did so. So I bit my tongue.

"You need to have a green card if you are going to be in the United States longer than *x* amount of time," she said, to which I replied:

"Look, I was born down there; I don't need a green card; I am not an immigrant; I am part of a *First Nation*, and this is the card that proves it!"

Upon hearing this her posture completely changed, she pushed my card to me, and said, "Well then,

you

are an American."
To which I said,
"*No*, I am not,

I

am a *Mohawk*."
I walked away from her. But as I was walking toward the door, she yelled across the border house to me,
"*You are an American*."
And I yelled back,
"*I am a Mohawk*."
And she yelled,
"*No*,

You are an American."
At that, I walked out of the din of surveillance and aggravation and onto the bus, sat down, and immediately wrote it all down. Once that was finished, I started a detailed letter to her supervisor and then found that I was too tired to write that one down. I never wrote that letter to her supervisor, but in documenting the interaction, I realized that ethnography in anger can have a historically and politically productive effect. This exchange sits in my "notebook" beside interviews, notes, and the emergent archive of stories of my own experience of the law, which articulates with the people that I was interviewing, observing, hanging out with, and then writing about.

The experience with this woman happened early in my formal fieldwork and remains, so many years later, the most aggressive exchange I have ever had crossing the border. As may be inferred from the moment above, voices were raised; there was palpable "tension." Her complete, summarizing disdain for what I was saying, expressed in "*You* are an American," registered to the tips of hair that I did not know I had at the nape of my neck. The assertion that I was other than Mohawk, or that this was anything less than a citizenship, was enraging and simultaneously had to be contained. I simply could not flip out. But she was snooty, authoritative, aggressive—everything, historically, politically, to dislike and to dislike with a vigor. When I crossed the following year from Vancouver to Seattle, I was asked similar questions (by another white woman, though less sneering) and instead of entertaining her line of questions, I simply asked her for her immigration papers, then waited for a response. She did not argue with me but sent me to the "room" where many people with red passports were. A white, male customs officer asked me if I "got myself into trouble with her," and I told him I have a right to ask either of them for their papers. Things became jovial; only I was not really joking. Either way, he then printed out the INS regulation 1952 for me to look at. I told him I know about it and our blood quantum is nobody's business, and he told me he went to college with a guy who said he was Indian but was not, and that is why blood quantum is useful. It protects everyone from dishonesty.

THE BURDEN OF PROOF

Further into my formal fieldwork I encountered this man, with sharp hair and relentless skepticism.

B. J. Riggs wanted to know where the letter was from my tribe stating that I am 50 percent Indian because, as he said while looking at my card in his hand, "these don't mean anything."

I told him that my "tribe" has a 50 percent blood-quantum requirement and that in fact this means that the card does "mean something."

He looked at me like I was an idiot and started flipping my card over and over in his hand. After my previous experience with the French-speaking American woman at the border, I knew that the card flipping was probably a *bad sign.*

"The burden of proof is on you to prove who you are—you know that, don't you? These cards don't mean anything."

He shifted gears, "Where are you going? How long are you staying? Where were you born? Do you have a birth certificate?"

"I was born in Brooklyn, New York. I am staying for a few weeks. Here is my birth certificate."

"This is what I need to see, this other thing here is useless." He pushed it to me across the counter and said, "Next time show me this." He folded up my birth certificate and handed it back to me.

Danny, an interlocutor and friend in his early thirties told me similar stories about being interrogated, being burdened with proving. I asked him very specifically if he had ever had difficulty at the border. His unedited responses follow.

"A MEXICAN STANDOFF"

At the JFK Vermont/Quebec border some years ago . . . I was crossing into the states on Christmas Eve. I flash my card to the old dude at the border, who proceeds to ask me my quantum. After giving the double digits, he wants to know if it is on my paternal or maternal side. When I tell him maternal, he informs me that my 50 percent needs to be on my paternal side in order to enjoy free circulation to the states.

He then (like all white people) takes the opportunity to talk about himself for a while and tell me how his grandmother was from "Kan-a-wa-ki" and how he should be entitled to a card, and why can't he have one.

Fucking nuts.

Finally, I hit him with my US citizenship and inform him that I am a US citizen by birth and would like to know under what provision is he denying me reentry into the country.

He concedes and lets me pass, grudgingly.

However, as I'm leaving his vision, he phones ahead to the Vermont state troopers telling them he believes I am smuggling something across the border. About twenty-five minutes later, the Vermont state cops pull me over and pull *everything* out of my car onto the side of the road, going through Xmas presents and everything at 2 AM.

Ultimately, my license was expired, and since the cops had conducted a search of my vehicle against my wishes, we agree to each look the other way and leave each other alone.

A true Mexican standoff.

"SLEEPLESS IN SEATTLE"

It was October 1998, and I was flying from Montreal to Vancouver on my way to Seattle to attend the National Association of Broadcasters annual convention. Traveling with me was my good friend J.D., also from Kahnawà:ke.

After making the long walk across the Vancouver airport to catch our departing plane, we were ready to make the standard pass through customs to enter in the US. Greeting us was a man in his late thirties, who wore a thick "NASCAR-style" mustache, had hair parted down the middle, and looked to be about twenty to twenty-five pounds overweight. He had the skin tone of somebody who had not worked outside of an office for at least ten years. As per the usual protocol, both J and I handed over our status cards when asked for a form of photo ID.

The customs agent was satisfied with J's and promptly handed it back to him; however, when he received mine, his tone began to change. He then asked me what my blood quantum was, and I responded, "Fifty percent."

"On your mother or your father's side?" he asked.

"My mother's," I responded.

He then took my card and sternly directed both J and I to take a seat. The agent then went into a back office and did not reappear as soon as I had expected.

After about twenty minutes had passed, it was clear that we were about to miss our connecting flight.

When he returned, he called me forward and asked if I had a letter from my "Tribal Council" stating that I was indeed a member of the community.

"I've never had any need for such a letter," I responded.

"Without that letter, I can't let you pass through."

He then went on to say that he was a "Cherokee," and in his "tribe" everyone needs a letter if they want to pass through the border. I told him I am not a Cherokee—I am a Mohawk, and my freedom to pass through the border is guaranteed by the Jay Treaty.

"Yes, I know about your 'Jay Treaty,' but that's only good for your area in New York State."

I was getting pretty upset by this point, realizing that this guy has his own membership issues and is now making very liberal interpretations of our right to free passage.

"Then you would know that nowhere in the Jay Treaty is mention made of our ability to pass exclusively through the eastern corridor" was my answer.

"Be that as it may, unless you show me something else, I can't let you pass through."

Realizing that I still had my CBC [Canadian Broadcasting Corporation] Reporter ID on me, I said, yes I *do* have one more piece of ID and it is issued by the federal government, indicating that I have passed through their security clearance.

I then slid the card across the counter, and he looked puzzled for a split second and swiftly disappeared into the back office again. This time I could see him talking with a supervisor behind venetian blinds.

J.D. just looked up at me from his seat and shook his head in bewilderment. Upon his return, he gave me back my CBC ID and said that his supervisor was satisfied.

As we left the desk though, his last words were "Make sure you get that letter from your chief, or next time it might not be so easy."

Fucking "Cherokees."

Ultimately, we were held for an hour and some change and were able to catch a connecting flight later that afternoon.

These stories join the multitude circulating in Haudenosaunee territories on border experience, border trouble, border nonsense, the "bullshit" that we go through when we cross the border. The ongoing "bullshit" referenced in the epigraph was heightened after 9/11, at the very start of my research, when our rights were constructed, along with those of others,[3] as a threat to national security and our forms of self-identification (and formal identification by the state) became subjected to greater scrutiny. "Status cards" issued by Canada and the United States attesting to our recognition as Indians would no longer suffice; our traditional "red cards" or passports deemed not up to security standard; our bodies, narratives, and arguments then folded into the seemingly newer threat to settler sovereignty and security—the illegal alien, the always-possible terrorist—rendering perhaps all bodies with color as border transgressors with the presumed intent to harm.

These post-9/11 anxieties have a deeper history. The legal underpinnings of these exchanges and the interpretive gymnastics that they entail in day-to-day border crossing will be contextualized throughout the course of this chapter. But suffice it to say for now that both Danny and I were committed to having our Mohawk identity and, by extension, our Jay Treaty rights, upheld from the moment we attempted to cross to the moment we finally did cross the border. This was made difficult by the interpretive spin on the Jay Treaty (as limited to the Northeast, as gendered, and racialized) that was put forth by particular guards.

Why are we so inspected? Why does Danny maintain and continue to assert this form of identification, and the law that confirms it, in the face of such inconvenience? Why would I do the same, and argue—with a stranger no less—loudly, vociferously, in public? Here we move from the textual domain of procedural, fetishized culture in anthropological productions of the Iroquois (as tradition) to another mode of representation. The Iroquois becomes, in the public eye, something else, "Mohawk," and that Mohawk is lawless—perhaps especially so after 9/11. Settler law is one of several keys to this interpretation, which, in these border-crossing stories, Danny invokes and the agents of the settler state ignore.

But this law also informs mainstream representations of Mohawk peoples as people without law, as people who transgress borders, rather than refuse them *lawfully*. These mainstream representations also inform national anxieties about sovereignty, about taxation, about lost revenue and lost subjects. Political subjects are, to some extent, supposed to stay still, or to move with permission, according to one law: settler law that authorizes Canada or the United States to govern. Yet when the settler law actually allows these subjects mobility, then their actions must be curtailed, especially perhaps in states of "exception," in what is presumed to be a time of danger so profound that rights have to be monitored, abridged, and suspended.

The continuity of Indigenous self-descriptions during these times and the defense of this identity as a Mohawk owe to a sense of self and to the history of Mohawk people's recognition *as just those people* in the law, but this is a rare moment when our law is dovetailing with settler law. Danny's sense of himself and the identity of his people are articulated to notions of a national or Confederacy complex and the *rights* that are guaranteed to Haudenosaunee people through treaty (Becker 1998). Although Mohawks such as Daniel are border crossers, they are not border *transgressors*, because they have this unique temporal and rights-based relation to the nation-states of the United States and Canada. This relation is temporal because the Haudenosaunee predate both political regimes. Their unique legal and historical arrangements with these regimes reflect the importance of this temporal arrangement. As the different voices and stories in this chapter explain, it is also because of this temporal relationship to these settler regimes that the geopolitical boundary of the United States–Canada border actually transgresses *them.*

Sovereignty up in Smoke

Danny and I have crossed the border all of our lives; people in these territories have crossed all of their lives. It was in the 1990s, however, that this was felt in the most onerous ways; we all seemed to be suspect and were treated as if we were either (a) not Indian and carrying fake ID that said we were; or (b) Indian and carrying something for resale on our person or in our cars and thus subject to greater scrutiny. These anxieties and perceptions have a deeper history, but in the mainstream Canadian media of the 1990s framed Mohawk travel and transport of cigarettes across the border as "smuggling" and, thus, as an abuse of a system of Indigenous rights recognized under Canadian law. The "problem" of smuggling was then constructed through the courts as wrongdoing by tobacco companies and as a question of how the United States, as a sovereign nation, could assist Canada, as a sovereign nation. The two governments therefore missed the larger, critical context of Iroquois trade practices and treaty interpretation across the borders of the United States and Canada, and the recognition of Indigenous sovereignty. In this way, Danny and I (and many others, innocent of these machinations) were caught up in deep webs of contemporary and historical misunderstanding, such as Franz Boas's classic study in "apperception," or sound blindness. The sounds are uttered, the words assemble, and something else is heard entirely. This is not because we pronounce them improperly; this is a problem in the listener, who, in this case, has "a wrong apperception" (1889, 52). It was not us; we were pronouncing things correctly. Rather, it was their perception that rendered us in particular ways. Only the compound of sounds in question is law, not grammar.

One of the primary ways Iroquois mobility and sovereignty was known to a larger public was through the mainstream press, which worked with a limited conceptual vocabulary of what they abhorred: savagery, criminality, and their own fear. A CBC documentary, *The Dark Side of Native Sovereignty*,[4] nationally televised in 1996, helped this interpretation along by subjecting Mohawk trade and traffic to intense scrutiny. Viewers saw Indigenous protagonists in a bustling, underground cigarette trade justify their participation through appeals in a system that had already constructed their activities as criminal or deviant. Through the television program's appeal to "tradition," to (special) rights, and to sovereignty, viewers saw the representations of these traders harden around the image of "smuggling." This was achieved through a chain of conflations that removed the practice and its practitioners from a larger field of exchange in which it occurred, that of smuggling on the part of tobacco corporations.

The role of "Big Tobacco" in illegal trade in cigarettes from Canada to the United States for eventual sale back into Canada culminated in a

Racketeering Influenced and Corrupt Organizations (RICO) suit in 2001, *Canada v. R.J. Reynolds Tobacco Holdings, Inc.*[5] This suit was filed by the government of Canada against R.J. Reynolds and others, a conglomeration of tobacco manufacturers, for conspiring to circumvent tax laws in Canada (*Canada v. R.J. Reynolds*). The company conspired to avoid paying Canadian taxes on cigarettes by exporting cigarettes manufactured in Canada—and sometimes Puerto Rico—to the United States, where they were then sold to distributors who transported the cigarettes back to Canada and placed them on the black market (ibid., 106–9). The Ahkwesáhsne Mohawk reservation and other Iroquois reservations factored more centrally into this plan when Canadian cigarettes were exported to distributors who transported the cigarettes back into Canada through reservations in upstate New York (ibid., 106–7). The cigarette-transport scheme also involved mail and wire fraud (ibid.).

Canada brought the RICO suit in the United States because many of the defendants and witnesses were based there, and "much of the alleged illegal activity took place there."[6] In the end, the circuit courts did not agree to collect taxes for Canada in the United States. In so doing, the court reinforced settler sovereignty—in an older, territorially based model—by not believing the argument that the defendants had been acting in good faith, based on their Aboriginal right to trade guaranteed to them by the Jay Treaty of 1794. Under the treaty, the defendants, as members of a "border tribe," were legally allowed to trade across the border as long as their goods were intended for trade with another Indigenous nation.[7]

In spite of the larger system of exchanges that created the societal problem of "smuggling"—namely, tobacco corporations willfully circumventing Canada's tax laws—it was Indigenous traffickers who received relentless public scrutiny, even when they barely appeared in the suit or the decision. The RICO lawsuit proved that there was something much larger at work than Indigenous trafficking in cigarettes, namely, different claims to sovereignty. In spite of their longevity in their territory as caretakers and sovereigns, Mohawk history, narration, and practice of this sovereignty were refracted through the prism of bourgeois capitalism. Social perceptions were filtered through a new understanding of government as an entity that accumulated surplus and distributed income accordingly. To this effect, documentaries and courts portrayed "rights" in a manner that wedded them exclusively to capital accumulation.

In the CBC's documentary, *Troubled Waters* (1993),[8] which preceded *The Dark Side of Sovereignty,* an Iroquois interlocutor asked, "In today's world, isn't money sovereignty? In today's world, isn't money freedom?" (ibid.). His question provocatively summarizes distributive models of capital and social hierarchy and demonstrates that those relations of production may enable or disable modes of tolerance in neoliberal states. However, when the political subject is Indigenous, citizenship takes on a temporal and economic form due to the societal expectation that Indians belong in a certain relationship to capital accumulation, that they be in another time (while simultaneously being within this world), and that they be poor (Cattelino 2008). This provocation, like those of other speakers in this documentary, exposes that very expectation as well as the legal proscription that Indians' bodies and their activities be contained on reservations.

The historian Philip Deloria characterizes the structures of reservations, Indian agents, and the historical practices of state surveillance in these spaces as a form of societal expectation that still shapes social relations, as a historically generated "colonial dream" in which "fixity, control, visibility, productivity, and, most importantly, docility" were realized (2004, 27). This dream was one of Indigenous pacification, containment, and demobilization. In order to be actualized in the present, this dream requires that Indigenous economic activities be watched, that there be a state-police presence in their community, and that Indians be passive in the face of this surveillance, regulation, scrutiny, and possible intervention. Consider, here, a response and a reflection on this expectation from a Mohawk named Kakwirakeron: "Are you talking about Canada, the RCMP [Royal Canadian Mounted Police], invading a sovereign Mohawk territory and using full violent force on the Mohawk? If you're talking about that, then they better think twice about that because the resistance here would be awesome. I think the people have really enjoyed prosperity for a long enough time and they have learned the lessons of Oka" (from *Troubled Waters*).

The narrative of the documentary *Troubled Waters* is set afloat by fears of Indian lawlessness: "Dust settles on the smuggling capital of Canada. Across the river, Loran Thompson is getting ready for another busy night.... Just across the river from Thompson's dock is Cornwall Island, located on the Canadian half of Ahkwesáhsne. Mohawks don't recognize the international border that cuts through the water. For them, it's all Indian territory and smuggling is a dirty word here. They call it sovereignty. They maintain a treaty signed almost 200 years ago [that] gives Mohawks the right to trade freely among themselves" (*Troubled Waters*). With one fell swoop, the director dehistoricizes the political and historical respatialization of Ahkwesáhsne through colonial boundary making. He renders this respatialization a simple matter of the refusal of Indians to recognize what is apparent, an international boundary that has been drawn through the water, which is in the minds of Akwesahsnero:non (people of Ahkwesáhsne) their water. The legal divestment of the water that belongs to them according to their understanding of territorial ownership then operates as a critique of their understanding of the space that they occupy. This becomes their (wrongheaded, misguided) "refusal to recognize."

If a refusal to recognize also involves using one's territory in a manner that is historically and philosophically consistent with what one knows, then it is an incident of failed consent and *positive refusal*: Mohawks refused to consent to colonial mappings and occupations of their territory. Such refusals, or failures to consent, require a legal response to contain those who refuse, a move that then incites settler anxiety about the containability of Indian bodies and practices. The fact that the territory and the people of Ahkwesáhsne are crossed by four state and provincial boundaries and jurisdictions, as well as an international boundary line that bifurcates their territory; that this territory was divided without their explicit consent; that their boundaries of this space are different from those mapped by relatively new nation-states and peoples—this was not up for discussion or analysis. It is simply the Indians' perceived misrecognition of boundaries (and the inability to contain their trafficking and their economic practice) that appeared to be the issue.

Discourses such as these two films are more than flattening and incorrect; they do significant political work to affect the public's sense of Indigenous rights and Indigenous commerce. But more important in this instance, they obscured the much larger economic imperative of tobacco corporations that relied on the "spectacularization" of Iroquois traders to hide Big Tobacco's illegal trade activities. This reliance is revealed by the facts surrounding the protracted period of cigarette smuggling, between 1989 to 2000, by Big Tobacco, as well as by later CBC attention,[9] police investigation, and the *R.J. Reynolds* decision. Mohawks and other

Iroquois transporters had a much smaller role in this "problem" than was represented in these early documentaries. Their relative insignificance was demonstrated in the R.J. Reynolds lawsuit and made public through the Canadian Department of Justice website, which stated, "The [members of the] Canadian Tobacco Manufacturers Council were also involved [and] were used to throw[ing] the Government of Canada off the smuggling trail. The government alleges RJR-Macdonald used the council to blame organized crime while pretending it was trying to stop smuggling. At the same time it is alleged that RJR-Macdonald was setting up a shell company in the United States to deceive investigators."[10] Yet the overemphasis on Indian activities was important in solidifying the fragile sovereignty of a settler nation-state—a sovereignty that, as I will show, requires, along with taxation, that Indigenous sovereignties be vanquished, if not eliminated. Shortly thereafter, in 2001, the Canadian Supreme Court would deny the Aboriginal right to trade guaranteed by the Jay Treaty of 1794.[11]

Indigenous "smuggling" was a refusal of settler dominion over territory, an assertion of the integrity of earlier agreements between sovereigns as well as an assertion of these rights. "Sovereignty" is articulated differently by Mohawks in their traditional trade practice, a practice that necessarily involves a grounded knowledge and deep critique of settler law. This sovereignty is misperceived as criminal, even when it is an explicit expression of treaty rights guaranteed to the Mohawks as a border tribe, or, as they would certainly prefer to be called, a "border nation."

Challenges to State Sovereignty: Lost Revenues and Failed Consent

In both *Troubled Waters* and *The Dark Side of Native Sovereignty*, "the problem" was not Indian; it was revenue lost to Canada. When Canada raised the tax on cigarettes to combat teen smoking in 1989 and then in 1991,[12] smuggling rapidly increased. By 1994, Canada estimated that it had lost $2 billion (Canadian dollars) in revenue and consequently lowered the tax to combat smuggling.[13] The public problem of cigarettes then morphed from a corporeal concern with the young citizen's body to a public concern over the nation's economy: "smugglers" were harming not only the former, but also the latter—the nation's pocketbook.

In the *R.J. Reynolds* case, one nation-state (Canada) acted as a person and filed a civil-action suit against an amalgamation of business interests within another nation-state. The suit was filed in the defendants' own territory, within their own legal system, in order to sue for damages under RICO for injuries incurred in Canada. Canada argued that an amalgamation of US and Canadian cigarette traders willfully circumvented Canadian taxation by smuggling contraband tobacco and cigarettes—via the Iroquois reservation communities in the Northeast—from Canada, across the international boundary line for repackaging, and back into Canada. In conspiring in these ways and in circumventing Canadian taxation, Canada argued, the tobacco company R.J. Reynolds and others "injured" Canadian property and caused additional damages and costs incurred by the investigation and legal proceedings. In ruling against Canada by upholding the revenue rule, which states that one country would not act as an enforcer of the other's laws, the Second Circuit recognized the sovereign status of foreign nations.

This scenario provides insight into the legal process of how Empire is negotiated, where legal and political territories are acquired, and how new boundaries and political subjects are decided through the space of courts. The terms—and the process—of political recognition are laid bare for analysis. This is a case in empire-building because its complicated legal reasoning both responds to and effaces, again, Indigenous people's claims to their "Aboriginal" right to trade, upholds and reinforces the singular forms of sovereignty (even where distributions in capital deterritorialize sovereignty) (Hardt and Negri 2001), and disables the very possibility of Indigenous participation in a contemporary trade network. In *R.J. Reynolds*, the possibility of a third, Indigenous legal system at work was not admitted into the analysis, thus solidifying settler sovereignty as normal, natural, and ultimately just.

In contrast, Mohawks interviewed in the films spoke of an alternative mapping of territory. Consider this conversation on transport, place, and the law:

> **Victor Malarek (VM):** So these boxes move out every night and they're headed for the Canadian side, but look what it says here—"Not for sale in Canada." Where are they sold?
>
> **Loran Thompson (LT):** Kanien'kehá:ka territory, Indigenous to the people of this country—the Americas.
>
> **VM:** But they end up in Canada.
>
> **LT:** Maybe to you they do; maybe to people like you they do, but to

people like me, nationalists of my country and my government, that word Canada to me is "Khanata"—a village.

VM: When you see this, "Not for sale in Canada," . . . you're not breaking the law?

LT: No.[14]

Thompson's arguments speak from Haudenosaunee legal and experiential history, a history that is punctuated by such exchanges and differential understandings of place and territory. Consider the history embedded in these remarks: "You are a cunning People without Sincerity, and not to be trusted, for after making Professions of your Regard, and saying every thing favorable to us, you . . . tell us that our Country is within the lines of the States. This surprises us, for we had thought our Lands were our own, not within your Boundaries" (Seneca Pine Tree Chief Red Jacket, cited in A. Taylor 2002, 66). More than two hundred years have passed since Red Jacket's address to Europeans in Iroquois territory, yet not much seems to have changed in the Iroquois perspective concerning the border. The central point of his lament and the opening epigraph to this chapter, although inflected differently, remains the same: the perception of territory that underpins Iroquois people's right to cross the border dividing the United States from Canada is radically different from that of either nation. These border utterances speak from the perception of the Northeast as a territory that belongs to the Iroquois, and as a place that was divided and is administered without their consent.

These narratives speak as well to the political relationships that underpin this territory, and to the difficulty that Iroquois people have had and still have in moving through the landscape of the Northeast in a manner that is consistent with their self-perception, and rights, as Indigenous nationals of that territory. Why is there such a radical difference between their self-perception and the ways in which Iroquois border crossings are administered? Why is there such incommensurability between Iroquois' perceptions of the treaty relationship and those of the regimes that now interpret it? What accounts, then, for the dissonance between Iroquois self-perception and the state's perception of them?

There are several factors at work in these disjunctions. The most significant are the different understandings of the proper relations that Iroquois and settlers have brought to their interactions through the past two hundred years. These different interpretations are brought to the fore in Mary Druke Becker's important article on Iroquois sovereignty through time (Becker 1998). Iroquois chiefs deployed the language of treaty—with concomitant notions of "father" when regarding the British—but did so insofar as these terms furthered their notion of the relation between the two as one of equals.

> Beginning in the late 1670s, the English and French began seeking territorial domination over larger and larger areas of land vis-[à]-vis one another. Each nation argued with the other that the Iroquois had agreed to become their children or subjects. The Iroquois had agreed to use the Iroquoian term for "father" when addressing Euro-Americans. This term was used because within the matrilineal Iroquois society a father was an indulgent, not an authoritarian, figure. The term was commonly used among Iroquois nations and by other Iroquois with whom they were in alliance. It implied a reciprocal relation in which care and aid were provided. It was not one which implied subordination. (Becker 1998, 988–89)

These understandings of the Iroquois and by the Iroquois are common to the different positioning and perception of Indians generally through time, and to settler-state formation and asymmetries of power that allow one perception of difference to become institutionalized through law, policy, and other forms of state practice. Indian tribes were first perceived as nations (hence the model of international treaty-making that marks the earliest period of their interaction with the Dutch, French, and English regimes) and were then perceived to be dependent wards who required protection from white unscrupulousness on the frontier (Becker 1998, 982, 992). Iroquois, in particular, have resisted their interpretive demotion in political affairs; yet, with the rise of the "welfare state," many perceive Indians on the Canadian side of the border as races, as clients (among many others) who need to be administered and managed.

With this transformation of legal perception in mind, what then is the basis in law for Iroquois self-perception, sense of jurisdiction, and movement across the border? It is largely the nation-to-nation, or "linking arms,"[15] metaphor of equality among people, reflective of the treaty relationship, that serves as an interpretive frame for Iroquois engagements with other nations, be they Indigenous or non-Indigenous (Becker 1998).

This is a notion anchored historically in arguments and deployments of the Two Row Wampum Treaty between the Iroquois and the Dutch,[16] manifest in reminders and interactions that have been issued in serial engagements in the national and international arenas over the past three centuries. But the most important among these treaties for cross-border articulations is the Jay Treaty of 1794.[17] It is this treaty that Daniel brought to the border guard's attention and which the border guard misinterpreted and then claimed as his own (erroneously, as a Cherokee).

This treaty would not bear upon Cherokee mobility, because their settlers were different. In 1794, the United States and Great Britain signed the Treaty of Amity, Commerce, and Navigation, commonly known as the Jay Treaty.[18] The US-British boundary had been established in 1783 with the Treaty of Paris, and, as a creature of the post-Revolutionary War landscape, the Jay Treaty then sought to delimit and establish jurisdiction along the Treaty of Paris boundaries and to harmonize trade between the countries.[19] In a concession to Indian nations along those boundaries, the Jay Treaty acknowledged and, as in the case of all early colonial legislation, codified within a particular time and space—and with concomitant attitudes and flows of power—the rights of Indian nations occupying areas near the US-Canadian border, among them the Iroquois Confederacy nations: the Mohawk, Oneida, Onondaga, Cayuga, Seneca, and Tuscarora.

In the Jay Treaty, the right to traverse the boundaries of the US-British divide freely and without levy was guaranteed for Indian people who were operating in what has been defined as their cultural traditional "nexus" of trade.[20] This is laid out explicitly in article 3 of the Jay Treaty:

> It is agreed that it shall at all Times be free to His Majesty's Subjects, and to the Citizens of the United States, and also to the Indians dwelling on either side of the said Boundary Line, freely to pass and repass by Land or Inland Navigation, into the respective Territories and Countries of the Two Parties on the Continent of America. . . . No Duty of Entry shall ever be levied by either Party on Peltries brought by Land, or Inland Navigation into the said Territories respectively, nor shall the Indians passing or repassing with their own proper Goods and Effects of whatever nature, pay for the same any Impost or Duty whatever.[21]

This explicit right to pass, then, implicitly leaves the legal regimes of Canada and the United States with the power to define who those Indian nations are and how that right to pass shall be rendered and respected. As well, and very critically, the regimes of the United States and Canada were bequeathed the power to choose whom they would recognize as members of these communities. It is prudent now to map out how these long-standing forms of recognition then speak to local forms of recognition and, more critically, how they speak to Indigenous notions of citizenship formation and territory. Connecting these discourses illuminates how legal interests and designations not only affect the possibility of movement, but how these interests also work to define, through identification practices, their own territory and boundaries (Torpey 2000). Such connections may illuminate as well how these identifications and legal and interpretive acts are reformulated in practice and how they are not only "resisted," but circumvented, denied, or refused.

Brushing up against the State: Transhistoric Narratives

> I was flying back to New York, and this guy at the airport wanted to know my blood quantum. I said 100 percent. He said, "Do you have a green card?" I said, "I don't need one. I am a North American Indian." He asked for proof of my blood quantum. I said, "Look at my Indian card[22]— I am an Indian; that is why I have one." He made me go to INS . . . the next day in New York City, and I was really mad but I went. This is the first time this happened to me in all these years. I went there and the guy said, "You are an Indian; you don't belong here—I am closing this case." I knew I didn't belong there. I went to the lawyer at the American Indian Community House the next day, and I got a copy of the Jay Treaty. Now I carry that and my Indian card with me whenever I cross. (R.J., in his sixties)

Before there was Danny, before there was me, and even before there was R.J. and the countless other people who do this daily, the Jay Treaty got its first legal test of Indigenous mobility and citizenship with the case of *United States ex rel. Diabo v. McCandless* in 1927.[23] With the passage of the Indian Citizenship Act of 1924, Indians in the United States were made citizens of the United States, and those in Canada who traveled and worked within the United States were rendered "aliens."[24] Although the Citizenship Act may have been regarded by some Native people as an affirmation of their equal place within the United States, the act was regarded by other highly independent, self-ruling communities—such as Hopi, Onondaga, and Ahkwesáhsne—as the imposition of a foreign form of citizenship and governance.[25] Citizenship criteria determined by the act omitted Canadian forms of recognition that afforded rights to Indians in Canada. Nonetheless, because Iroquois on both sides of the border had histories of crossing the border and knew that this passage was a right recognized by the Jay Treaty,[26] they believed that they had a right to pass through the Canadian-US border as Indigenous nationals rather than as "aliens."

Paul K. Diabo was, by all legal reports, 100 percent Iroquois, Indigenous, and not, therefore, an "alien,"[27] except, of course, under the terms of the Citizenship Act. More specifically, he was a Mohawk ironworker from Kahnawà:ke who traveled down to the United States to work, as did many other men from the community. He had worked on and off in the United States for ten years and had both passed through the border and worked in the United States with no difficulty. Yet he suddenly found himself arrested and deported in 1925 as an illegal alien. Diabo petitioned for a writ of habeas corpus on the grounds that as a member of a North American Indian tribe, he was exempt from immigration laws as guaranteed under article 3 of the Jay Treaty. The US District Court for the Eastern District concurred and held that the right to cross the border was in fact an Aboriginal right, a right that was inherent—one recognized and confirmed, not created, by the treaty:[28] "The rights of the Indians are [not] in any way affected by the treaty, whether now existent or not. The reference to them was merely the recognition of their right, which was wholly unaffected by the treaty, except that the contracting parties agreed with each other that each would recognize it. . . . From the Indian view point, he crosses no boundary line. For him this does not exist."[29] The court's decision was confirmation throughout Iroquois country that Iroquois rights were legally recognized, affirmed, and active, in spite of the major setback that the Citizenship Act posed for the particular form of recognition that they desired—as sovereign nations.

Both the Citizenship Act and the Johnson-Reed Immigration Act of 1924, which included exclusionist measures against both Native Americans and Asians, were especially onerous for the Iroquois because they represented the twin imposition of (first) alien status, with its difficulties for Iroquois travelers and workers from Canada, and of (second) foreign citizenship, with its links to foreign-governance structure. These laws, as well as band-council governance, were resisted in Iroquois communities on both sides of the border, as any form of foreign citizenship meant the dissolution of traditional governance and membership and the growing power of the settler state within Iroquois communities.

These resistances to, and struggles with, state forms were not limited to a few periods and places. They had also been felt in Kahnawà:ke in 1884, with petitions against the Canadian Indian Advancement Act of 1884;[30] in Ahkwesáhsne in 1899, when the traditional chief Jake Fire was shot and killed by Royal Canadian Mounted Police for demanding their removal from the community in respect for traditional Mohawk governance (Mitchell 1988, 118); then at Six Nations, for the imposition of an electoral band council in 1924; and the American side of Ahkwesáhsne in 1924, with the United States' Indian Citizenship Act.

The Indian Defense League of America (IDLA) was formed at Tuscarora in 1926 by Clinton Rickard specifically to address the cross-border rights of Iroquois peoples (Rickard 1995b: 48). The IDLA was inspired by the work of the Deskaheh (Levi General) at Six Nations and embodied the effort to assert Iroquois sovereignty and to affirm Iroquois treaty rights.[31] Deskaheh worked tirelessly to get Six Nations recognized as a member nation within the League of Nations. But, in 1924 Canada began to forcefully enforce its Indian Act of 1876 (whose imposition at Six Nations was avoided because of the Indians' "civilized status" relative to other Indians), supplanting the traditional chiefs and band-council forms of governance in his community (Deskaheh 1991, 41–47), and seizing the wampum belts.[32] When Deskaheh's struggle to gain international recognition failed, he made a radio address explaining the Iroquois position vis-à-vis land and sovereignty, exhorting Americans to "know their history" and argued for an understanding of citizenship as a colonizing technique. Of this he argued,

> Your governments have lately resorted to new practices in their Indian policies. In the old days, they often bribed our chiefs to sign treaties to get our lands. Now they know that our remaining territory can easily be gotten from us by first taking our political rights away in forcing us into your citizenship, so they give jobs in their Indian offices to the bright young people among us who will take them and who, to earn their pay, say that your people wish to become citizens with you and that we are

ready to have our tribal life destroyed and want your governments to do it. But that is not true. (Deskaheh 1991, 48–54)

He died days later in the home of Clinton Rickard on the American side of the border on the Tuscarora Indian Reservation. The circumstances of his death were symbolic of his struggle and for the struggle of Iroquois peoples at the time. He was exhausted and sick from the struggle in Geneva, and the medicine being delivered to him from Six Nations did not make it across the border because of immigration restrictions (Rickard 1995b: 48). His final words before he died on the Tuscarora reservation were to "fight for the line," meaning fight for the Iroquois people's right to cross the border (ibid., 51).

In the fifty years following Deskaheh's death, the Immigration and Naturalization Service, the courts, and the border guards variously interpreted Jay Treaty rights and applied law to Indigenous and non-Indigenous peoples who crossed the border. Citizenship Act interpretations were at times in direct conflict with Canadian forms of recognition. In 1933, Canada adopted more political forms of recognition at the border, with its own terms of Indian admissibility. These forms of recognition in Canada confounded border guards as they dealt with individuals who were non-Indian and had Indian status conferred upon them by the Canadian state, such as non-Indian women who married Indian men; they likewise applied a separate set of rules for Indian women who married non-Indian men. In a series of interesting situations, predicaments, and decisions, border guards and the Immigration and Naturalization Service then had to stretch immigration law and the Jay Treaty to deal with white women who had Indian cards and wanted to cross;[33] Indian women who did not have Indian status in Canada and wanted to stay within the United States;[34] and, in one the of the earliest test cases of the Jay Treaty, with two non-Indigenous Canadians.[35] These arbitrary gymnastics account for the gendered and raced questions directed to Iroquois people today as border guards attempt to recall laws of recognition at work in both countries.

Borders of Blood

With the passage in 1934 of the Indian Reorganization Act, blood became a legal marker of Indian identity in the United States at the federal level,[36] and the INS determined that the amount of Indian blood that Indians from

Canada had to possess in order to gain passage into the United States was 50 percent.[37] At the border, this requisite was largely ignored in favor of more political forms of recognition, in line with Canadian practice. This persisted until the case of *Goodwin v. Karnuth* in 1947.

Dorothy Karnuth was a full-blooded Upper Cayuga from the Six Nations Reserve near Brantford, Ontario,[38] who was disenfranchised from her Indian status due to her marriage to a white man.[39] She did not have the political recognition that was necessary for her to remain in the United States, according to immigration practices. In her case the courts gave the concept of Indians born in Canada a raced definition. The INS soon revised its immigration manual: "The words 'American Indians born in Canada' . . . must be given a racial connotation. Thus an alien born in Canada who is of American Indian race is entitled to the immunities of this section regardless of membership in an Indian tribe or political status under Canadian law" (M. Smith 1997, 131, 147–48). This blood-quantum requirement was hardened into INS policy in 1952, with the Revised Citizenship Act of that year and then upheld in *Akins v. Saxbe.*[40] The blood-quantum requirement was not consistent with Canadian forms of recognition, forms that were based on the preexisting and somewhat sanguine model of the Victorian bourgeois family, but it was clearly consistent with the racialization of identity that had long been occurring in the states and was hardening around issues of immigration.[41]

The racialization of Indian identity in the United States correlates to the differing conceptions of Indian relationships to the state and to Indian citizenship through time. These were conceptions of recognition that moved Indian tribes (as they are known in the United States) away from the semisovereign status of "domestic and dependent nations" and into the conceptual and legal ambit of racialized minorities. Here we see the biopolitical project of recognition, which sees governable populations based on bodily attributes rendered as "races," trumping a prior and ongoing, if not strangulated, political order of sovereignty. Much like the East Indians who immigrated to Canada (Mongia 1999),[42] Indians in the United States and Canada appear completely outside of the frame of US citizenship, from which the US Constitution excluded them by virtue of their perceived incapacity for civilization and taxability (Smith 1997, 133). However, unlike the East Indians in Canada, Indigenous peoples within the United States were not geographically distant people, or at that time, foreign people who represented reprehensible or anxiety-provoking cultural differences to the American or Canadian legal eye; they were, from their earliest moments of interaction, recognized and Indigenous sovereigns, not foreigners seeking to immigrate, nor citizens.

This initial exclusion, which was based on the semisovereign status, or the "independent" status of Indians and the taxable standard of citizenship, was in contrast to the deliberate exclusion of African Americans and Asian Americans in that it was not yet based on racialized criteria (Smith 1997, 135). However this nonracialized standard of difference and recognition for Indians would soon change (ibid., 136). Because Indian exemption from the more racialized ambits of exclusion was most likely in reference to their "nontaxable status" within the geographical parameters of the United States and to the membership they possessed within internal nations, the diminution of their separate status—and concomitant political authority and recognition—was directly related to the application of more racialized forms of recognition and to US citizenship.

This diminution began with the Dawes Severalty Act of 1887, which granted US citizenship to Indians who rescinded their tribal membership and their Aboriginal rights to land and who accepted the apportioning of their land into fee-simple plots.[43] During this important transitory period, tribal membership was maintained as important, but in the space of "neither this nor that," or between the legal categories of citizen and ward in the courts.[44] Citizenship is, in this rendering, a political identity rather than a racial one, and, as such, Indians were citizens only in geographic "spots."[45] More racialized forms of recognition began in part with *Mosier v. United States*,[46] which acknowledged blood to be the proper form of identification for Indians.[47] In this decision, blood took precedence over other forms of recognition that were at work—and at work simultaneously— in the United States at this time: wardship, citizenship, tribal membership, and, during the twenty-five-year waiting period mentioned above, allotment and aptitude.[48] The American recognition of blood or quantifiable notions of race (or difference) was not completely consistent with Canadian forms of recognition, but was consistent with the racialization of identity that had long been occurring in the United States through the legacy of slavery and through the courts.

The landscape of recognition in Canada was, and still is, different from that in the United States. Yet in some respects, it is quite similar. Unlike the racialized interpretation of crossing in the United States, Canada would take an extreme culturalist position in interpreting the Jay Treaty.[49] When Ahkwesáhsne grand chief Mike Mitchell tested the Jay Treaty in 1988 by going "the other way"—from the United States to Canada—to renew trade relations with the Mohawk reserve community of Tyendinaga, his rights to trade within Mohawk territory were not upheld. In his trial, archaeological evidence was used to deny the Mohawk claim to an Aboriginal right to travel and to trade with other Mohawks and trade north of the St. Lawrence River. Based on the culture test laid out in *Van der Peet*, the 1996 Canadian Supreme Court decision that defined Aboriginal rights based on cultural practices that were in place *prior* to settlement,[50] this trade north of the St. Lawrence was deemed not to be a significant part of Mohawk culture and thus not a right to be upheld by the Supreme Court of Canada: "The border marked by the Saint-Lawrence River is absolute: while changes to the way trade is carried out are permitted, the Court explicitly refuses to apply the same dynamic reasoning with regard to the territory on which such trade takes place" (Denis 2002, 113, 123).

These different interpretations regarding boundaries and territory are part of an interpretive process in Canada of using especially static and culturalist methodology to mete out recognition. Note that here it is "culture," not sovereignty or historic agreement, that is the legal test. One sovereignty, as we see from RICO, cannot test the other. Culture is allowed to change, but elements within in it must maintain the same value and meaning through time, and apply to collectives that are recognizable to the state based on that state's criteria for Indigenous difference— difference that is constructed as "recognizable" as cultural practices affixed in a certain moment in time. The practice must remain evident to the juridical eye and to the expert eyes of archaeologists, historians, and anthropologists, and it must be evident through time. This expert juridical frame for recognizing rights to territory has real implications, as well, for the ways in which Indians born in Canada exercise their rights to cross back to Canada and to conduct more contemporary forms of trade. As the contemporary border-crossing challenges and negotiations in this chapter evidence, there is a constant form of contention between Iroquois and all settler regimes that they encounter.

The Savagery of Indigenous Sovereignty

The visibility of Indian governmental bodies through the form of arrests and through the nationally televised documentaries of *Troubled Waters,* in 1993, and *The Dark Side of Native Sovereignty,* in 1996, served as spectacles that would obscure the larger modes of production and exchange at work. These larger machinations involved tobacco conglomerates willfully circumventing the law in order to derive surplus from the sale of untaxed cigarettes. The lost revenue and associated law-enforcement costs then traversed the boundaries of provinces, states, and finally nation-states, begging the question of whose law applied. These are issues that begin with the territorial premise of sovereignty as dominion over a place and people but that, more specifically in this case, are applied extraterritorially through the form of revenue and in particular, the revenue rule.

Although the revenue rule stated that "one sovereign will not enforce the tax judgments or claims of another sovereign,"[51] the problem was not cast in these terms because the problem, in the early and mid-1990s in Canada, became something else through the focus on Indians as the visible smugglers. The role of Big Tobacco was yet to be revealed and remained invisible, unnoticeable in the earliest public scrutiny of tobacco smuggling. Iroquois nationals and, in particular, Mohawks—and their sovereignty— were, by contrast, very visible. Their border-crossing history, as just narrated, was less visible.

Consider here the Canadian Border Service Agency's summary of the events leading up to *R.J. Reynolds*: "While Canada knew that smuggling was occurring along its borders, it was not aware of Defendants' [Big Tobacco's] participation in smuggling. Canada recognized the devastating impact upon Canadian society and the integrity of the Canadian regulatory framework. Thus, Canada augmented efforts to control tobacco smuggling and embarked upon an almost decade-long effort to eliminate the growing smuggling problem."[52] Perhaps because of an unawareness of the corporate defendants' position, the "smuggling problem" in an earlier iteration was conflated with Indigenousness, and Indigenousness with Mohawks. Mohawks were then equated with lawlessness, and lawlessness with Indigenous sovereignty.

Indigenous sovereignty carried the residue of savagery. As a perception rooted in a deep history of Occidental reasoning, reasoning that constructs our notion of sovereignty, Aristotle (and his progeny) have perceived savagery as a condition of beastlike association that is defined as being without law (Aristotle [350 BCE] 1995). As the discussion and analysis of public texts on smuggling illustrated, it was Mohawk invocations of sovereignty and the practice of sovereignty through their exercising of the right to cross based on the Jay Treaty that made their move toward "savagery" and "lawlessness" possible in the public mind. This representational chain of equivalencies and conflations reduced sovereignty to aboriginality and, in this, to racialized and temporalized bodies and locales. These bodies were reduced to entities that were legally confounding and spectacular; the entities became newsworthy in their failure to conform to economic norms, to nation-state boundaries, and to consent to citizenship by conforming to taxation regimes.

To be taxed is to be a citizen (Isin and Turner 2003, 5); to evade this is to be a savage, improper, or lawless citizen. The publicizing of this "lawlessness," as with the nationally televised documentaries discussed above, incited national anxieties and fiduciary norms around taxation that then took the shape of public concern. However, to be an Indigenous person in Canada is also to occupy a different space for citizenship, one that from its inception "evades" taxation because of the legally defined status of "wardship" that recognized Indians occupy. This legal status has been called "citizens plus" in liberal policy,[53] a naming that sought to capture the perceived duality of their legal category: they were citizens of a "first nation" (the Aboriginal one) and also citizens of the nation-state that now frames that first nation (the settler society). This policy did not take into account the way the category of citizens plus also signified to Indians an executive or settler fiat: the recognition was a one-sided recognition, a legal event ensconced in time and in law that signaled the descent of their ability to be recognized as Indians and the strangulation of their governmental systems. Indigenous governmental systems were not recognized; what was recognized was the differentiation of those systems according to criteria defined by first Britain and then Canada.

The conservative Canadian think tank the Mackenzie Institute examined the issue of cigarette smuggling. Its researchers derived their concern over cigarette smuggling from these histories of spatial and legal containment of Indians. They asked questions and sought to find their own answers, answers that lay within Indigenousness itself, particularly within Iroquois Indigeneity, as the main Indian protagonists in this issue who possessed special rights guaranteed to them as a border tribe that exercised distinct Aboriginal (cultural) and treaty rights.[54] Of this issue the Mackenzie Institute wrote, "While smoking for pleasure was practiced by other Natives and Europeans, this would have been seen by many [eighteenth-century] members of [the] Confederacy as vaguely sacrilegious. Leaf tobacco is still used for traditional purposes. When the Jay Treaty was signed in 1794 to allow Natives to bring goods across the border without paying taxes, king size, filter-tipped menthol flavoured cigarettes were a long way off" (Thompson 1994).

The Mackenzie researchers' questions and answers animated a volley of conflations and representations and added to the anxieties in Canada about the sincerity of Indigenous culture and the North American Free Trade Agreement; taken together, these impressions seemed to induce a panic. Elizabeth Povinelli attributes this type of panic to the temporal precariousness of settler nations, the demands that the politics of recognition place upon settlers and Indigenous peoples vis-à-vis the history and the courts (2002, 2–4). Although she does not note that precariousness is also the work of settler sovereignty, she warns that this panic signals the potential for that sovereignty to be undone.

Conclusion

This chapter began with an invocation of white men and "bullshit," a pairing of terms with a deep provenance. Yet much of this chapter mapped out the more recent nineteenth- and twentieth-century genealogy, filtered through the border-crossing history of one First Nation with territory that predates the United States and Canada, and so is caught up in the United States and Canada. What is the bullshit that this interlocutor spoke of? It is the mess of settlement as it inscribes itself in territories, territories that belonged to others. This is part of the process that Patrick Wolfe and others have spoken about, of taking land. When I stand at the border guard's counter and present myself in terms that are *not* cadastral, that are not in Mishuana Goeman's words, "spatialized" into settler terrains or colluding easily with one fully recognized citizenship or another,[55] I am pulling up these histories into this critical moment of translation, and possibility. *Will I get to cross, to get where I am going? Can I get through this and have the moral sense of what is right or wrong, upheld? Will I have this political authority that I answer to respected? Will I lose all respect for you? Will I keep cool if I do?* The same applies to Danny, to R.J., to countless others who slow down lines, sit in detention rooms; who get sneered at, otherwise inspected, or completely demobilized when they do not proffer up the easy answer. The problem is, an easy answer does not exist in the history that upholds these ethnographic moments, the perception of Mohawk mobility as already a crime, a contravention of the fixity of place, borders, and settled states. In one case, the crime, in fact, was committed by corporations in an unwitting collusion with the optics of the settler state, optics that then used Mohawks as the spectacle that obscured a multinational corporation's deep lawlessness, contravention, and cunningly planned crime. This chapter has moved through representational practices of a settler nation-state, dwelled within case law, and ended with history. As we saw from the earliest moments of this larger narrative on Iroquois mobility and constraint, Danny's body, R.J.'s body, Red Jacket's lament, and my tense exchanges are tied up with deeper structures of understanding, of apprehension, of anxiety, of states attempting to talk to each other through border guards, through legal decisions, through practices that then put Indian bodies (once they are agreed upon as, in fact, Indian bodies) and Indian polities in place.

I mentioned a deep provenance between white men and bullshit. The representational history of Indian "lawlessness" does not have its beginning with cigarette "smuggling" in the 1990s. Its genealogy extends back to the earliest moments of recorded encounter, when Indians appeared to have no law, to be without order, and thus, to be, in the colonizer's most generous articulation of differentiation, in need of the trappings of civilization. "Law" may be one instrument of civilization, as a regulating technique of power that develops through the work upon a political body and a territory. Designating "savagery" was required for the forceful imposition of law, as was designating brutishness. So the law in Canada—and to a less focused and less encompassing extent, that in the United States—has attempted to define and regulate Indian behavior, to protect, and, in different iterations, to confine and contain the Indigenous in certain spaces. The 1876 Canadian Indian Act, when compared to the 2,500 pieces of legislation that make up the rubric of federal Indian law in the United States, is a uniform body of law that has sought to do all of the above. It is very much about achieving a state of lawfulness and containment, which is an ontological state of political subjecthood, one that is highly regulatory and does significant legal work upon the territories, bodies, and cultures of Indians in Canada. Its structuring presupposition is that Indians reside somewhere between ward, citizen, and people presumed to be savage who must have their savagery recognized first, in order to be governed. *R.J. Reynolds* and related decisions revealed the ways in which law regarding Indians was a failed episode of consent, consent to a form of sovereignty that is clear and that unambiguously accords with territories of conquest. It also fails to regulate fears of lawlessness while uncovering the role that "Indigenous savagery" has had in furthering settler capitalism. Finally, it diminishes Indigenous rights to trade and to act as sovereigns in their own territories.

SIX

The Gender of the Flint

Mohawk Nationhood and Citizenship in the Face of Empire

44. The lineal descent of the people of the Five Nations shall run in the female line. Women shall be considered progenitors of the Nation. They shall own the land and the soil [the clearing]. Men and women shall follow the status of the Mother.

—Wampum 44 from "The Constitution of the Five Nations," Parker (1916)

Sovereignty and the Spectacular

In the summer of 1990, then prime minister of Canada Brian Mulroney worried about matters other than cigarettes. But, he worried about Mohawks just the same. At that time Mohawks and allied individuals were pushing against settler encroachment so vigorously that a "Crisis" of epic proportions ensued. "The Oka Crisis" was a seventy-eight-day armed Indigenous resistance to land expropriation. It was a spectacular event that pronounced the structure of settler colonialism in Canada, illuminating its desire for land, its propensity to consume, and its indifference to life, to will, to what is considered sacred, binding, and fair.

Relentless media coverage "spectacularized" this event and, in the minds of many Mohawks there, saved their lives by relaying their armed refusal to an international audience via television and print news media. Here I want us to consider one official, state discourse among many on the motives and the reason animating the Mohawk refusal at Oka. In one of his interviews with the press, Prime Minister Mulroney explained to a CBC journalist that the Warriors who were encamped behind the barricades at Kanehsatà:ke were not a traditional Iroquois society.[1] In fact, they were criminals and terrorists. As such, there was no authorizing text for their action, besides vice and violence.

Brian Mulroney spoke with the expertise of Lewis Henry Morgan when he pronounced on the content of the cultural sincerity and integrity of the Warriors. He even took the authoritative discourse further, and as a head of state he implied their motives were aberrant to the politics of the place that they were defending, the bodies of the dead that they stood before, and the directives from Mohawk women that they acted upon to defend territory. These directives, the philosophical tradition that shaped them, and their right to act were aberrant to the settler nation's configuration of a birthright to act. This society, these men, Mulroney said, were criminals and they were terrorists, and to add perhaps a territorial affront to Canada's injury, some of them, he said with great certainty and solemnity, were "not even Canadian."

The Oka Crisis of 1990 is the most recent act of "domestic warfare" in Indian-settler relations to date. The incident received massive coverage; it was spectacular, an event of seemingly epic proportions. I am starting off this chapter on gender and territory with this story to ask deeper questions of the structure of settler colonialism, its systemic relationship to gender in particular and to the governing auspices of authenticity and colonial expectation in configurations of "the problem of membership." In spite of what Brian Mulroney said about the Warrior society, I start this part of the story of membership here because even more than precedential reasoning and the law of settlers in the grounded history of the border we just read, the Oka Crisis illustrates the violent, vigorous defense of territory and the centrality of Mohawk women to this process.

Iroquois women are too often and to easily imagined simply as "caretakers of the land" and "mothers of the nation" in a way that is stripped of its contemporary valences, instantiations, and meaning.[2] As well, they are imagined in a way that occludes the ongoing effects of white, settler patriarchy in their communities and in their lives.[3] With Oka we see the empirical face of that caretaking: women who called a peaceful protest and then an armed refusal against further dispossession. And we have here women who then *managed* that refusal during a seventy-eight-day armed standoff. But with this massive refusal there was a flip side. In the midst of it, they were still contending with their own ongoing struggles against the state and their band councils. Some women were still suffering the burden of disenfranchisement: the snaking, dividing, and yet organizing logic of raced and gendered heteropatriarchy manifest in the Indian Act, which sought to divest Indian women from land by divesting them of their legal rights as Indians.

As earlier chapters explained, "out-marriage" appears to be the problem: its ulcerating effects and legacies, with people left juridically adrift outside of the legal territories of their nations, outside of the normative space of their parents' homes. Their bodies were placed juridically beyond the reserve, outside of the grasp of its particular rights, even when it is inside. We saw this with "C" in chapter 4, his interview on the legacy of "C-31," and his own refusal to narrate its effects. Yet, out-marriage is *not* the problem. Like the "crime" of smuggling, this form of conjugal relation is spectacularized, this time by Mohawks, as a social offense, and then by the mainstream media as the community's illiberal transgression against a new normative order based on "human rights" rather than white, settler patriarchy. The transgression, however, masks what makes it so—a white civil and legal order that is from its inception in Mohawk and Iroquois territory, intent upon eliminating them.

I was in Montreal interviewing a woman from Kanehsatà:ke. As anyone who watched the evening news or spoke to people in Kahnawà:ke or Kanehsatà:ke could see, during the Oka Crisis the women were the primary negotiators with the Sûreté du Québec[4] and then the Canadian armed forces. However, what was not apparent was the level of fear the presence of women caused in the armed forces of the state. Here she told me,

> **A:** You know in 1990 the police and army were more scared of the women than they were of the men. . . .
> **Q:** How did you know that? How did you . . . ?
> **A:** From firsthand experience! [*laughs*]
> **Q:** Tell me how . . .
> **A:** Starting from the beginning on July 11 when we were raided there were about nine to ten women that went to the police . . . and the police were like "this" [*gestures nervously*] and from the beginning they were more afraid of the women because the women were like, right in their face . . . and it had to do with their machismo stuff, like they wanted to hit us, but they couldn't; they were intimidated by the women.

They even said, because it was the women that were in the front, like on July 11, they had told the girlfriend of one of our guys—she was non-Native—the sq guy said to her, "These are not normal people, because usually when we come in dressed up the way we were, and we shoot tear gas, and shoot grenades at them, people *run*," but these people just kept coming back—they are not normal . . . and it was the women that met them.

It was indeed the women who "met them," and it was also the women who hailed this action, who started the peaceful protest and then managed the standoff in the Pines. They did this regardless of blood quantum, clan, or reserve (there were women from Kahnawà:ke there, as well as a few women who had traveled from other reserves, other parts of Canada). Their articulation of rights was one that refused either the blood-based, individualist, or more collectivist discourses of governance in play.

The Oka Crisis is of a piece, strangely, with C-31. This is because of the centrality of territory and women to both, and their status as symptoms of the logic and practice of settler-colonial elimination. Oka represents an overt push to eliminate rights to land, while C-31 is a legal bestowal of the state to rerecognize what they had legally eliminated. Oka designates a disappearance, C-31 a reappearance. Both of these events are linked through a state apparatus of eliminations but also through the different citizenship projects that they reveal and that they pronounce in part, through these state-driven attempts to dispossess, to repossess, and to govern the content of Mohawk political orders.

Narrating Oka

The Mohawks of Kanehsatà:ke were never in a proper status of wardship vis-à-vis the federal government. Thus their land was vulnerable to expropriation, and their reactions to those expropriations vulnerable to interpretations that considered them to be acting in unreasonable ways. Prior to the summer of 1990, they had endured two centuries of sustained land expropriation. The Mohawks of Kanehsatà:ke did not sit passively as their land was taken from them; they petitioned Ottawa, they petitioned Quebec, they suffered incarceration for those petitions, and finally in 1990 their women resorted to a peaceful protest that became decidedly militarized. When their months of peaceful protest did not effect a response from Ottawa regarding the most recent land situation, which involved extending the neighboring town of Oka's country club golf course directly into Mohawk land, the Warrior society convened at Kanehsatà:ke with AK-47 assault rifles.

Carl Schmitt argues that the power of the sovereign allows him to determine what is needed (2005) and act accordingly, and so the mayor of Oka, Jean Ouellette, attempted to act as a sovereign. He acted in accordance with what in his mind was needed. In doing so he incited a state of exception that distributed its effect through a ratcheting of tradition through a ratcheting of Iroquois political theory, and through a maelstrom of meanings that were sieved and mediated through the evening news, saturating the viewing world with two centuries of misrecognitions. There was, in this state of exception, no monopoly on violence; nor was there a dense, recognizable moral cachet to reveal what the utilitarian "good" was. The depth of this grievance, the philosophical and geopolitical purpose, was unclear. In fact, everybody in certain moments looked really bad—some for more sustained moments than others. One thing that was for sure, however, was that the land that was to be used to extend the golf course nine more holes was and still is precious to the Mohawks of Kanehsatà:ke because it held both the bodies of their dead as well as Pines that were sacred to them. So, when the traditional "Warrior" society convened at the behest of the women in Kanehsatà:ke, Indigenous people from all over Canada and the United States caravanned to Quebec in support of the Warriors and for an answer to the "land problem," which was then conflated with terrorism or criminality. Both were depicted by the masked, camouflaged Mohawk Warrior—a symbol not of the Kaianere'kó:wa or gendered forms of power and alternative forms of political authority and legitimacy, but of a contemporary, militant, and lawless savagery. The Warriors at Oka became the synecdoche for Mohawks in general and were, in the minds of the Progressive Conservative government of the time, defying the laws not only of the state but of reason itself. They defied the social and political presumption of universal rights in Canada: citizenship. They defied settler citizenship and they defied land expropriation, highlighting their comingling. This affront to the organizing principle and attendant sensibility of membership to Canada incited Mulroney to further say of the Warriors (and this in reference to those who were born and raised, it was noted, repeatedly, in Brooklyn, New York) that "some of them are not even citizens of Canada!" (Obomsawin 1993).

So it was. And it was true. These were men and women with differently defined citizenship, and some were born in Brooklyn and some in Detroit. They assembled and took up arms, doing so in part because they saw the failure of the rights that Canada offered them, the limitations on those rights as tied to land. They did what they did in part because of their own constitutional framework, which decrees that they have to defend their land, their nation, and their Confederacy from encroachment, but also because of the vulnerable and contested nature of the title to their land, land they could never properly or improperly own.

Indians in Canada can never own land in a full sense, in a Lockean fashion, even when they have been encouraged by the state to farm it in preparation for title. According to the Indian Act—the text that recognizes them as juridical beings with particular rights and possibilities (the primary one being civilization), the act of Congress that is *the* governing document of their lives—reservation land is held in trust by the Crown for their "use and benefit" until they are properly civilized and made citizens. As of 1947 they are citizens of Canada (and 1924 in the states), and the Mohawks at Kanehsatà:ke were an exception to the exception that the nation-state found itself in when they took up arms. The "law" revealed itself again to be precarious and fragile, never properly extending itself to them or their territory, enunciating in those moments a colonial past that refused to stay there, historically, *there* in a "before" state. Suddenly the highest number of troops in the history of Indigenous-settler relations in North America was deployed to Kanehsatà:ke, as this was the most unambiguous form of exceptional relations, that of warfare. There were 2,650 soldiers deployed to handle fifty-five Warriors.

I want to think now about what the law failed to contain in those moments. This was a seventy-eight-day armed standoff, one that resulted in three deaths: a Sûreté du Québec officer, a Quebecois resident of Kahnawà:ke, and an English Canadian who died from teargas poisoning outside of Kanehsatà:ke. Three instruments of law arrived: the Sûreté du Québec, the Royal Canadian Mounted Police, and finally 2,650 regular and reserve troops from the Thirty-Fourth and Thirty-Fifth Canadian Brigade Groups and the Fifth Canadian Mechanized Brigade Group. These were brought in at the height of tension, when Quebec premier Robert Bourassa requisitioned the assistance of the Canadian forces in "aid to the civil power" by invoking the Emergencies Act. The state of exception was official, and colonial law was strangely, violently, and very precariously reinscribed. Simultaneously, the Canadian viewing public and negotiators were forced to listen to sound bites that issued from the Kaianere'kó:wa. This was a "watershed" moment so disorienting in this history of Indian-white relations in Canada that capital had to be released immediately to address, redress, assuage, and some would say silence the booming but very reasoned Indigenous critique of dispossession. Money was released by Canada to evade deep historical accountability, presumably to assuage the pain of territorial loss and violence once things came to a strange and immediate close. Afterward, the federal government released $5.2 million to buy the land in question (to be held in trust for Mohawks), and another $51.2 million was released for a five-year royal commission to hold hearings around Canada on the issues of land, sovereignty, and Indigenous rights.[5]

The Mohawks burned their weapons (rather than buried them), peacefully surrendered, and were immediately incarcerated. This was a state of emergency that was not a state of exception for all. Luana Ross argues that for the United States, genocide has never been illegal (1998, 15). In a similar vein, legal scholar Sora Han argues that "along side the newest images of America *at* war (over there, back then) there is, still, an image of America *as* war—even as this image is effectively invisible under the War on Terror's visual economy" (2006, 232). Han writes from the vantage point of the "War on Terror," over there. Yet I wondered at the time if Canada fancied itself the United States? In a review by Giorgio Agamben (2005) of the labor of constitutionalism and precedential reasoning that works to actually conceal (rather than protect) the suspension of individual and collective rights in times of emergency, we see a suspension that in fact produces constitutionally sustained, *legalized* illegality; this is totalitarianism by law. This is a totalitarianism and an analysis that in this sociological case became precise and correspondent, aligning perfectly, it seemed, with what was unfolding. Oka was a moment that was (and is?) coterminous with the space we understand to be indigeneity, constructed by and symptomatic of the structure of settler colonialism itself.

Giorgio Agamben's legally sanctioned no-holds-barred space of "exception" has alluring conceptual attributes when accounting for times of crisis, but is simply not surprising or, perhaps, innovating when considering the case of Indigeneity and settler colonialism. As well, one does not have to dwell exclusively in the horror of a concentration camp to find life stripped bare to cadastral form, ready only for death in a biopolitical account of sovereignty. This is structural, not eventful, like many others; the Indigeneities of the Mohawks of Kanehsatà:ke necessitate techniques of power that work upon them to foment the exception, and in this to proliferate state sovereignty. This productive power occurs through the ways in which law must respond to their actions because they are themselves always a subject of failed juridic containment. As with the people, the land in Kanehsatà:ke was that problem writ large because their reservation was so improperly configured; the land was in a state of continued expropriation; their actions were ignored, vanquished, or cause for incarceration. They recognized again that they were in their own constant state of historical emergency. This was what Jeremy Waldron and other political theorists sometimes gloss as "historical injustice" (1992, 2002). For the people of Kanehsatà:ke, it was most specifically, most grievously, a sustained problem of constant land expropriation. Furthermore, they could not achieve a colonial contortion that would allow a recognition and some degree of protection. Their land did not appear the way it should because it was expropriated; it would not and could not appear in a manner that would afford it proper recognition or protection; it did not appear to be theirs for use and occupancy, making it even more vulnerable to expropriation.

Rather than a reservation or reserve that was consistently occupied by Indians, this reservation was a "checkerboard style," with Mohawks on some patches of land and whites on others, living right next to them. This checkerboard represented competing property regimes: civil law versus Indian Act wardship, a system that harkened back to Kanehsatà:ke history in the colonial era as a seigniorial land grant that the Mohawks (and Nippissings and Algonquins) inhabited and which, according to standard historiography, was supposed to begin in 1721 with their movement up to the Lake of Two Mountains from Hochelaga (an Iroquois village in Montreal). It was in Hochelaga, or Montreal, or Tiotià:ke where they split from other Mohawks and moved, with one missionary in tow, up north.[6] There they were to be protected by the seignior, and later the Sulpician monastery that slowly, devastatingly sold it off, bit by bit, until the 1970s (Gabriel-Doxtator and Van den Hende 1995). So it was that Canadians (some of whom were sovereigntist Quebecois) held title to land that was originally Mohawk. This is an extended, imperial moment because everything about it foments Empire. Reservations are often imbricated in these extended, imperial moments, where theories of praxis elude them unless it is to decide their relationship to sameness and difference defined by a Canadian normative center in their claims to land and liberty in the courts. In order to exercise territorial rights, they must be in possession of this territory prior to Canadian settlement and they must then pass the legal culture test of *Van der Peet*, in which they demonstrate that the territory they claim is tied to their cultural practice as defined in the moment of settlement (what has been called "frozen rights").[7] These practices must be in accord with their (colonial) moment of beginning, when they were first seen, or recorded, or made use of their land in ways legible to outsiders. But the situation in Kanehsatà:ke seemed extreme even for the extreme: how to claim and protect what is so improperly configured (in even the most colonial sense—the demarcated, bounded, wardship-status space of the reservation) in order to protect what is left from further encroachment? Theirs is an unusual political topography for reservation land in Canada and was a topography that aligned more with the postallotment landscape in the United States, where one will see in reservations such as Lac du Flambeau in Wisconsin—which Gail Guthrie-Valaskakis (2005) documented and theorized from—whites living side by side with Indians. Such a topography is unusual for Canada, as reservations were generally not subject to privatization or termination, as was the case in the United States. The result in Kanehsatà:ke was an exceptional configuration, and their diminished possibilities for claiming an already diminished juridical sovereignty so that no proper claim for even wardship status could be made.

I am speaking of the Oka Crisis only to situate this discussion within a larger moment in Canada or series of moments around the *longue durée* (although it is really short durée) of colonialism, which may appear as an exceptional "event," but is in fact deeply structural. Recall that settler colonialism requires an Indigenous elimination for territory. This elimination (and its pushback, its refusal) is manifest in relentless crises of recognition, crises that have been enabled only by the juridical strangulation of Indigenous governmental forms, philosophical practices, and gender roles. Colonial techniques such as the Indian Act of 1876 limit Indians (note the word "Indians" here, as there are also two other Indigenous groups in

Canada: Métis and Inuit) to spaces of reservations and bodies of certain substance and practice. Conversations around historical injustices take on both a corporeal and territorial cast, but have been central in defining for Canada a sense of itself as less than perfect, less than what the United Nations index would have people think it is because every five years or so Indians take up arms, block bridges, and kill themselves in protest, or, if they are women, they simply seem to "disappear."

The "phenomenon" of the disappeared women, the murdered and missing Native women in Canada, is not a mystery, is not without explanation. Sherene Razack (2002), Beverly Jacobs[8] and Amnesty International (2004, 2009), Andrea Smith (2005), the filmmakers Christine Welsh (2006) and Sharmeen Chinoy (2006), as well as countless activists and heartbroken, devastated family members who have marched and petitioned, have all documented, theorized, and written about this disappearance, which is explained by Canada's dispossession of Indian people from land. This dispossession is raced and gendered, and its violence is still born by the living, the dead, and the disappeared corporealities of Native women. The disappearance of Indian women now takes on a sturdy sociological appearance: six hundred to nine hundred "missing" in the past decade, gone from their homes, murdered on the now-legendary "Highway of Tears" in Northern British Columbia,[9] off streets or reservations. Indian women "disappear" because they have been deemed killable, able to be raped without repercussion, expendable. Their bodies have *historically* been rendered less valuable because of what they are taken to represent: land, reproduction, Indigenous kinship and governance, an alternative to heteronormative and Victorian rules of descent. Theirs are bodies that carry a symbolic load because they have been conflated with land and are thus contaminating to a white, settler social order. So it is that they must be eradicated (A. Smith 2005). They are considered inviolable; in Andrea Smith's language, they are "rapable," as Native women are constructed as "immanently polluted with sexual sin . . ." already-violated (10). So they suffer disproportionately to other women. Their lives are shorter; they are poorer, less educated, suffer more from illness, and are raped more frequently; and they "disappear." Their disappearance thus is not an unexplainable phenomenon; like Oka, it is symptomatic of what administrators have called in Canada (and sometimes in the United States) "the Indian Problem." This problem is a problem of arms, of smuggling, of disappearing (if you are a woman), of political insistences (*this is mine, not yours*), and citizenships of refusal rather than consent. This problem is the structure, actually, of settler colonialism. It has beneficiaries as well as subjects.

Citizenship and reason have a history of entanglement in Canada and in other places of course, whereby only those who are fit to be recognized are admitted into the body politic—the settler state. The Oka Crisis is interesting for this reason (and many others), but I do not wish to speak more about what happened at Kanehsatà:ke. Rather, I wish to mark it as the "public face of nationalism" for Mohawk people and then embed other stories and takes on the interior negotiations and frontiers of Mohawk citizenship and nationhood within several gestural moments that Oka suggests. One gestural move was a discursive one, by Prime Minister Brian Mulroney, to disarticulate Mohawk claims to land and kin from the soil by saying that Mohawks are not citizens of Canada. This was laughable to Mohawks, as they are citizens of their nation; the defense of the Pines was an enactment of that historical obligation to territory and to each other. However, it rang true and was criminal to Canadians because in their eyes some of these Mohawks were in fact born in the states, were from sundry places such as Brooklyn, and thus had no business and no *reason* to be there. Furthermore, they were acting in an *unreasonable* manner (i.e., using force). Yet these Mohawks, and all Mohawks with whom I have worked in order to better understand the contours of citizenship and nationhood, think, feel, and often act otherwise, in accordance with texts and philosophical frameworks such as the Kaianere'kó:wa. They also form notions of citizenship from their experiences as travelers, workers, and Indigenous nationals in their own theaters of recognition, or refusal; in the affinal space between each other; according to another political authority; according to their knowledge of each other; and according to their responsibility to their territory, the bodies of the dead, their families.

Their political assertions, such as the one at Oka, force us to think beyond the politics of bestowal, in which sovereignty is *bestowed* rather than asserted, and then acknowledged as inherent. The politics of bestowal and atonement are favored by contemporary political theorists and politicians over the politics of assertion, acknowledgment, and radical reformulation of the grounds of governance. Mohawk assertions prompt us to reorient questions from "what do they want?" and "how do we accord them rights in a manner that is fair to all (and does not offend our sensibilities)?" to a more practice-based approach to politics *as* culture and law making in the face of Empire and its violence. Their actions, when contextualized, force us to ask how one is to define a citizenship for one's own people, according to one's political traditions while operating in the teeth of Empire, in the face of state aggression. And in considering this case and the adamant refusals and work that Mohawks undertake to defend their territory, to maintain that territory and in doing so, undo these expectations of docility, of assimilation, of a roll over to dispossession, we may reveal the presumption of consent with citizenship and citizenship with Empire. Because Mohawks insist that they are not citizens of Empire, they force us to ask how nations may exist without recognition, in states of strangulation; how one may construct and maintain citizenships after a century of colonial impositions that sought to remove not only the right but the cultural and political procedures to do so . . .

In this chapter I start an analysis of membership with the Oka Crisis in order to examine the cultural and lived contours of citizenship formation among the sister community to Kanehsatà:ke: Kahnawà:ke. Their citizenship project moves through several spheres of political authority and normative claims, as they must assert their independence from the United States, Canada, and the province of Quebec while simultaneously asserting their loyalty to their history and tradition as Haudenosaunee. They must maintain these allegiances while negotiating continuously for forms of political recognition (and affirmation) from settler regimes that have both created the problems with which they find themselves grappling and which will afford them some space for resolution. Because they are recognized by and at times antagonistic to the state, this is a tight normative spot to be in. How does one assert sovereignty and independence when some of the power to define that sovereignty is bestowed by a foreign power?

In order to understand the process of citizenship formation in light of all these factors—recognition, refusal, acquiescence, traditionalism, a history of domination, and various other articulations of power—I have examined how people constructed, deconstructed, or invoked "the nation" from the "ground level" of their experience. I look from this perspective because it is "top down," or statist forms of recognition, that many believe have created the dilemmas in which they find themselves, and it is the grounded forms of recognition that produce the authoritative nexus within the community that make, refuse, create, endure, withhold, or in various other ways *affect* the will of others. This particularly Iroquoian form of *authority* and *power* within the community that I will be working through is Iroquois' own space of recognition, if we were to call it something, a space shaped by political authority that does not derive solely from the state, but is drawn from their own traditions, their interpretations of that tradition, their shared archive of knowledge of each other, their genealogies, and their relationships with each other through time. It is that authority, which, were they to let go of it would cause them to "panic" (in Elizabeth Povinelli's parlance) and leave them with nothing but the desires and expectations of the state to govern their conduct, a slim authoritative pool for them to draw from. And were they to recognize this authority, it would induce competing obligations to perform their Indigeneity in ways that are politically effective, convincing, and pleasing, inducing a public sympathy for their "plight," which they would not, as we saw with Oka, perform. The state did not want Indians to remember, let alone act upon, other political traditions and authorities, to pick up weapons, to stand ground on their ground. This was not the "culture" that multiculturalism sought to protect and preserve. This, rather, was sovereignty and nationhood, something that was and still is to say the least an uneasy fit within a state that wishes to be singular, even when it imagines itself "federalist." Precontact nations are not "confederateable," as settlement requires a new political tableau or one made of parts that can be assimilated.[10] Povinelli (2002) theorizes the contradictions within this political imaginary as the dilemma of late liberalism, a social fact so structuring that it induces a panic in all—settlers, Indigenous people, and the state. I am interested in the ways in which alternative, Indigenous citizenships may move polities away from this panic, from these seductive inducements to perform for the state, and the way they do a different kind of work through a narrative and memory-based process of constructing and affording rights to each other.

The scrupulous and unwavering attention of Kahnawa'kehró:non to the issue of political membership within their community raises questions not only about the content of citizenship and political identity itself, but also about how local forms of knowledge and experience intersect with more global, historical, and, in particular, colonial forms of power. So what is this, specifically, that I speak of; and that I speak of after the cigarette crisis, after the Oka Crisis—crises, I would argue, in settler sovereignty and security? I will speak again of women, death, and rights.

Narrating Territory and Rights

> Even a dog could be buried in Kahnawà:ke, and we [the women who lost their Indian status upon out-marriage] could not! (Mary Two-Axe Early, ca. 1983)

The transition from property holder and status giver to a rank that is, upon death, beneath that of a dog requires a sudden and swift shift in power. In spite of the grinding force of the state evidenced by the Oka Crisis, both the wampum that opened this chapter in epigraph form and the utterance of Mary Two-Axe Early cited above tell us that notions of status and rights, and the complex of both that constitutes "political membership," must be tied up with something more than the power of the state. Why? Canada does not bury members in Kahnawà:ke; families do, and they do so in accordance with Mohawk Council of Kahnawà:ke (or traditional Longhouse) rules on membership and jurisdiction. Thus, the decision that allows dogs to be buried in the community and not women (who had lost their status) and *then* to cite this as a matter of injustice, references something deeper than the state. There is another story, another working even of *value* at play. There is evidence here of a local and Indigenous notion of "the utilitarian good" that is historically driven and striving to be consensus based, attempting to recover and manage the vicissitudes of lawful and unlawful forms of dispossession that are borne by women today in various forms: dispossession of their rights as Indians, of their land, and of their lives. The agency exercised within the community, then, is an agency and instrumentality that work upon these notions "on the ground," notions that work in some relation to notions of territory.

In spite of these very complicated valences, "membership" has been conceived and represented as a gendered, raced, place-based project and "problem" that is particularly virulent in Kahnawà:ke. Recall from various points in this book that we understand it as gendered and raced because of the rules in place in the Indian Act that decreed that Indian women lose their rights upon their marriage to non-Indian men and that non-Indian women who married Indian men would gain status as Indian. This was summarized in chapter 2. Recall from much of the cross-border history in chapter 5 that such "magical" acts of the state configure gender and race membership in ways that accord to British laws of property (and civility). However, these moments of recognition go beyond the Victorian notions of marriage and property law, when what was "Victorian" became particularly American and phenotypical. We see this working of race through more contemporary juridical decisions through the Canadian Human Rights Tribunal case of Peter Jacobs (Canada 1998).[11] Peter Jacobs was described as a phenotypically black man who was raised as a Mohawk of Kahnawà:ke and was denied his rights as a Mohawk by the Mohawk Council of Kahnawà:ke based on his lack of blood quantum.

The Jacobs case—in which a lifelong resident of the community, adopted and then raised by members and married to a member, was denied member rights—received much coverage in the press at the time. This coverage rendered the problem of membership in a narrow, blood-based way, a manner that, in its appeal to "race" as a transcendent and readable category of difference (blackness), was a matter of *claiming* rights and *rendering* justice. As this was a problem that invoked universal categories of offense (discrimination), justice was to be rendered by state intervention and adjudication. Justice was *not* to be determined by the community at hand, as it was they (in their assertions of sovereignty) who were, in fact, unjust. It should be noted that the problem of membership was and is not particular to Kahnawà:ke, it applies to Indian communities across Canada.[12] The Jacobs case moves us to the juridical site of impasse, where "tradition" has a hard time being heard, but was in some ways the basis of his argument—but this is a different sort of "tradition," I will argue, than the "tradition" of Morgan et al. Jacobs was active in the Longhouse at one time, he was a deeply cultural member of the community—here I mean, culture in an everyday sense—he was, he *is*, someone whose life aligned perfectly with the lives of Mohawk men: attending Billings High School off the reserve, participating in the Longhouse, attending an all-Native college in Quebec, serving in the American armed forces, marrying a Mohawk woman from Kahnawà:ke. How could his adoption status (his natal status as a non-Native) undo all of that? As I listened to his testimony before the Canadian Human Rights Commission, it was striking—as striking as the disconnect of "Richard" we read in chapter 2—how thoroughly imbricated and *of* the community Peter Jacobs was then, and still is.

A traditional woman whom I interviewed from another Mohawk community answered my questions on Mohawk identity, nationhood, and territory in this way:[13]

> **Q:** Please give me some words to describe Mohawk people; how would you describe Mohawks to someone that does not know us?
>
> **A:** Strong, peace loving, funny . . .
>
> **Q:** Are these qualities the same for women as they are for men?
>
> **A:** These qualities are more pronounced in women.
>
> **Q:** Please tell me what nationhood is to you?
>
> **A:** This is the disappearance of the boundaries between our reserves. In the ideal world, we would move through our traditional territory with no impediments, we would restore our relationship with the land as women. We would be free to do these things and not stay on the "ghettos" that they call reserves.

Territory is a large issue in her discourse on identity and nationhood and was throughout the course of the interview. She wanted to see the traditional territory of Mohawk people, which extends down from Kanehsatà:ke into the Ohio Valley, restored. In relation to this territory, she said, women are "the caregivers and own the territory, and the caregivers of the children and keep the communities going while the men are away." This is a neotraditional argument that takes the "traditional," precontact role of women and transposes it onto the contemporary. I will offer more of this cultural discourse momentarily. However, it is first worth considering the links to territory and to actual membership practices of the discourses already presented with reference to the living manifestation of settler colonialism in the Oka Crisis.

Here we are not yet finished with blood quantum or ideas about purity, as women still seem to carry the burden of this shift. Thus local membership options—such as matriliny, blood, and (in the case of one interlocutor in my data set) formal Canadian citizenship[14]—should also be viewed as adaptations, and somewhat sensible ones, to a colonial scene. Iroquois membership prior to the ascent of the settler state on the Canadian side of the international boundary line was about clan membership, and clan membership was transmitted through the woman's line. Particularly in light of the importance of women as clan bearers and as landowners in traditional Iroquois communities, blood quantum and the disregard for these *traditional* lines of descent—along with hooking ideas about nationhood to colonial forms of membership—seem especially problematic and self-defeating. If Iroquois women were the "mothers of the nation," then how could the nation continue without them in authoritative, structural positions of power?

To imagine and write an ethnographic or ethnohistorical scene that is innocent of colonialism and the effective properties of its project is simply to ignore the power relations inherent in any scene. This sensibility of indifference is unconscionable for the living and striving of Indigenous interlocutors; it is a sensibility that produces notions of lost worlds, worlds of yesterday, of perfect timeless tradition, that sets up an impossible burden of proof for Indigenous claimants today. To imagine such worlds is to fetishize them, and to fetishize them is to dominate them—to exercise dominion over their representation and possibly their territories and their lives. I am working against the reifying tendencies of that paradigm in my work. Thus, in my accounting of the institutional disempowerment of women (and their children), I have also to account for the "settlement of space" in Canada, a settlement project that was predicated upon the gendered occlusions and exclusions that work to transform not only land and its meanings to Indigenous peoples but the boundaries that they are found within.

So how indeed could this "sudden and swift" shift in power occur? Land diminished rapidly; resources dwindled; being Indian mattered differently, and became hinged, perhaps, to a notion of decision making and loyalty to the community land base. Thus being Indian and having status became tied to notions of personal and individual responsibility. Women were told, "If you marry out, then you have to leave."[15] Interlocutors told me, "I always knew what would happen if I married out" (mind you, one woman in my data set purported to *not* know this). And perhaps this series of admonitions worked, in concert with the diminished land and resource base in the community; the visual and auditory spectacle of actual community women having to leave and of families divided strangely according to colonial logics of exclusion, to create a sensibility of closure, and perhaps a new "common sense" of blood connection to a shrinking territorial base. These adaptations were tied as well to notions of territory that moved along with labor and travel beyond the confines of Kahnawà:ke. It is to this new "diasporic" space that disenfranchised women and their children, along with the shifting community of travelers and workers, would have to relocate. In this way, policy and cultural practice forced a new, gendered territorial imperative; this is especially the case if the women remain committed to the community and to their identities as Mohawks, transmitting this identity to their children. They may have had to leave the community proper, the bounded space of the reserve, but their activities in Chateauguay, Brooklyn, Ottawa, or elsewhere may have oriented them toward home or a re-created "home" away.

How does this predicament manifest itself in the present? This excerpt is from a woman who awaits recognition:

And so when we come out and we are [talking] about the things [that] are going on with the community, I am sure that the band council is not . . . going to Ottawa and telling the minister everything that he's doing to the people over there. You see, and yet he is saying "We are providing the services, we're doing everything that we're supposed to," but only to the few that they select. Now what about the rest of the population?

Now you've got people living off-reserve, because the community has rejected them—those people are not necessarily familiar with the daily activities that are going on in the community, so what they have done is basically removed themselves from having to deal with those situations on a daily basis. . . .

I mean life is hell there! I mean, it is not the best, I'll be the first to say it, living there; you gotta be damn tough to live there. And in order to survive there, you have to be really tough. Now some people might have gotten tired by it, and decided, "I'm gonna go live off the reserve where I won't have to deal and face those things on a daily basis, where somebody's telling me, 'Leave, you don't belong here,' facing the discrimination on a daily basis." Which is what we encounter.

I encounter it daily there; you never know what's going to happen from one moment to the next. I mean water and sewage is one thing, landfill is another, getting slapped in the face [when I got] my letter from the Education Centre . . . saying that they are not accepting me so that I can go ask and beg and plead to the Department to get it. . . . I never got rid of it—certificates of possession, with letters of rejection . . .

I mean at every turn we are getting slapped in the face—every single turn—which should be normal things that we should be entitled to for the past seventeen years. And the federal government has been: "Well, sorry."

Now if anybody is going to . . . want us to trust them, they have to jump over a lot of loops to do that now, and hurdles, because there is no more trust. There is no trust in the councils, and there is no trust in the federal government because both have reneged on their responsibilities.

So, now we are sitting back, and this is why we are taking the position that we are taking, and this is why we are *angry*. I mean, I lived hell for *x* years, my whole entire life getting slapped in the face at every turn. I grew up in the city, them telling me "Go back to where you come from." I go to the town,[16] they tell me, "Go back to the city you don't belong here." Where the hell do you go? And then when you do decide to make your decision—your stance on where you are going—you still get slapped in the face daily. So life is not a bed of roses over there, but I choose to live there because it is my *right*.

I didn't get the land that I am living on by *buying* it; it was passed down from generation to generation within my family, and I am being told I am third generation, I am white, and I have no right. That is what I am being told, and yet I inherited that land; I never bought it; it has been passed down from generation to generation.

This narrative moves us through the historical spaces that one must simultaneously occupy to manage the question of rights and justice as a historically excluded woman of unambiguous Kahnawà:ke Mohawk descent. We can cull from her narrative that she is first constructed as a claimant upon the community as a nonstatus Indian (or in the eyes of some community members, as a non-Indian). As such, she is also being constructed as a claimant upon the resources of the community. Within her narrative, we can see that she experiences aggression from others in Kahnawà:ke, where she is told "to go back to the city." And the city, she makes clear, is also not a welcoming place for her. She wants to stay on the reserve in spite of this because it is her *right*. Now this notion of "right" that she is working with is an interesting one. It includes what she is owed by her Bill C-31 reinstatement of status and, as she makes clear toward the end of her narrative, to her position as a landowner. Her status as a landowner is owing to her descent from people who were property owners within the community. She is not directly invoking the notion of an Iroquois woman's role in presettler society as a caretaker of the land, but her argument is tied to the commonsense transparency embedded in the parentage of her right as a person descended from people who lived and owned land in the community. Thus it is her right to remain there. This for her is obvious; it is commonsense; and it is what she leaves us with, along with the dissent that greets her claim to this right within the community: "I am third generation, I am white, and I have no right."

The following ethnographic moments will map the boundaries of this moral community, a national one at that, and do so from the ground up. They stem, in part, from the territorial imperatives of Iroquoia and of colonialism. These imperatives are ones in which the "clearing" and the "forest" of traditional Iroquois cartography and mental mapping have been shifted in some spots. Kanienke, the land of the flint, or Mohawk territory, has had its boundaries undermined and then redrawn by a larger, national community with its authority and power vested in the Crown and then the state. The Oka Crisis showed us what that redrawing looked and felt like and the role that women played in that refusal, but also the role that they played conceptually to the state and to their own people. I would now like to redraw these settler mappings differently.

As I moved across the borders that divide reserve from city, state from state, and country from country, during my fieldwork, I collected narratives about the practice of membership and the historical problem I have just detailed. The following utterances will touch upon, in different ways, alternative conceptions of political membership in Kahnawà:ke and the larger body of the Mohawk nation (spread out across six different reserves in Ontario, Quebec, upstate New York, and urban areas). Consider now these propositions and how they shift and change as we move through different locales, from the reserve to the city.

CLEARING I

When interviewed in *NOW* magazine, an alternative weekly in Toronto Ontario, Ida Goodleaf, a Kahnawà:ke Mohawk, offered her thoughts on the blood-quantum debate on the reserve. At the time of her interview in 1994, the debate over membership requirements in the community was in "full swing." The blood-quantum requirement of 50 percent was on the books, but was not ratified by the federal government. Consternation and conflict abounded within the community. The local and outside media sought to document and discuss the "racial" requirements for membership in the community and its implications. In response to her interviewer's questions, Ida Goodleaf said, perhaps defensively, "People have got to understand that this little postage stamp [the reserve]—I've got to fight for it. . . . I only want to keep my rights and what rightfully belongs to us, and anybody that is 50-percent Indian. If we had let that go [the land, the membership requirement], we would have already lost our rights" (quoted in Sero 1994, 15).

This discourse is from the reserve. It clearly pronounces the reserve to be in a diminished state—"this little postage stamp"—and a site of protection, of a place that must, in her mind (and the minds of others), be protected against encroachment by those who do not have sufficient blood quantum. Like the previous narrative, in this story rights—the right to be there, to hold property, to have further rights *as Indians*—are central. Here, we see the rights-based geographic and raced flux that the previous interlocutor laid bare; recall her narrative, which essentially said: "I go to the city—they say go to the reserve. I go to the reserve—they say go to the city; you don't belong here." The conditions of not belonging are determined by a degree of blood that is to approximate lineage and can be discerned by people in Kahnawà:ke. Blood quantum has always been a way of talking about lineage—descent from people who themselves were imagined to have 100 percent Mohawk blood, who were on the band list, and could be reckoned by others as Indians who were from and of that place. The rights that this woman speaks of would perhaps approximate collective rights, rights that belong to a group larger than herself, contrary to the model mapped out by the geographic and rights-based flux of the previous interlocutor who does not seem to belong anywhere, and yet has individual rights to property.

PERCEPTION OF WOMEN'S ROLES

In 2002 I interviewed the Kahnawà:ke Mohawk who helped to draft the first blood-quantum requirement rules for the community. We were in Montreal, and when our meal had wound down I asked him, "What do you think of blood quantum? What is the legacy of C-31 in Kahnawà:ke? What about the role of our women in deciding membership?" He told me, "Look, I am 'hardline' on this issue, I believe that blood is part of identity. But I also believe that women are part of that too, they should be the decision makers; that is the way it was before white people got here, and that is the way it should be. Women should be in charge—they know what is going on in the community; the men have no idea—they are away all the time."

One sees how gendered even the exclusionary discourse can be, how tied it can be to ideas about "traditional" and actionable theories on gender (women simply are in charge) and the contemporary experience of that role of women in lives lived in the Longhouse structure of the past and transposed onto the life of the reserve today. "Men are away all the time" is a reference to the labor of ironwork, done almost exclusively by men, for the past century. It takes them down to New York City, almost always across the border to the United States, where French language is not required, anti-Indian racism is less apparent, there are US dollars, and, historically, a greater monetary exchange and greater work opportunities. This is what he is referencing and why "men are away all the time." The conundrum, then, of gendered exclusion based on blood quantum is not addressed; there is no recognition that the descendants of women, and those women themselves who the Indian Act made white in the eyes of the state, are afflicted by exclusion. This man maintains a commitment to blood as the basis of recognition and rights, with shades of the more collectivist and territorially protectionist model of rights instanced by Ida Goodleaf in her *Now* interview.

THE FOREST

Eventually my research took me "away" from the reserve, the surrounding cities, and the suburbs, down to the "forest," to the place of men (it seems), to New York City. I found myself leaning against a bar in Greenwich Village, talking to the ironworkers who had just finished up a day of bolting and welding on the new student services building at New York University on West Fourth and La Guardia. I was interviewing a Mohawk man from Ahkwesáhsne.

"Hey, L, tell me, what is the ideal form of membership for us? What do you think makes someone a member of the community?"

He looks at me squarely in the eye, and doesn't answer. Instead he says,

"Well, can I ask *you* something?"

"Sure . . ."

"When you look in the mirror, what do you see?"

"When I look in the mirror, what do I see?"

I repeat this out loud. The question hangs awkwardly and stubbornly between us. The silence between us is louder than the song by Kate Bush and Peter Gabriel that fills the bar. He pushes me,

"I asked you, Audra, when you look in the mirror, what do you see?"

My stupefied silence is audible, and somewhat embarrassing even now, when I replay it on my minidisc recorder. I finally answer him, I say,

"I see a nice person, L."

"Well, that is who we are, then—that is the answer to the question."

These utterances and narratives gathered and produced during fieldwork testify to the shifting content and positioning on the question of membership and citizenship *within* the political membership. Here we have different notions of rights, and what rights *should* be like, as well as the gendered valences of their form, their role, and the implications of this to contemporary territory. The story of Oka, a defense of territory, flips and opens into a gendered specificity. We started this story with a traditionally inflected responsibility to territory that spoke through the whittling language of Aboriginal rights but, in its execution, tipped the settler state into questions of citizenship, of rightful (rights-bearing) belonging to place, and, if pushed enough can lead us to think about nation-state formation: Whose land is this; whose nation is this; how is it that we are here if these people who were here first, who have this different constitution, are pushing back, refusing the encroachment, refusing the ongoing dispossession of their land? They did what they did because they were and are not Canadian citizens, indeed. They did what they did because of a responsibility to their territory, the bodies of their dead who were buried within that territory, and the fearful spectacle of that responsibility to the military arm of the state as it views Mohawk women, Iroquois women, fulfill their mandates to the territory, to act.

The particular history of Indian women and territory in Canada factors into this analysis of territory and citizenship as the central subject of historical and legal exclusion, a subject whose (dangerous) Indigeneity was legally eliminated upon marriage to a non-Indian man. When she left her moral and "racial" community, she joined "civilization" through heterosexual practice. "Civilization" and citizenship (and geographic banishment from her family) was then achieved through the legal union with a non-Indian man. This completely counters Iroquois perceptions of gender roles (and thus a woman's access to institutional power) within communities where women are the carriers of the names, the owners of the land, the ones who appoint chiefs. These narratives pivot through the different ways in which these roles and responsibilities punctuate territory and how they mark it, but also how "rights" are subject to ongoing deliberation and debate.

The final narrative, a conversation I had with an ironworker in a bar, flips it all back into my face—gender roles, legal status, informal status—as he pushes me to define myself. I am struck now at how completely indifferent I was to gender and to responsibility, and defined myself in completely attributional terms that are not part of official discourse. "I see a smart person," " I see a funny person," "I see a person who is ethically challenged by these policies that are unfair." These transcendent qualities such as "nice" and "funny," when intertwined with a just genealogical con-figuration and authority to act on that configuration, may be the things that matter the most to the project of moving away from the choking grip that settler colonialism has on Indigenous governance and, consequently, membership and citizenship.

Yet there is no place in the formal political discussion for qualities; roles, history, and tradition are the terms of appeal. And it is no wonder; those were the very things that the Indian Act and its gendered imposition upon communities sought to change. During the course of my research, I attended as many community meetings on membership as I could. During one of these meetings, I witnessed a Kahnawà:ke woman stand up and read a prepared statement to the councillors, who are sometimes known as "elected chiefs." Here I paraphrase her letter: "Why is it that we as Mohawk women were important, that we owned the land, gave children their clans, and now we cannot even own land or build a house in this community?" This woman's mother is Mohawk and is from the community, and her father is non-Indian. Because she is not married to her Mohawk partner, she remains a "C-31" and off the band list, in spite of having grown up in the community, having a partner in the community, and having children with that Mohawk partner. What she reminds the community of in these moments and within a Mohawk Council of Kahnawà:ke meeting—what some traditional people would say is an authoritative space of Canada and of colonialism—is that "as women we had power; why do we not still have power? Why do we, as a Mohawk community, uphold non-Mohawk ways of recognizing descent?" And, further, "Why are women such as myself, who carry the clan with them, not recognized by this official, land-granting body of this community?"[17]

The discursive shifts in power that opened up my discussion on gender and citizenship suggest to us that membership within a political community is more than a consequence of location, a matter of luck and birthplace. It is more than a set of participatory practices, as in a matter of civic citizenship. Membership is a social, historical, and, in the case of this study, *narrated* process that references personal and collective pasts while making itself over, parameters and boundaries and all, in a lived present. As a social, historical, and narrated process, gender is necessarily bound up in and speaks of and from the power that accrues to the settlement of space. Although membership is made over, the stories and practices in that remaking may reinterpret and subvert the metahistories (and fictions) of the state(s) in which one finds oneself; the narratives of membership may work to build a sense of nationhood not from the signs and symbols of the state, but rather from the words and interactions of the people—words and actions that are issued in the everyday moments of exchange, from epiphenomenal moments such as the Oka Crisis to seemingly mundane moments in a bar. Building a nation from the "ground up" also occurs in the ethnographic moment documented above, where gender and colonialism intersect and are subverted by the bodily and discursive person who is doing the reminding: the Mohawk woman who is telling people how membership *was* and clearly how it *should* be.

Feeling Citizenship

There is a difference between what is prescribed and what actually should be, and that is being worked out in the day-to-day life of the community. This difference between "membership" and "citizenship" was made clear to me through the course of an interview with a man in his early twenties, "C" whom we met briefly in chapter 4. He is a lifelong resident of the community, yet the situation regarding his own membership is difficult.

Q: Are you a citizen of Canada?
A: I live and work, for the most part, within the territorial boundaries that Canada has unilaterally set. For the sake of ease, when crossing the

border, or in discussion or signing any forms, for the sake of simplicity, and, as I said, ease, and to get things done with rather quickly, I will say I live in Canada. I will say I live in Canada, [that] I am a Canadian citizen, for simplicity's sake,

That is not how I *feel*, and when it could be avoided I never say that. But of course when I am crossing the border and they ask where I live, or if they say "what country" I will say "Canada" just to avoid any problems. Of course anywhere else I never say that—that is not how I feel. I am a Mohawk of Kahnawà:ke, not a Canadian citizen.

Q: What does that mean, to be a Mohawk from Kahnawà:ke, 'cause you said, "I will do this for the sake of ease." It is more like this citizenship of convenience.

A: Yes, "convenience."

Q: You know, it is like, "OK, don't give me a hard time, I was born . . ." Well, actually they were born in our territory, but now it looks like we were born in their territory.

A: We will say it was theirs, to avoid problems . . .

Q: So there is this citizenship of convenience, and then you also said, "This is not how I *feel*, but this is what I have to do, just in this situation," so what then is this other thing, the "feeling citizenship," is that a *feeling* citizenship?

A: Within Kahnawà:ke?

Q: Yeah, the idea, "I am a Mohawk from Kahnawà:ke?" is that your *other citizenship*? Is that your *other* . . .

A: That is my *primary* citizenship; that is my main citizenship. Canadian citizenship is sort of an ancillary citizenship, which I invoke to avoid hassle. I don't consider myself "Canadian." As I said, I am a Mohawk of Kahnawà:ke, and I feel that that is where my citizenship lies. If one would like to go even further, I could say, "I am a Mohawk of Kahnawà:ke of the Confederacy," although I see myself more limited to Kahnawà:ke. . . .

Q: Why is that?

A: I see no working, legitimate Confederacy to be a part of. It [would] be different if there was a true, governing, recognized body, but there is none that I am aware of, so I limit my citizenship to "Mohawk of Kahnawà:ke," perhaps a bit further the "Mohawk nation," but no Confederacy. In my eyes it's nonexistent.

Q: Would you be interested in that form of citizenship if it were possible, for us?

A: If it were possible, yes!

Q: If there were those operational—you are probably thinking about institutions? If we had our clans back up? If they were . . .

A: Not really, but a system of nations associated together for the betterment of all Aboriginals in that group. . . .

Q: Iroquois?

A: Iroquois. That I would agree to—I feel that in a way is what we should be; it isn't agreeing to anything new and extraordinary; it is just the way it should be. . . .

Q: There is this "citizenship of convenience," [but] your "primary citizenship," that "feeling citizenship"—what is the content of that citizenship for you? When you say you are a Mohawk of Kahnawà:ke, what does that mean to you?

A: That is where I associate with most, because that is where I've grown up; that's where my feeling and loyalty lie. I have . . . what is the word I can use? I have a *bond* with the community; that's the life that I know; that's the society, the setup, the whole setup to the society, the way life evolves and revolves around certain institutions in the community, is what I am used to, and that's how I feel that my citizenship lies there; that is the life that I know. . . .

This interview pinpoints the very crux of this chapter, the arc of my argument, the very point of this book. In spite of the rules of the state, in spite of the governance structure that attempts to implement them (or not implement them, or find an alternative to them), there are other workings of citizenship. This is that "feeling citizenship" or "primary citizenship," the affective sense of being a Mohawk of Kahnawà:ke, in spite of the lack of recognition that some might unjustly experience. In some ways we could see these as Lauren Berlant's affectively structured citizenships, but they are not articulating to the United States, an encompassing frame for her analysis and critique (1997). C's is in active and attached disaffiliation from the state—"for the sake of convenience, I am a Canadian"—yet he was unrecognized by his primary space of self-articulation—the Mohawk Nation as instantiated by a tribal or band council governance system. Even so, he maintains a sense of himself as *still* belonging, and indeed he does belong to the community, in spite of the fact that they do not *legally* recognize him. He is distanced from the settler state as well. Here he elaborates further on the bite of that exclusion, the ways in which it cuts through, in some ways, his "feeling citizenship":

Q: Tell me what you think our ideal form of . . . Are citizenship and membership the same thing?

A: From my understanding, and whomever I ask, I get these gray, cloudy answers in return, so I am not quite sure. I am a *citizen* of Kahnawà:ke, but I am not a *member* of Kahnawà:ke. I am not on this mysterious list that no one seems to have any information about.[18] So although I dearly love Kahnawà:ke, there are many positions I will never be able to hold until this membership issue is cleared up, so I don't know much about it, other than, I don't think it to be fair. There are those who leave the community, as I said—we all come back to Kahnawà:ke, but there are those who leave for twenty-five years and they come back and they're a member, and they will have all these opportunities that I won't, even though I've never left. I don't think that's fair. But I think there's a distinction—one could be a citizen without being a member.

Q: Interesting, and that citizenship is based on. . . . Let me push you on that then—how is that different; explain it to me?

A: Citizenship is—as I said—you live there; you grew up there; that is the life that you know. That is who you *are*. Membership is more of a legislative enactment designed to keep people from obtaining the various benefits that Aboriginals can receive. So I am a citizen; I live there; that is who I *am*; yet, I cannot be a member because of these laws, which I feel is unfair. If I had been there my whole life, I should have the same opportunity to run for Council that anyone else can. Yet I cannot.

Q: Do you think that's because of public sentiment, the Indian Act, is that because of . . .

A: I don't know what you know, or what others know—this is an area that I can't get straight answers from; no one seems to know.[19]

"No one seems to know" was laced through much of his discourse on C-31 and on his own predicament. However, people do seem to *know* the different forms of recognition that are at play in the exercising of rights, and that knowledge translates in the "feeling side" of recognition. I want to return us now to the community meeting that I discussed prior to this interview in order to compare the difference between my interlocutor's critical point on the difference between "citizenship" and "membership."

At the same meeting at which the woman read her letter to the community and to Council—a community member with an especially complicated membership, but with an official membership no less—stood up and made an impassioned speech about the perils of blood quantum and its similarity, in his mind, to Nazi policies on race purity. During his narrative, a woman sitting near him said loudly to the woman sitting next to her, "He shouldn't even be here" and then repeated herself, louder. When he reached the point in the trajectory of his argument about how Mohawk identity was about clan and language, not blood, she said even louder to no one in particular, "Then speak in Indian." This discursive challenge to his authority to speak on matters of culture was testament to the unfairness of the situation presented by these different cases. What I wish to suggest is that these *living, primary, feeling citizenships* may not be institutionally recognized, but are socially and politically recognized in the everyday life of the community, and people get called out on them—there is little room or toleration for an inconsistency in one's own situation and what is considered just—hailing at that moment, that which makes it unjust: the Indian Act, for example. One who has rights that another does not because of gender inequality and then pronounces on the "best way" in spite of his or her privilege will get pushed, discursively—will get reminded. The challenge to the community is to harden these pieces of knowledge, these critiques and these possibilities into a membership policy that may accommodate the simultaneity of these experiences, these different trans-historic discourses (and people), so that these "feeling citizenships" may then become *lived* citizenships for *all*.

These feeling citizenships are narratively constructed, hinge upon sociality, and are tied in ways to the simultaneous topography of colonialism *and* Iroquoia—where certain women reside outside the boundaries of the community because they have to, and others remain in; where the forces of social, primary, "feeling" citizenships may work to enfold all into a narrative frame of collective experience. The narratives that connect these people deal heavily in the currency of "who we are, of who they are, of what rights we should have, of what we shall be in the future." They are a relentless process and practice, as Mohawks come up against the state and against each other, as they enfold each other into ambits of critique, refusal, care, and ambivalence in spite of forces that would have them completely banished.

I wish to argue here that the case of political membership is one that narrates "who we are" while archiving the living legacy of colonialism through recitation and reminder. These narratives are more, however, than colonial recitations of exclusion; they embed *desire* in ways that speak between the gulfs of the past and the present, whether this might be, as we have seen, for traditional modes of governance within the nation-state of Canada or the Mohawk nation (itself a member nation in the Iroquois Confederacy), for a limited form of self-government within the boundaries of the community, or for an abstraction such as justice. No matter what the final object of that desire may be, the narratives of citizenship in this study are laden with desires that want in some ways to affect the differentials of power that underwrite notions of nationhood and citizenship away from the politics of recognition and into other unfolding, undetermined possibilities. This desire is made from the intimacy, the knowledge, and the messiness of everyday life, and from the bonds of affection and disaffection that tie people into communities and communities into nations, even if they are unrecognizable or unrecognized.

Interruptus

How to stop a story that is always being told? Or, how to change a story that is always being told? The story that settler-colonial nation-states tend to tell about themselves is that they are new; they are beneficent; they have successfully "settled" all issues prior to their beginning. If, in fact, they acknowledge having complicated beginnings, forceful beginnings, what was there before that process occupies a shadowy space of reflection; it is allowed a blue future-life in cinematographic narratives such as *Avatar,* a ghostly prior-life in horror films, and a deeply regulated life in law and economic distribution. Indians, or Native people, are not imagined to flourish, let alone push or interrupt the stories that are being told. In this book I have documented and theorized an ongoing interruption of the story of settlement. The life that I document and theorize from is not only biological and does not only belong in the statistician and census taker's ledger, or the geneticists' tableau. This is political life that, in its insistence upon certain things—such as nationhood and sovereignty—fundamentally interrupts and casts into question the story that settler states tell about themselves.

I started this book with three claims and three recent events that signal a form of Iroquois, or Haudenosaunee, sovereignty today. First, I asserted that one sovereignty can be embedded in another; second, that refusal is an alternative to recognition; and finally, that Indigenous politics require a deep historical accounting to contextualize the processes that appear anomalous, illiberal, or illogical, and get conflated with pathology, economic desperation, and depredation ("smuggling") in the public eye. Much of the political work Native people do is structured by the claims that settler colonialism places *upon* their land, their lives, and their aspirations. And so a "problem" such as membership, along with the signs of illiberality that are actually various refusals to this logic and structure, required this sort of accounting. Thus, much of this book is concerned with how these people have been known, how their history has been understood, and thus how they are not only comprehended but *apprehended* in these literatures. These are assemblages of ideas, Said's sturdy consolidations of knowledge that do particular things that have a life beyond the text, that bleed into newspapers, curricula, and Indian and non-Indian homes to affect our understanding of "these people" (cf. [1978] 1994). As such, the book is as much an archive of knowledge constructed and executed in a particular way as it is an ethnography, in a classic sense, of a place and a people, seized for apprehension, ready for control. The book, in what it refuses to disclose, however, does not make contents available for the control of classic ethnographic subjects, unless perhaps that subject is governance itself.

Three empirical cases of expulsions, passports, and lacrosse set this book afloat. These cases led us to the larger frame or grammar of action that embeds Mohawk discussions of membership, the movement of Kahnawa'kehró:non across borders of every sort, and their unwillingness to participate in nation-state formations. These cases led us to the work of unmasking, archiving, and assembling ways of knowing in order to "get at" the problem, but also to demonstrate how knowledge can be complicit with the imperatives of settler colonialism by giving us a particular sense of Indigenous people: if not "vanishing," then certainly pathological, illiberal, or acting in a racist way. Some of this book dealt explicitly with the question of writing, of how to write about this.

Recasting Membership

Fifteen years after the start of my formal research, membership still matters. The membership code is fundamental to political organization (to nationhood) and is so elemental, in fact, that it represents the right, simply, to have a right. And yet, this right is the very thing that was taken away from Kahnawà:ke by the Indian Act and by Canada as that nation-state came into being. This was taken from Kahnawa'kehró:non along with the *authority* to govern according to Iroquois norms and practices, and then written over with patrilineal descent, with electoral practices, and with band governance. Its imposition upon Mohawk regimes of governance made these problems of membership in the late nineteenth century,[1] and has completely governed the ongoing attempts to render justice within this community, to move out of this framework and into another, fairer, more just modes of recognizing each other.

But let us return to the signposts that inaugurated this book, signposts that are used to illuminate a territorial space of argumentation. The first signpost, that of the expulsion of non-Natives, references exclusion, but it also signs from an agreed-upon place, "Kahnawà:ke," which is a particular kind of place: a reserve or "reservation." These are juridically and jurisdictionally demarcated spaces of Indigeneity in the United States and Canada. In the United States they are considered "semisovereign," and in Canada, under the auspices of the Indian Act, they are "land held in trust for the use and benefit of Indians." There is a territorial referent, tied to specific people, tied to authoritative and juridical charters, that this sign carries with it; that referent is to diminished and protected space that those specified people occupy by right (exclusively) of conquest. Yet this "conquest" is fundamentally a failed one, as those people survived and remain not only Indigenous or Indian, but specifically Mohawk and in possession of their own philosophical and governing charter, the Kaianere'kó:wa, or "Great Law of Peace." They assert this charter as a basis for their actions, and do so often. However, the conquest manages a semiotic density that carries its ongoing property interest in law.

So the land that these people occupy is diminished, but also has with it a simultaneous other history or understanding, which is simply, that this is the northern part of traditional Mohawk hunting territory and thus, is part of our traditional territory. Maps have not always imaged that territory properly. Yet the first signpost, which seems to be all about a tragedy of exclusion, is also full of this territorial story, one that is partial, unfolding, and appears in newspaper accounts and television coverage to be deeply illiberal. What is originally a shortage of land becomes a shortage of civility (tolerance, really), or it is that shortage of civility that is spectacularized and may then obscure the shortage of land. This is a story of "Indians behaving badly." And more seriously, they might say "cruelly"; and the modifier may become the noun—these are *cruel Indians.* They are evicting (white) people! To add semiotic density to this narrative, the subject of one newspaper article is a former Olympian and simultaneous veteran (of sorts) of the Oka Crisis who was bayoneted by a Canadian soldier in her departure from the site of the largest deployment of state troops in the history of Indian-white relations—at the age of fourteen.

We see this history of hers condensed and narrated repeatedly in the newspaper accounts of her notice by the Mohawk Council of Kahnawà:ke that she must leave her community if she expects her non-Indian partner to cohabitate with her on the reserve. That she was seven months pregnant at the time only adds to the disconnect between her past, a past that is absolutely imbricated in the collective history of this reservation (and several others), and this reservation with a broader history of land expropriation and state violence. Her story is also imbricated in failures—a failure of tolerance on the part of the Band Council and of the Victorian model of the family (a heterosexed, domestic partnership), if raced *or* framed as a nation in such a way. Her partner is white. They are perfect; they are athletes even (perfect, modal bodies), but for his whiteness. The language of "tradition" was deployed by the council at that time to exclude her and her partner from rights to residency.[2]

The reproductive capacity of the nation, then, will be borne by this woman alone, structured by a residency law in such a way, with a certain kind of raced and exclusive cruelty. Others within the community—perhaps among the fifty petitioners from the community who presented the Mohawk Council of Kahnawà:ke with their grievance against her violation of the Kahnawà:ke Membership Law when she built her house on the reserve—would argue that this is their adherence to a long-fought-over, long-fought-for law. This event also emphasized the *right* to have a law that protects their diminished land base and a law that represents the will of the people, in this context the Kahnawa'kehró:non who vote in Mohawk Council of Kahnawà:ke elections.

There is a sympathetic ear for the story of the almost-evicted woman, whose biography also references resistance in a deep way to the ongoing struggle over land and rights in Canada. There might not have been such interest in her predicament or care for her plight thirty years ago; nor would that have been the case forty years ago, when Indian women and men were deeply divided politically over the terms of marriage and recognition *within* communities. It is unclear and perhaps unfair to attempt to ponder how allied Mohawks would have been to her plight at that time had there not been an attempt at gender parity made by the double gender exclusion within the community. Neither men *nor* women can marry out since the moratorium on mixed marriages in 1981, which has been added to by the 50 percent blood-quantum regulation for marriage and member-ship in 1984. Both of these requirements were applied equally to men and women on the band list after 1984. Exclusion is no longer the sole domain of women. Yet this case carries with it echoes of an earlier time, when only women were being told to leave. Earlier chapters have unpacked the con-text for this requirement. However, both requirements prompted the orig-inal question that guided the research for this book: "What is a Mohawk to oneself and to others?" A prosaic question, it is frighteningly modern, flirting clearly with the certainty of essentialism (the "is"), but one that was raging when I started this research, and a question that I found repeated in official correspondence between the Caughnawaga Indian agent and Ottawa,[3] and in oral history. This was a question that has raged for the past 150 years of writing and remembering in the community. There has been, as Gerald Reid (2004) has textualized for us in his book on Kahnawà:ke, a serious distrust and dislike of outsiders (*especially* as property owners) within the community since the first Indian agent started sending reports to Ottawa in the 1850s.

However, the question itself articulated a deeper set of anxieties than it did beginnings, "Who are we now; who shall we be for the future?" Retro-spectively, these questions *are* deeply modern but signal a fear of disap-pearance, to be on the receiving end of an eliminatory story, disappearance at the hands of global capital, and an ongoing settler project that attempts to move Indigeneity away, to eliminate it (Wolfe 1999, 2006; Seed 2001, 29–44). In light of that eliminatory logic and its practices, reservations are these protected spaces of "unfreedom"; they are the topographic and deeply carceral remainders of what is left: deeply winnowed territories (disappearing land, not Indians) whose diminishment and simultaneous-ness preservation *for* specified peoples make the question of *who* shall be within them, who shall live upon them and access their resources, gain even greater traction. In this context of diminishing land, the chances for the failure of equivalency—of perfect justice *failing*—increase as does the move toward incivility and exclusion. The question that has surfaced at various times in this book—"How do we include who *should* be here with what little we have left" (diminished territory, limited resources)—appears again. So we have "the problem of membership."

The second signpost similarly references land but also an assumption and an assertion of the *right* to travel through land properly. Access to land in this actual story is tied to charter, to governance, and then to identification. The three young men traveling from the climate change conference in Bolivia were tied to the place of Kanienke (Mohawk Territory), clan members of the Iroquois Confederacy whose passports attest to this lineage and this place within a larger spatial order of things and people. Their story narrates a *willful* detainment in a faraway place in order to assert this other form of emplacement and, more deeply, another authoritative nexus for referencing this emplacement. That they refused Canadian forms of identification and rendered it a kind of treason that must be marked—with recourse to the recent notion of Scott Lyons (2010) regarding the "x-mark"—a textual mark made by Indigenous peoples within a field of historical and political possibilities that are, from their inception, deeply constrained. Like the treaty signature that he works from, these are marks of *assent* rather than *consent* that were made in light of conditions that were not ideal and that were not entirely of their making. They are part of scenes of mistranslation in which Indian signatories signed their "X" with the best intentions, the best understanding that could be rendered in moments of total difference, but that would make a lasting, historical mark.

The third signpost, "lacrosse," is as also an x-mark, but of overt refusal. This is a different time and a different space, and the lacrosse players are different from treaty signatories in that they have a command of the theater in which they are being apprehended, the space of recognition that they are flipping back, questioning, not signing on to. Like the treaty signatories of Lyons's analysis, the lacrosse players are acting out of traditional political authority, but the chances of mistranslation and misapprehension now are diminished because of shared language, because of the conditions of settler colonialism through time. They are not at its beginning; they are feeling its arc. As such, the young men are not being excluded from the nation-state; they are refusing inclusion within it. They are asserting rights based on a prior agreement—treaties between the Iroquois, the Dutch, the French, Great Britain, and the United States. Similarly, the game of lacrosse becomes a sign of a radically *contemporary* failure to remember

Fig C.1 The translator Kanentokon Hemlock with Kahnawiio Diome and Tyler Hemlock in El Salvador after the Climate Change Conference in Bolivia (2010). Photo courtesy of Kanentokon Hemlock.

the past, to honor those treaties by the *present* United Kingdom. Thus, to assert the past agreement in the present, many sovereigns call up the x-marks on those agreements, insist on prior equivalencies, and then make this actionable. But sovereigns must be willing to pay a price when those connections do not achieve the desired outcome. This price is demobilization, not being able to compete. However, this may not be a price at all if the gains exceed it. Here the gain is the assertion of the principle, the sign of the other political authority, vibrant and insistent, and the suggestion of possibilities beyond the horizon of what we may think is a "good" or a "gift"—travel, competition, winning, the givenness of citizenship, the givenness of settlement.

For one moment (or five days, to be exact), in 2010 Americans and Brits (Canadians less so) had the shorthand story of Iroquois sovereignty narrated for them repeatedly: "We are not Americans; we are not Canadians; we are members of the Confederacy. There are treaties signed between nations that we still honor. We are a Confederacy of nations. Why would we then travel on the passports of a government that is foreign to ours?" Recall Tonya Gonella Frichner's quote from the beginning of this book: "We

Fig C.2 Iroquois National Lacrosse Team in New York City (2010). Former and present executive directors Percy Abrams and Deborah Waterman hold Iroquois passports. Photo courtesy of Percy Abrams.

are representing a nation, and we are not going to travel on the passport of a competitor." Viewers watched as the Iroquois Lacrosse Team waited at John F. Kennedy airport for clearance from the United Kingdom and did not receive it. Viewers heard New York State senator Hillary Rodham Clinton work "on her end" to offer a one-time exclusion to post-9/11 security requirements so that they could return on their documents, their Confederacy-issued passports that referenced the Kaianere'kó:wa, the "ancient" governing agreement between the Five and then Six Nations that brought peace to their people and organized them into a system of clans, chiefs, and clan mothers, in the "new world's first federal system" (Morgan [1851] 1996, 8) and, some have asserted, "democracy" (Bruce Johansen 1996). The passports were signed by their chiefs and issued (the press told viewers repeatedly) in handwritten form, a form not up to security regulations (and thus unrecognizable as legitimate).[4] X-marks as well, these contemporary signatures attempted to move the prior forward. They were intended to move the Kaianere'kó:wa forward, out of the past, into the present, and into the border guard's hand; into his head, into the state's imaginary of their body politic and its imaginings of admissible bodies—bodies attached in a secure manner to a recognizable, or in this case (presently) unrecognizable, political order.

These were the contemporary refusals that inaugurated the book, which is one story (among many) of Kahnawà:ke as it moves in time, through time; as it is constructed; and as it manages not only the problem of membership, but its own relationship to territory, to others, to itself. In doing so I wanted to take what may be perceived as stubborn and wildly inconvenient (the principle of one's own passport, for example) and place it within a context of comparison and connection across the geopolitical boundaries of nation-states that take themselves to be settled, to be secure, to be stable in their history and their purpose. The sovereign assertions assembled as signposts were deliberately used to mark a conceptual territory that we would then walk through the course of the book. I wanted to set the stage for understanding how the assertions of autonomy and difference via membership by Kahnawa'kehró:non could be appreciated within the shifting boundaries of their own community. I also sought to problematize a vast literature as it pertains to people who have their own living, national histories and who necessarily upset the conceits and premises of settler states: that Kahnawa'kehró:non would, as Indian people and as a condition of their Indigeneity, lose their territory and disappear; and that these states are therefore, somehow, new and beneficent.

Citizenship, Nationhood, and Membership—Pasts and Presents

I introduced the problem of membership and recognition itself as a technique of colonial rule, but also of historical consciousness and of citizenship. I emphasized this linkage between consciousness and citizenship because the people of Kahnawà:ke wed their desires for control over membership with a desire for sovereignty and a notion of nationhood. Much of that nationhood is driven by their awareness of their history as Mohawk people, their sovereignty, and their struggles for recognition of that sovereignty in the Northeast. At times, though, their notion of nationhood is driven by their refusal of recognition, their refusal to be enfolded into state logics, and their refusal, simply, to disappear. Thus, historical consciousness is critical in making and maintaining the link between nation and citizen. Membership "proper," or the form of membership that is linked to legally belonging in a band or a first nation, like other jurisdictional issues, affects reserve communities and serves as a trigger for them to articulate these desires in discussions around membership and the practices of nationhood. However, it is not to be confused with citizenship in either the nation-state of Canada or the abstract or material Mohawk nation. I have asserted at different points in this book that Kahnawà:ke's situation as a single-nation community within both the Iroquois Confederacy and the nation-state of Canada confounds and confirms common understandings of nationhood. This is owing to their unique positioning as an Indigenous precontact community with its own national history, colonial histories, and postcolonial visions for the future, a positioning that I have come to understand more forcefully as fundamentally interruptive both to themselves and to the settler states within which they find themselves. Other Mohawk single-nation reserve communities—such as Ahkwesáhsne, Kanehsatà:ke, and Wahta—might share the same self-identification process since they share similar histories of territory, political organization, relocation, resettlement, and adjustment to the theater of settler colonialism. I examined the history of land, membership, and meaning in Kahnawà:ke and Iroquoia to give a sense of Mohawk nationhood (and its linkages to the Iroquois Confederacy) as a territorial and semiotic imperative. I also undertook that review to provide a sense of the Mohawk as possessing a national history that takes place above and beyond the traditional territory of the Mohawks in the Valley. In precontact times, the Mohawk Valley in what is now upstate New York was the home of the "Keepers of the Eastern Door." This is also the place from which the precontact Mohawk nation emerges and, in some ways, returns to and re-creates through ceremony and political discourse. Events within and beyond Iroquoia—such as the American Revolution, the settlement of the Northeast, the vision of Handsome Lake, and the fur trade—all bore on the movements, migrations, and meanings of the people of Kahnawà:ke.

In chapter 2 we met an interlocutor who identified himself as descended from *that* place, the pre-present-day Kahnawà:ke of the Mohawk Valley. His claim to be descended from that place reminds us of the slipperiness of the reserve and the historicity of peoples who are descended from places, the continuity of consciousness in spite of colonization and Indigenous mobility, and the problem of recognition both within communities and between researcher and subject. Data from that ethnographic scene illustrated the ways in which recognition, which came to the fore at different times in this book, is made real in places away from the reserve and from the time of the reserve, which seems in that context, to be a present time rather than a past time.

Two problems now come to the fore from this discussion: first, the ways in which a "single-nation" reserve community may think itself and, second, how that upsets larger understandings of nationhood as a territorially circumscribed phenomenon and of citizenship as a state-driven project. Both of these problems are made real by the space of reservations, the legally and temporally fixed place of the reserve, and the colonial effort to affix people and their identities juridically to these places through forms of band membership (with its original, Victorian connotations). And both of these problems are made real by the presence, persistence, and insistence on an alternative membership, a citizenship per se that exists within and beyond the space of the reserve and in other places and spaces. Although affixing people and their identities to place has meaning on the ground in day-to-day life, my data suggest that people do not need to affiliate with states or, for example, with band councils (such as the Mohawk Council of Kahnawà:ke) in order to think of themselves as members of a nation-like polity. This self-ascription is legitimated in their personal history, the broader legal matrix that they may move through, and the meanings that accrue to treaty, as well as the discursive work of their everyday lives. We saw this most clearly around the axis of border crossing, which is fraught with juridical overlays, constraints, proliferations, and alternative assertions.

Throughout this book I have argued for an understanding of Kahnawà:ke as a community possessing a consciousness of itself as a nation in spite of its location in the place and space of the reserve and as a nation within the place, space, and present time of Canada—as a sovereignty within multiple sovereignties. In order to come to this understanding, we need to situate reserves as manifestations of the colonial imperative to disappear Indians as polities, acquire their territory, and then reserve what is left in order to protect and assimilate them into spaces on Crown land held in trust for them. Yet these are much more than protected spaces; they are places of deep meaning to those who derive from and live within those spaces, and we must recognize, if anything, that deep meaning derives from the history that their members (and nonmembers) share. Thus part of their citizenship and political consciousness stems from another time, a past that is very much alive in the present and a past that gets pushed forward into the present.

Kahnawà:ke's history, hence, moves through several places and times as a single-nation community. It began as a Mohawk village in the Valley, some of whose people moved north to find temperance from alcohol, participate in the fur trade, and seek respite from troubles in the Confederacy. The people within this village came north as Mohawks but also blended with Abenaki, Huron, and other "mission Indians" who were already in Sault St. Louis, the original seigniorial land grant. Eventually, the culture that dominated there was Mohawk, and diplomacy was conducted according to Iroquois protocol. Their continued consciousness of being a nation, or a nation-like entity, within a reserve would be a sensible adaptation both to the movements they made from the Valley as well as their distance from, yet relatedness to, the Confederacy. At the same time, this self-consciousness of being a reserve-nation was a sensible adaptation to what was happening to the south of them and to the colonial scene itself, which demanded, to a certain extent, the making of lists, the fixing of names, the rendering of "legibility," and the congealment of identities around certain spaces. Kahnawa'kehró:non had their precontact experience within the Confederacy to draw from in asserting their difference and autonomy from these restrictions, but they could also, to a certain extent, use those colonial restrictions to protect what resources (both semiotic and material) they had as a reserve community.

From a sample of thirty-six interviews (see appendix), my field notes, court transcripts, official documentation, and public statements to the press and to other media, I established that (1) an alternative form of citizenship is being worked out through the everyday lives of community members, (2) historical memory is important, if not critical to this alternative form of citizenship, and (3) colonialism and "traditionalism" (as a self-conscious imperative) coalesce into these frames of reference within and beyond the boundaries of the reserve. How are these processes worked out, and how are they relevant to other studies of Indigenous or subaltern peoples? As we saw in interview data, a clear distinction is being made by some interlocutors between *membership* and *citizenship*. Membership entails formal recognition by the Mohawk Council of Kahnawà:ke (and in all cases, the state), whereas citizenship entails something else, a complex of social belonging, of family, of intracommunity recognition and responsibility. This is not to say that there is not overlap between membership and citizenship, or that one does not inform the other. As we saw with the Band Council meeting, these forms of recognition (and processes) are in a dialectical tension with each other. We saw the ways in which these different forms of recognition inform each other when two interlocutors made the same "cultural argument" regarding membership in the community but were received differently. There are also grounded, intranational, intracommunity forms of recognition at work. One of my interlocutors described a "feeling citizenship" or a "primary citizenship," a notion that is very useful for helping us to think about forms of social belonging, forms of social recognition, and recognition that does not necessarily entail a juridical or state form of recognition. In other words, some may feel themselves and be recognized by others to be a *part* of the community, and they may be social members of the community, but they may remain unrecognized and without legal rights as legal members of the community. This feeling citizenship, rooted very deeply for some in the place of the reserve proper or in their web of relations, may be an alternative (or a complement) to state forms of recognition that are afforded through *band membership.*

We saw feeling citizenship, or the intracommunity forms of recognition, at work at various times during this book, in interviews and through narratives from community meetings. But this form of recognition clearly is not experienced by all. Recall the narrative of the woman from the consultation meeting with the federal government who said that she was told she didn't belong at the reserve, to go back to the city; when she was in the city, she was told to go back to the reserve. Her narrative here evidences a form of recognition by outsiders and other Mohawks that is place based (reserve vs. city) and anchors that moment (of recognition) for her stubbornly within a site. The stubbornness of these conflations (white with the city, Indian with the reserve) ignores the webbings and tendrils of feeling citizenship and raises the question of why this form of recognition is at play for some and not for others. Does the legacy of C-31 cut so deeply that if one is removed beyond a certain point in time and attempts to return, there will be no place for him or her in the social web of recognition? I would argue that this may be true for some and not for others, and it shifts through the kin groups of the community, each with its own authority, interpretive framework, and story of home. So, although she may be perceived by some on the reserve as white, others may perceive of or *recognize* her as a cousin, auntie, or neighbor. This form of recognition still matters, but presents a challenge to the meting out of membership. Can the authoritative frames of these families and their stories of recognition be marshaled into a membership "policy" that works? In her narrative this woman predicated her feeling citizenship strongly upon *rights* of inheritance and property. This rights-based form of feeling citizenship—a form of membership that is the last, but necessary, resort for some of these women—is one that may appear to upset the balance of more social forms of recognition (even where they are present). This may place an impossible burden upon women who await a return.

We can see from my data that certain forms of rights (namely, C-31 and the cases that were before the Canadian Human Rights Tribunal) carry with them the residue of state imposition. The presence of the state through these forms of "rights" may diminish the social claims that women have upon the community. Whether the answer to these vexing questions— as some of my interlocutors strongly indicated—lies in reinstating women to their rightful, presumably *traditional* place in governance has yet to be seen, but this option is clearly on the minds of the membership and the citizenship.

Future Interruptions

The critical question of how grounded forms of membership are gendered and racialized must be taken up in further ethnographic works on citizenship and national belonging. To encourage and facilitate the investigation of such issues, this book has also sought to demystify the dominant, authenticating paradigm for research in Iroquois studies. As a single-nation community of "praying Indians," Kahnawà:ke has *not* figured significantly into this paradigm for research. I identified the reasons why and argued that until the underpinnings and assumptions that guide research are revealed and analyzed properly, further progress in research cannot take place, as communities will continue to be constructed, analyzed, or ignored for their failure to meet the extraordinary expectations and authenticating desires of researchers. This was my silent plea for an anthropology of Iroquoia—and by extension an anthropology of and with Indigenous peoples—which takes into account the history of anthropology, settlement, and power relations *at once*. Further research with other Indigenous communities dominated by similar authenticating paradigms might take up similar themes in order to unmask the history that constrains ethnography in the present. Until then, the very urgent, the very deep and lacerating issues that these communities and nations are dealing with—membership, taxation, land expropriation, resource extraction—will appear anomalous, their responses illiberal and pathological, unless this web of comprehension has been accounted for. Until then, settler colonialism will not arrive on the scene either, which is, in historical and anthropological terms, unconscionable, as it accounts for much of what we and our interlocutors are dealing with.

The gendered and racialized forms that rights and their narratives take in settler-colonial settings (and in specific frontiers and sites, such as the border) force us to ask further questions not only of the grounded, everyday life of *feeling citizenship* but of the limits of reciprocation in communities. Why do some people feel a part of a polity, and why is that reciprocated with recognition when the feelings of others are not? What are the limits of recognition and reciprocity of feeling? The new membership code extends back three generations and to the limit of three great-grandparents. There are provisions for residency status, for language, and other "cultural" forms of affiliation in case of missing lineage. Both the counting of great-grandparents and the cultural provisions represent sharp departures from the 50 percent blood rule and should bring even more people back, or afford formal recognition to those already in place without recognition. Is this enough, or is this too much? It is still too early to say, and this is still a deeply contested process, but the provisions force us to ask of the histories that inform these policies, and the calculus of misrecognition on the ground, how do these processes work?

Elizabeth Povinelli's book *The Cunning of Recognition* (2002) takes on this critical question from the vantage point of the state and of the law in settler and Indigenous Australia. Similar engagements of such processes on the ground would greatly enhance our understanding of this political and historical process, will, and memory in the everyday lives of Indigenous peoples within and beyond the territorial limits of their reserves and/or living in communities that are not recognized legally. I have started this on-the-ground look for one Indigenous community in North America. This project required that I move through these other theaters of apprehension—history, law, and, cartography—in order to understand how it is that they came to this question, but also how it is that they came to be known. I do this simply so that they be known fairly. Further works that engage membership, belonging, and citizenship ethnographically should continue to do this contextualizing work, but also to move through the boundaries of legally demarcated spaces into the affinal space of reserve-based communities as well as nonrecognized communities, into "Métis" families, and into what were previously understood as "urban" communities (strangely without family, culture, or national contexts). Further, this ethnographic work should trace and track the workings of belongingness in these spaces. "Cultural citizenship" research studies do move in this direction, but they unproblematically conflate American (or state) citizenship with a sense of will, a desire on the part of their interlocutors to be enfolded within the rubric of state recognition, if the state is stretched properly to accommodate difference (Rosaldo 1994, 1997; Flores and Benmayor 1997). This framework is of little use for Indigenous peoples, whose memories and consciousness and relationships with the territory of what is now North America demand that the state accommodate *them* instead. My data suggest that there are alternatives to this multiculturalist framework in the minds of its "subjects." Further work should trace those alternatives in other communities and among other peoples.

Continuing research might also investigate the cultural contours and connections between Indigenous citizenship projects and their relationships to each other, both within and beyond the territorial limits of reserves. Renya Ramirez (2007) has started to do this important work vis-à-vis the critical concept of the "hub" in Indigenous California, and more work will certainly elaborate the analytic possibilities of this concept. The reserve system, the bounding of space and people—as the research of Deborah Doxtator (1996) demonstrates—is accommodated in Iroquois communities by the dynamic frame of clan and its membership system. Jon Parmenter (2010) has now elaborated this dynamism onto a seventeenth-century territorial theater of mobility throughout the Northeast, completely upending the previous way of understanding Iroquois as largely sedentary peoples. Wedded to Doxtator we see that this dynamism owes not only to adaptations to the reserve system but also to the role of nations, to the traditional culture of kin obligations within the Confederacy itself. Doxtator argues that Mohawks are dominated by more restrictive, or contracting, tendencies in relation to land and membership, and this lends itself to a more patrilineal bias in forming membership *in the colonial scene.* This was borne out in the data from Tyendinaga and at Six

Nations and, I would suggest, in Kahnawà:ke as well. Further research deploying Doxtator's theoretical framework and Parmenter's findings, as well as the arguments within this book, would greatly enhance our understanding of the material and semiotic relationships between Iroquois clan, land, band membership, gender, and meaning in both the periods of the nineteenth and twentieth centuries and into other geopolitical literatures and problems. How are other people undergoing the stresses of settler colonialism in their territories adapting to this structure? Do they configure themselves similarly, as nations within states that are refiguring their land and their systems of descent, of property, of gender formation, and of governance? More important, however, might be the question of their politics and their strategies within these scenes of both national and international disavowal—where "recognition" and now "reconciliation" appear to be the only options on the table, false choices if ever there were some, for remedying not just specific, historical issues of "wrongdoing" but our understanding of time and of justice itself. Choices are not choices if they are bestowed rather than self-generated.

In this book, there were clear articulations between the juridical and discursive history of an imposed, international border and the community's efforts to formalize membership in ways that might or might not enable it to exercise rights that guarantee passage across that border. The border, with the interpretive gymnastics that it entails for both its crossers and its administrators, is a site that requires investigation far beyond what I, or other investigators north of Mexico, have been able to do so far. Further work should look at the panics over Indigenous sovereignty manifest not only in the 1990s, but also after the post-9/11 securitization of the border. Future ethnographic work should also investigate the relation between the recognition policies and practices of border nations (such as the Blackfoot, the Ojibway) and their process of crossing. Further work on the gendered, racialized policies of ICE (Immigration and Customs Enforcement, formerly the INS), citizenship practices, and experiences will contribute greatly to studies of citizenship formation, the state, and the nation for the memberships of these territories. As such, we might ask how differently gendered peoples at different points in time were affected by the implicit assumptions of border guards. We might ask how ICE processed or coded "deviance" and other forms of difference and used it to deny or allow passage, and how those decisions and policies referenced a larger (or diminished) citizenship project in either state. Further research must then balance the study of state process with the grounded interpretations and practices of the citizenry, and it must take political subjectivity and all that it entails—emotive, affective, performative, and narrated forms of belonging (or not belonging)—into their analysis and critique of recognition, and into productive ambits of refusal.

Appendix

A Note on Materials and Methodology

This book follows on the heels of several studies done in the community during the past century, and of specific books written in the past two decades, as well as articulating to films written and directed by community members. Much of the research that was done in the community proper had been dominated by the discourse of five to ten community members since the time of David Blanchard's unpublished dissertation (1982). The field changed significantly since the mid-1990s, with the publication of Gerald (Taiaiake) Alfred's three books: *Heeding the Voices of Our Ancestors: Kahnawake Mohawk Politics and the Rise of Native Nationalism* (1995), *Peace Power and Righteousness: An Indigenous Manifesto* (1999), and *Wasase: Indigenous Pathways of Power and Freedom* (2005), all of which drew from the experiences of a more diverse group of people. Donna Goodleaf's book *Entering the Warzone: A Mohawk Perspective on Resisting Invasions* (1995); Gerald Reid's book, *Kahnawà:ke: Factionalism, Traditionalism, and Nationalism in a Mohawk Community* (2004); award-winning local journalism such as *The Eastern Door* (published weekly and available online: http://www.easterndoor.com/) and *Iorì:wase—News from the Kanien'kehá:ka Nation*, another award-winning weekly news source, which is published online (www.Kahnawakenews.com) and also in print have also shifted the scholarly and public understanding of the community. The ongoing vitality of the radio station, K103 Kahnawà:ke (http://www.k103radio .com/), which has a wide listenership in the community proper but also in the surrounding communities of Chateauguay and parts of Montreal, also provides a contemporary source. In 2001 the community started its own TV station, Kawatokont TV (KTV), which regularly broadcasts news and ongoing regular programming in Mohawk and English. The concentration and circulation of artists and curators from Kahnawà:ke—Ryan Rice (curator, Institute of American Indian Arts), Skawennati, and Carla and Babe Hemlock—all have a strong presence within the community and beyond (notably curating, writing art criticism, and producing work both individually and collaboratively). Their visual practice and, in Jolene Rickard's formulation, "visual sovereignty" (1995a) communicate the concerns of the community and its aesthetic practices to the broader world of Indigenous and critical visual art. All of these modes of communication and representation have made for a more publicly accessible and more diversified archive of the community from when I first started doing this work in 1996. In the past six years, there have also been three documentaries directed and produced by young women from Kahnawà:ke: Tracey Deer's films *Mohawk Girls* (2005) and *Club Native* (2008), as well as Reaghan Tarbell's *Little Caughnawaga: To Brooklyn and Back* (2009).[1] Each of these films deals either explicitly with issues relating to membership or, in the case of Tarbell's film, the spatial history of movement to and from the community to Brooklyn. They are visual windows into the very processes that are documented in this book.

In relation to the second wave of work done in the community (Alfred 1995), I deliberately sought to expand the geographic frame of inquiry beyond the space of the reserve. In doing so, I also sought out other people to talk with. Because of this, my sample is more stratified along class, age, education levels, employment, residency, and political orientations. Approximately half of my sample moves back and forth to the reserve proper for either ironwork or other forms of work or education, and all except two are connected either by kinship or by other forms of belonging to an Iroquois reserve. The total number of men in this group was twenty-three (63 percent); the total number of women was thirteen (36 percent). Of the men, 15 would be considered working class, 2 were professional, 1 was self-employed, 3 were students, and 1 was a civil servant. The women included 1 professional, 1 student, 1 self-employed, and 9 retired or homemakers. Two people in my sample, 1 male and 1 female, were either non-Indian or hard to situate. Of these two, 1 was retired and 1 was a professional. Most of these people were from Kahnawà:ke. I also interviewed people from Kanehsatà:ke, Ahkwesáhsne, and Cattaragus (Seneca Nation). I interviewed one person who claimed to be of Kahnawà:ke descent, but it was difficult for me to determine how. I have included some of that interview in chapter 2 because it illustrates in some very curious ways the very problem of recognition *within* the community, the ways in which consciousness operates in claims to Indigenous identities, and the ways in which territory may be reconfigured to align with different histories. I also included this data to illustrate the problem of recognition between researcher and subject.

The people I initially talked to formally included people I knew to have certain positions on membership, people I knew were affected by policy in certain ways, and people who sought to influence policy in certain ways. For example, I sought out someone who might self-identify as "traditional," and thus might have a clan-based vision for membership, as well as someone who might not or might be more sympathetic to "blood quantum" as a form of determining membership. I also sought out those who were middle-of-the-road on their position, or people I understood to move between or be simultaneously sympathetic to different political orientations. I looked for people of various statuses (on the band list, on the federal list of those who regained Indian status via Bill C-31, those who were unclear or ambiguous), people who were travelers or who grew up away from the community and returned, and people who had never left. I did not rely entirely upon on my own knowledge, family, or friendship group for this research (and thus had to be introduced to people), but I "rolled out" from an initial set of ten. None of my original ten interviews were family members, and one of that ten was an acquaintance whose phone number I already had. I moved to my final set of thirty-six largely by asking "Is there anybody else that you think I should talk to about this?" I deliberately did *not* interview people I knew had been interviewed repeatedly by others, either by the press or other anthropologists or researchers. However, I did complement my interviews and ethnographic vignettes with "official data" and data of the public record, such as newspaper articles, court transcripts, and information available from official sources on the Internet. In this way I was able to "fill in," at times, pieces of this story I knew existed but was either reluctant to gather myself (for reasons discussed throughout this book) or unable to represent for privacy issues. I was also able to represent some of the more "accessed" discourses on nationhood and membership that way. Thus, the situations and narratives of some of these more public (and positioned) figures are considered alongside my own interviews or ethnographic field notes and ethnographic reconstructions. I have also included my own experiences. I found the questions "What is membership?"; "What is citizenship?"; "Is there a difference?"; and "What is your ideal form of membership?" to be very useful for most of my interlocutors, but even saying the word "membership" made some people uncomfortable. One ironworker in Manhattan said to me, "I don't want to talk about that; you should talk to ——; he is more political; he likes to talk about that." Because of the sensitivity of the subject matter to some, I complemented all of these interviews with data from participant observation, or witnessing, and have used my field notes to support what could not be transcribed or was left unrecorded. In some cases, in particular with women, I found it much better to simply abstract from my field notes and recordings (which I had permission to make). The public statements that they made at community meetings, to the press, and to the government in consultation spoke volumes about the situation in which they found themselves regarding membership and saved the extreme discomfort of interviewing them directly regarding their experiences as disenfranchised community members. They appear to be underrepresented in my sample, but their public utterances are far from so. I did not want to retraumatize or victimize them by asking them to share their stories of exclusion during my fieldwork. Because I was invited to participate in meetings of the Quebec Native Women's Association with the federal government and to record and use the data generated there for the purposes of this project, I conducted no face-to-face interviews with these women. I did, however, interview some of their children.

Researchers have written about the difficulty of doing fieldwork on sensitive issues and the problems that this poses for them in terms of both the safety of their interlocutors and their own comfort level and safety (Ginsburg 1988; Landsman 1988). During the course of my fieldwork I did everything I could do to *not* make people uncomfortable or to jeopardize their sense of safety, their well-being, and their self-consciousness. Membership and, in particular, its strong associations with blood quantum, has multivalenced interpretations within the shifting boundaries of the community, and I would argue all are valid and some extremely difficult depending on one's personal and familial situation. Membership and the practice of using blood quantum as a requirement for legal rights have been described in community meetings as a form of "lateral violence," the members of the community in favor of blood as a "southern court," and individual members simply as "white" or "half-breed" and therefore ineligible for status. All of these interpretations are not only hurtful and damaging personally but very real to their interlocutors and have a serious context that must be treated carefully or not treated at all. As decontextualized statements can mobilize into larger meanings, I did not wish to amplify them through the research by asking people "so, who is Indian" or even to be *in the neighborhood* of this question.

Suffice it to say for now that my engagements did not allow in any way for a proprietary or possessive stance with regard to narrating Mohawk life. As this was at times an ethnography of uncomfortable processes, I turned off my (now antiquated and somewhat embarrassing) minidisc recorder when I was asked to do so. I did not write up notes if my interlocutors were explaining things to me that might either jeopardize them or diminish the claims of others. I relied on the public record to discuss the harder edge of membership experience (i.e., court cases and hardline blood-quantum discourse). I revealed the names of my interlocutors only if they wanted me to. The ethical barometer for this research was set not only by the Social Sciences and Humanities Council of Canada guidelines, but also by the commonsense questions that should guide the work of anyone doing research in their own community: (1) Can this knowledge be used to hurt anyone?; and (2) Can I go home after this? In chapter 4 I staged an a posteriori argument for the position of this research—one of "ethnographic refusal" rather than "decolonizing methodology" or "radical indigenism" (Tuhiwai-Smith 1999; Garroutte 2003; Simpson 2007)—which were in deep and simultaneously rapid circulation when I first wrote up the results of the initial research as a dissertation. Subsequent thinking on this position made me reconsider what to call what I did—how to argue for a method, the protective method I used, that was tied to the political processes under inquiry. I also sought a way to respect and honor the individual privacy of people and the ethics of collective representation within deeply asymmetrical fields of power. I was not willing to have this research or this book harm either individuals or the broader community, and so chose a different writing style in accord with insiders' sensitivity to this issue, the ongoing vilification of Indigenous political life in the press, and my own deep wish for a less intrusive, more critically inflected anthropology of colonialism and Indigenous North America.

Throughout the course of this research, I moved through the spaces of Manhattan, Brooklyn, Kahnawà:ke, Chateauguay, and Montreal. I interviewed one interlocutor on very specific matters in Ottawa via e-mail. I crossed the international border over twenty times and include my own experiences doing so in chapter 5. I have crossed the border my entire life, in cars, on buses, and had my first flight alone into Dorval International airport at age seven to see my grandparents and my extended family. "Explaining" my particular status as an Iroquois person at the space of the border and arguing my rights were done from rote memory and near verbatim recitation of elements of the Jay Treaty of 1794 for much of my life until "fieldwork." It was not until I was formally doing research for my dissertation that I realized how intimately connected my conversations with border guards were to the law and history of settler sovereignty in the United States and Canada. I could not resist including them in the study.

Notes

Chapter 1. Indigenous Interruptions

1. Mohawk words and place-names have been harmonized as much as possible to official phonetic and lexicographic conventions. What was once Caughnawaga, Kahnawake, Akwesasne, has been changed to "Kahnawà:ke," "Ahkwesáhsne" and so on, to reflect this. I am grateful to Teyowisonte Deer of the Kanien'kehá:ka Onkwawén:na Raotitióhkwa Language & Cultural Center for help with this.

2. I know of two women that have done ironwork, one Abenaki and one Iroquois, but neither from Kahnawà:ke.

3. There are many popular and scholarly accounts of this journey. See Joseph Mitchell 1959 [1949] for the most popular account. For a sociological and largely quantitative study of this, see Bruce Katzer 1972, 1988; the paradigmatic documentary *High Steel*, directed by Don Owen (1965); and *Spudwrench: Kahnawake Man*, directed by Alanis Obomsawin (1997).

4. Joseph Mitchell "The Mohawks in High Steel," in *Apologies to the Iroquois: With a Study of Mohawks in High Steel* (1949), ed. Edmund Wilson (New York: Random House, 1959), 3

5. The Kahnawake Mohawks use the older spelling of the community (revised from "Caughnawaga") and are part of the Iroquois Lacrosse League. They have won the prestigious "Presidents Cup" Senior B Lacrosse Tournament six times in their 13 year history.

6. There are eight PhDs: Political Science (Gerald [Taiaiake] Alfred), Educational Psychology (Kahawi Jacobs), Educational Administration (Frank Deer), Public Health (Treena Delormier), Religious Studies (Christopher Jocks and Brian Rice), Anthropology (myself), Interdis-

ciplinary Studies (Kahente Horn-Miller). There are one ED (Donna Goodleaf) and two MDs (Ojistoh Horn, Kent Saylor). There have been three medical doctors in the twentieth and twenty-first centuries: Dr. Patton, Dr. Jacobs, and the late Dr. Montour. There are at least three lawyers (Trisha Delormier-Hill, Mary Lee Armstong and Kevin Fleischer) and many people that hold master's degrees and certificates of various sorts from McGill University and Concordia University. Almost all teaching positions at all schools are held by people from Kahnawake.

7. See Reaghan Tarbell's *Little Caughnawaga: To Brooklyn and Back* (2008) for an in-depth examination of the significance of this event to Kahnawa'kehró:non today.

8. In 1985 it was determined that their rates of diabetes were more than double that of white American population of the time—12 percent of the adult population was determined to have the disease. This was based on research that Louis T. Montour and Ann Macaulay did in 1981 [with] adult men and women, the first study of diabetes rates in any Indian community in Canada at the time. They published these findings in the *Canadian Medical Association Journal*. There is a terrific body of research that documents the results of a participatory research project between medical researchers and the community that involved children and their parents: the Kahnawà:ke Schools Prevention Project. It charts a decline in the incidence of the disease in 2007, when the last published paper on its incidence appeared. Horn et al. 2007. More generally, see www .ksdpp.org, accessed March 5, 2013.

9. A magazine store that carries international newspapers and journals.

10. My biological grandfather is Sam Simpson, who passed many years before I was born.

11. "Indigenous" is the broad language that captures the category of precontact peoples residing and claiming their ancestral territories postsettlement. The people I work with refer to themselves as Mohawks, Kanien'kehá:ka (People of the flint) Onkwehonwe (Original People in Mohawk, or Indian), Indians, and Natives. My use of the category of Indigenous is to attach their politics to a more global movement centered on Native politics. They do, however, use the term "nationhood," as opposed to "tribe," to describe their political form, identities, and aspirations.

12. The Membership Report, "A Review of the Membership Law" from the Membership Department in the Social Development Unit of the Mohawk Council of Kahnawake states that there are 6,154 on the local registry. There are 3,301 considered "nonmembers," who theoretically await reinstatement to the local registry. We may understand these people to be former members, descendants of former members or descendants of present members who lost their local membership perhaps due to out-marriage (they would account for most of the discrepancy between band list and the roll, as they would still be on the Federal

Registry). See http://www.kahnawake.com/org/docs/MembershipReport.pdf, 2007, accessed 08/18/2013.

13. I am a Kahnawà:ke Mohawk in active kin and political relation to the community at hand, and I work and live primarily off-reserve.

14. The name means "People of Kahnawà:ke."

15. These movements counter the dominant framework within Iroquoian studies for apprehending their spatiality as either (a) demobilized and reservationized "slums in the wilderness" (Wallace [1969] 1972) or, as put forward by the new argument in literary history, (b) demobilized and static in situ social formations contra Abenaki mobility (Brooks 2008). Both of these arguments are based on a postrevolutionary discourse of the Pine Tree chief Joseph Brant (136–39). Broad claims are made about Iroquois identity, spatiality, and political perceptions of space based on secondary source materials and the experience in the case of Brant, who, though politically significant, moved to a reserve in the province of Upper Canada granted by the Crown in recognition of Iroquois service as military allies in the Revolutionary War. Both Anthony Wallace and Lisa Brooks make these assertions based upon limited data (in particular a secondary archive) and do not consider either the philosophical dynamism in Iroquois political culture (manifest in the creation story and epic narratives such as the founding of the League). For the operationalization of Iroquois philosophy manifest in the creation story and put to work analytically by Deborah Doxtator, see her dissertation (1996) on three Iroquois communities (and their movements between each other). For a different but significant counterposition to this framework of Iroquois stasis from the seventeenth century, see Jon Parmenter 2010.

16. My notion of refusal differs from that of Sherry Ortner's very useful consideration of the literature on resistance and agency, which, in the hands of historians, has paid excellent attention to the possibility of movement against "power" but has left the subjectivity of historical actors, their motivations, and their contestations with each other unconsidered. She argues that an antidote to this sort of anemia (my rendering, not hers) would be ethnography, which would capture more substantively than poststructuralists the subject effects of force. She sees this as a form of refusal by analysts rather than subjects in contestation with each other and the wider world (1995: 184–87). For a cognate and helpful consideration of the range of analysis deploying this term in Americanist (and Native American in particular) anthropology, see Jessica Cattelino 2010a. I am indebted to and very grateful to David Holmberg for bringing Ortner's rendering of ethnographic refusal to my attention.

17. A notable exception in political science and theory the edited collection by Duncan Ivison et al. (2000).

18. See, for example, the fetishizing gaze of Iroquoianists analyzed in chapter 3 of this book. Early ethnologists and anthropologists were not very good about

taking account of Indigenous intellectual and philosophical traditions on their own temporal terms. Nor did they account robustly for the early stress and strain of colonization on Indigenous political culture, looking instead for cultural purity where it simply could not exist and extending this to a theory of immanent disappearance (see Morgan [1851] 1996; Boas 1911; for secondary cases and analysis in Australia and the United States, see Blackhawk 1997; Wolfe 1999; ben-Zvi 2007. Political science and political theory have used Indigeneity as a test claim to moral and "pragmatic" limits of reparation (Waldron 1992.) However, the deep history of Indigenous people, land tenure, and culture as imagined by Western political theorists (and protoanthropologists) as, in short, savage foil for European notions of civilization and sovereignty is too long a citational list, but for foundational works see Locke, Hobbes, Rousseau, and critical, secondary readings by Tully (1993), Pagden (1982), Arneil (1996), Nichols (2013), note 35.

19. There has yet to be a challenge to the form of sexuality recognized in the Kahnawà:ke Membership Law. This should not be taken to mean that there are not individuals from the lesbian, gay, bisexual, transgender, queer/questioning (LGBTQ) and same-sex couples living in Kahnawà:ke, or that this form of affection and romance is not tolerated. Challenges to the law have been based on its presumably raced provisions, not its heteronormativity. I am highlighting the normative heterosexuality of the Indian Act and the Kahnawà:ke Membership Law in both the 1994 and 2003 versions because it presumes this configuration of conjugal love, and this presumption has a Victorian genealogy that similarly affects the legal and affective arrangements of all Kahnawa'kehró:non.

20. The revised Kahnawà:ke Membership Law, accessed 8/18/13, www.kahnawake .com/council/docs/MembershipLaw.pdf.

21. There are also other clans present within Kahnawà:ke, such as Snipe and Rock, as the community was originally a composite of Abenaki, Huron, and other Haudenosaunee and captive peoples (see chapter 2)

22. There are notable exceptions to this trend. See Michael Levin 1993 and Gerald (Taiaiake) Alfred 1995.

23. The recent spate of public apologies by former settler-commonwealth states (United States, Canada, and Australia) in the face of historical injustice presents an interesting twist to this assertion. My current thinking on the apologies is that they are in fact a technique to keep a thin historicity in place and ape the logic of the contract, which is time sensitive and heuristically (and legally) cancels out all further claims to harm. I am indebted to the important analysis by Sherene Razack (2002) of the murder of Pamela George and her explicit exposition on contractual thinking in white settler politics in Canada, and to the analysis by Robert Nichols (2005) of Hobbes's and Locke's formulations and the Iroquois and Indigenous position as people outside of, yet central to, contract theory. Nichols (2013) extends this argument on contract into a close reading

and analysis of Jeremy Waldron's argument on the practicality of superseding historical injustice and its articulation to the contractual thinking in settler governance.

24. See Greg Horn, "Canada Prevents Mohawks from Returning Home on Haudenosaunee passports," *kahnawakenews.com*, June 1, 2010, accessed August 18, 2013, www.kahnawakenews.com/canada-prevents-mohawks-from-returning -home-on-haudenosaunee-passports-p798–1.htm.

25. For an overview of this analytic in anthropological literature of North America, see Jessica Cattelino 2010a, 2011 and North American history, see Hoxie 2008. More broadly, the richness of this analytic and its transborder and transtemporal articulations may be found in the journal *Settler Colonial Studies,* which although international, publishes many articles that are rooted in North American cases.

26. Charles Taylor's cases are derived from Canada and so are germane to this book, but his reading is from what most would consider the true foundation, Hegel, in the *Phenomenology of Spirit* on subject formation and the now canonical "master-slave dialectic." See the philosophical rereadings of Hegel by Fanon (1967), Alexandre Kojève (1969), Alex Honneth (1995), Kelly Oliver (2001), Elizabeth Povinelli (2002), Patchen Markell (2003), and Glen Coulthard (2007).

27. Morgensen's analysis of the Indian Act that attempts to flatten and erase political specificities in Canada is especially apropos here (2011, 62–64).

28. Patrick Wolfe argues that assimilation itself is the most efficient settler colonial technique of elimination, for "in neutralising a seat of consciousness, it eliminates a competing sovereignty" (2011, 34).

29. See Alyosha Goldstein (2008) for an analysis of self-abrogating legal decisions and their relationship to the unwillingness of the United States (along with Canada) to withhold from signing the United Nations Declaration on the Rights of Indigenous Peoples, enacted in 2007.

30. Time does not permit me to engage fully with Byrd's excellent parsing of the distinctions between historical intention and political trajectory with her use of the term "arrivants" to distinguish between those who "settle" against their will (those enslaved are difficult to imagine as "settling" and thus dispossessing) and the moral issues of intent and effects (2011). For related pieces see also the discussion by Malissa Phung (2011) of this in the context of Canada and by Dean Itsuji Saranillo (2008) in Hawaii. Patrick Wolfe offers a critical elaboration of the manner in which the structure of settler colonialism as also structuring identities relationally to Indigeneity in his transcribed and published conversation with Kēhaulani Kauanui (Kauanui and Wolfe 2012, esp. 239–42).

31. The literature on political recognition is concerned largely with identities and state power. This literature does not deviate from the axis of the state even though the impetus for recognition itself is, in Hegelian terms, between two, unequal people (master and bondsman). Patchen Markell has described the

translation of this issue into the terms of justice as a "thick form of respect" (2003, 7).

32. Fanon is reading the slave's apprehension of a global economy structured on the extraction of his labor through absolute force, through nonconsent. My argument is indebted to Glen Coulthard's reading of these texts in his article "Subjects of Empire" (2007).

33. Coulthard takes this from Fanon's story of a white girl who sees him on the street and says, "Mama, see the Negro! I'm frightened, frightened!" This is a scene of recognition that Fanon (writing as himself) relays and a gaze within that he "turn[ed] away" from (Fanon [1967] in Coulthard 2007, 444, 54–6). This was an intense moment of object formation (subject *as* object) that could have been potentially devastating in its diminishment, but it was not; it became an occasion to move outside of the politics of recognition into self-authorization and subject formation, again, by "turning away" from the demeaning little girl and "inward and away from the master" (ibid.).

34. See the analysis by Alyosha Goldstein (2008) of the legally and temporally based notion of "laches" (legally defined as a "reasonable amount of time") as operationalized by Supreme Court justice Ruth Bader Ginsburg in her decision on Oneida land claims in what is now New York State. For an argument regarding its nonprecedential nature and danger to Indigenous treaty claims, see Kathryn Fort 2009. I am grateful to P. J. Herne for calling this article to my attention.

35. The Associated Press, July 10, 2010, accessed October 17, 2012, www.cbsnews.com/2100–500290_162–6686478.html.

36. For this history see Price, "Pride of a Nation."

37. The province of Quebec is home as well to a deep and at times militarized independence movement that has been institutionalized into a political party, the Parti Quebecoise. Their history is tied to seventeenth-century French labor and servitude to a monarch and the Catholic Church, and then British (and Anglophone) subjugation. The subsequent liberation of the Quebecoise occurred through a "Quiet Revolution" and military action understood as "The October Crisis" in 1969. As an officially francophone province within a bilingual confederation and with a history of some animus toward the British and, some would say, Indigenous sovereignties, there is an *uneasy* participation in federalism. That the northernmost tip of Mohawk territory is overlaid in a zone of political activity of this sort makes for interesting politics, to say the least. Subsequent work in anthropology and political science might take up the different sovereignties at work in this space. For key works on Quebec sovereignty see Pierre Vallières's seminal *White Niggers of North America: The Precocious Autobiography of a Quebec "Terrorist"* (1971) and analysis by the sociologist (and sovereigntist) Hubert Guindon (1988). For anthropology on the nationalism of Quebecoise, see Richard Handler 1988. For recent work that considers

Quebec sovereigntist claims within the frame of settler colonialism, see Sandra Hobbs 2008 and Bruno Cornellier 2013.

38. The "father" of the "Warrior Society" in Kahnawà:ke, Louis Hall died in 1993. See www.louishall.com/bio/hisstory.html (accessed August 27, 2010), a website with his paintings and sketches, his written work, and a biographical entry on his life maintained by his niece.

39. This is what Mary Mathur called, in the early 1970s, "self-conscious" tradition-alism (1971, 1973).

40. This is Hall's spelling of "Kaianere'kó:wa" or Great Law of Peace.

41. There is one unpublished M A thesis on the history and significance of Louis Hall's (now) iconic "Warrior Flag" to the communities of Kahnawà:ke and the Mi'kmaq community of Esgenoopetiji (Horn-Miller 2003). Thanks to Janine Metallic for helping me with Mi'kmaq spelling.

42. Métis is the category of people descended from French and Scottish trad-ers and their Cree wives and partners in what are now the Canadian Plains. They narrate themselves as descending largely from the "Red River" region of Saskatchewan and speak a distinct language: Michif. They are understood in the historical literature as "half-breeds" and maintain a distinct identity from (status) Indians, to whom they are sometimes related. They are without Indian status, as their ancestors accepted "scrip" in exchange for land and were immediately enfranchised. Along with Indians and Inuit, they were recognized in the 1982 Canadian Constitution as distinct peoples. There is an ample legal and genealogical literature on them and a significant emergent literature on the forms of recognition they afford to each other and their terms of recognition by the state (Andersen 2008, 2011).

43. These numbers are from September 2005 and are available at www.sixnations .ca/MembershipDept.htm, accessed October 9, 2012.

44. The legal status of Kahnawà:ke women who "married out" and lost their Indian status remains in limbo, with significant numbers waiting to be put back on the band list. This is in spite of their traditional status as clan bearers.

45. The Confederacy includes both the "precontact" Iroquois Confederacy, or Haudenosaunee, and the postcontact Seven Nations Confederacy, of which Kahnawà:ke was a "central fire." The member nations of the Iroquois Confed-eracy are the Mohawk, Oneida, Onondaga, Cayuga, Seneca, and Tuscarora nations and the member nations of the Seven Nations Confederacy were the Canadian-side "mission communities" of Ahkwesáhsne, Kanehsatà:ke, Kahnawà:ke, Oswegatchie and Odanak/Becancour, the Algonquin and Nippiss-ing at Kanehsatà:ke, and the Huron of Lorette (MacLeod 1996, xi). In discussing the form and function of the Wabanaki Confederacy, Frank Speck lights upon, in far more depth, the "Seven Nations" Confederacy (although it is not called as such in his article). His information is based on the memory of Newell Lyon, of Old Town, Maine. He witnessed the procedures of the Confederacy as a

child. He describes a landscape of warfare with losses so great that the Ottawa were asked to intervene on behalf of the Mohawk and create a peace with the Abenaki, Penobscot, Passamaquoddy, and Mi'kmaq. Their resulting peace was between these four nations and the Mohawk at Oka and Caughnawaga, and included neighboring nations. The Ottawa named Caughnawaga the "central fire" of the Confederacy, and it was to that place that the nations convened and "regular meetings were held among delegates from the allied tribes where their formal relationship was maintained by series of symbolical ceremonies . . . wampum procedures, the condolence, the election of chiefs, the sending of delegates, and functions in general which characterized the internal operations of the Wabanaki Confederacy [a postcontact, post–Seven Fires phenomenon], the whole fabric of which was manifestly modeled after the pattern of the Iroquois League" (Speck 1915, 493–94). The Seven Nations have been referenced in historical work (Jennings et al. 1985, 192; Calloway 1995, 35; Fenton 1998, 519) and the popular history of the Penobscot where Caughnawaga (Kahnawà:ke) was the site of the Great Fire Council (Eckstorm [1945] 1980, 158–59), as well as in the community and web-based historical archive of Darren Bonaparte of Ahkwesáhsne, www.wampumchronicles.com, accessed August 19, 2013, which testifies to the contemporary social and political meaning of the Seven Nations to "northern" Iroquois.

46. This text is from the Mohawk of Kahnawà:ke's official website, www.kahnawake .com, accessed 2003, and as such may be viewed as an "official" statement on the meaning of the Two Row Wampum Treaty by the elected council of the community.

47. The term "citizens plus" was first coined by the Alberta Indian Federation in response to Pierre Trudeau's proposed *White Paper* in 1969 (Denis 2002, 125).

48. Much of this is changing, however, with recent works in Native American studies and anthropology that are less interested in the salvage paradigm that dominated the anthropology of Native North America. Cognate works within political theory, government, anthropology, and Native studies now take sovereignty (Fowler 2002; Barker 2005; Biolsi 2005; Bruyneel 2007; Moreton-Robinson 2007; Cattelino 2008, 2010b); petitioning and international activism (Niezen 2003; Silva 2004; de Costa 2006); race and racialization (Moreton-Robinson 2004; Biolsi 2007; Kauanui 2008); and violence and history (Smith 2005; Blackhawk 2006) as points of analysis, and also as windows into larger theoretical and sometimes applied issues within communities and settler societies themselves.

Chapter 2. Land, Meaning, and Membership

1. I do not wish to have this person subject to scrutiny and am keeping the book in which I saw his name and his name confidential.

2. Ganienkeh is land reclaimed by Mohawks near Altona, New York in 1974.

Please see Gail Landsman's *Sovereignty and Symbol: Indian-White Conflict at Ganienkeh* (1988) for an ethnographic account of this process.

3. Scholarly literature on Kahnawà:ke has touched on issues of membership and jurisdiction but has emphasized a fractured and factionalized impasse in community communication (Dickson-Gilmore 1999a); the assertion of nationalist consciousness (Alfred 1995); interpretations and expressions of tradition and change in Longhouse ("traditionalist") culture (Jocks 1994); early twentieth-century assertions of traditionally and electorally based notions of difference within the community (Reid 1999, 2004); and the relationship between internal discussions over membership criteria and Western democratic and legal theory (Dickson-Gilmore 1999b; Paine 1999b; Simpson 2000). All of these contributions to Kahnawà:ke's history and contemporary cultural analysis are united in their focus on largely institutional expressions of "culture" and a tacit acceptance of "the reserve" as the social limit and even the boundary of the community. These institutional approaches to culture persist despite the importance of discourse and narrative to the construction of identity, as well as the centrality of settler colonialism to the problem of membership. And the geographical limit of the reserve persists in these studies despite the well-known presence of Kahnawa'kehró:non in American cities such as Brooklyn, Detroit, and Boston. Some popular and scholarly literature of the past century has examined the discursive and recursive links between urban centers and the reserve. Most popular is Joseph Mitchell's widely read essay from the *New Yorker*, "Mohawks in High Steel" (1949, in Wilson 1959). It is largely owing to Mitchell's essay, and successive but sporadic articles in *The Brooklyn Bridge* (Duffy 1999) and the *New York Times* (LeDuff 2001), that Kahnawà:ke, ironwork, and Brooklyn have been conflated in the popular and scholarly imagination. In the scant anthropological work conducted in the community during the last century (Voget 1951, 1953; Postal 1965; Blanchard 1982), few have taken on the question of the connectedness of Kahnawa'kehró:non among varying locales, except for Bruce Katzer's largely quantitative study of Kahnawà:ke ironwork (1972).

4. There is a conceptual placeholder for people like me who have lives within and outside of the geographic space of the community. My point ethnographically is not to belabor my place within the community or in any way overemphasize my relationships with people, people who are my friends, family, and sometimes friendly and not-friendly acquaintances and strangers.

5. Jon Parmenter's analysis of seventeenth-century Iroquois mobility locates clan and ritual protocol at the center of Iroquois action, reconsidering colonial "misreads." Here he reminds us, as perhaps we should be reminded when examining these two quotes, that "the notion of the temporary abandonment of core cultural values and the need to reclaim them through renewed dedication to ritual practice represents a common trope in Iroquois traditional thought" (2010, 181–82). As such, lamentation, invocations of grief, and immanent loss

may be recast as vital expressions of political culture and especially so within the context of war, encroachment, and settler occupation.

6. "Credit Union."

7. See Kim TallBear's comparison of American and Canadian federal modes of reckoning Indian descent and apportioning recognition. In her discussion of lineal descent vis-à-vis blood quantum she argues, "Lineal descent is not non-essentialist. It is differentially essentialist" (2011, 73).

8. Mohawks of that time called the settlement Kentaké.

9. My intent here is not to remove Kahnawà:ke from the experiences of other Iroquois of that time. The Mohawks of Kahnawà:ke are bound to the terrific and tumultuous period of Iroquois military and social history in the Northeast of the seventeenth century. I have to limit my discussion to events and processes that frame or are historically salient for a contemporary examination of membership. For a deeper military history in relation to migrations out of the Valley, see Trigger 1985, 273–74.

10. The king of France deeded this land, the seigniory of Sault St. Louis, to the Mohawks in 1680. Jesuit priests were named as the trustees of this seigniorial land grant. Over the years they leased and accepted rents on behalf of the Mohawks, but they also acted unilaterally and illegally to sell off large sections of the reserved lands against the wishes of the Mohawk owners. The result of this is a complicated, long-term land-claim negotiation process for those lands, involving parts of the neighboring communities of St. Constant, St. Mathieu, Delson, Candiac, La Prairie, Ste. Catherine, and Chateauguay with the government of Canada. I took part in the oral history research for this claim when I was an undergraduate. None of that information is found in this book. I am grateful to Taiaiake Alfred for helping me with this summary of the land grant.

11. Discussions of the seaway (Ghobashy 1961; Alfred 1995) focus on the material and political prima facie aspects of its construction. However, the expropriation of the land has to be examined for its social and symbolic dimension. Stephanie Phillips has started this work with her master's thesis on the seaway (2000). It has been asserted in the literature that the relationship *up until this point* between Canada and Kahnawà:ke may be viewed as a balance between integration and accommodation. One view of this period asserted by Alfred is that the Indian Act and band council governance threatened neither Mohawk nationhood nor the perceived nation-to-nation relationship between Canada and Kahnawà:ke (1995, 55). Gerald Reid's archival work locates resistance to the act itself in 1884 (2004).

12. As noted above, I researched oral history pertaining to Kahnawà:ke's compensation suit for seigniorial lands lost to church mismanagement and mendacity. As part of this project, I conducted interviews with people who had been "relocated" from the riverfront. These data, compiled in the "Oral History of Land the Seigniory of Sault St. Louis," are property of the Mohawk Council of

Kahnawà:ke. To date, Stephanie Phillips has written the most comprehensive piece on the meaning of land lost to the seaway expansion (2000).

13. Much of Fred Voget's article maps out the profound anxiety that people in "Caughnawaga" had over intermarriage, loss of land, loss of culture, and loss of rights because of incursions by outsiders and the State itself (1951)

14. Frank Cassidy and Robert Bish (1989).

15. Recall the specter and threat of enfranchisement noted in Voget's fieldwork in the late 1940s, in response to potential amendments to the Indian Act.

16. The Twinn Case involved three plaintiffs: the Sawridge First Nation, Tsuu T'ina, and Ermineskin First Nations. The case was against former band member Agnes Gendron and twenty other women of the bands in northern Alberta who had lost their status and were supposed to be reinstated onto their band lists with the passage of Bill C-31. The band refused to uphold their "rights" as granted by Canada and would not put the women (and their children) on their band lists. *Windspeaker*, a national Native newspaper in Canada, printed sections from a press release issued by the three bands after the decision of the court came down, stating that the judge's decision "incorrectly treats Indian status and band membership as synonymous, even though he was aware that the plaintiffs never challenged a return to Indian status of anyone, and only challenged returns to band membership to the extent that *the government rather than the bands made the decision to grant membership*" (Sawbridge, Tsuu T'ina, and Ermineskin First Nations 1995: emphasis mine). On July 14, 1995, Judge F. Muldoon of the Federal Court trial division dismissed the bands' claims that their rights to determine membership (as protected by section 35 of the Canadian Charter of Rights and Freedoms as Aboriginal and treaty rights) should take precedence over the revised Indian Act (Bill C-31). See Bruce Miller 2011 on the claims of bias against Muldoon.

17. With her exemplary study, Tiya Miles does much to chart and nuance with great historical depth the transitions of race and recognition in early eighteenth-century Cherokee life (2005).

18. See John S. Milloy [1983] 1991 for the definitive history of the various acts that eventually culminated in the Indian Act of 1876.

19. Deborah Doxtator's dissertation documents land transactions at Six Nations, Tonawanda, and Tyendinaga. Her research at Six Nations documents how the traditional government in place (Six Nations Council) from 1847 would not even allow husbands from any other communities to hold land in their names or receive annuities (1996, 246). She further adds that as early as 1790, the Seneca chiefs at Six Nations had given a small piece of land to Ebeneezer Allen for the well-being of children he had with a Seneca woman, but that he was selling it. "The council sought to prevent Euro-Canadian men from holding reserve and to avoid any claim on the collective land base even if it meant denying the property rights of their Six Nations wives" (ibid., 248). Further, although

there was tolerance for civil unions, intermarriage was viewed as grounds for removal of Six Nations women from their registry.

20. Based on my admittedly suppositional analysis, there is a profound need for more gender analysis and clan research on this historical period in Kahnawà:ke and beyond.

21. See Cori Simpson 2008 for an oral history of the figure of the Indian agent in from late 1800s to 1973 in Kahnawà:ke.

22. See John S. Milloy (2008) for the broader picture of what Milloy calls "Indian Act colonialism" following just after Canadian Confederation in 1867. This piece emphasizes the policy-driven attempts represented by the various acts to assimilate Indigenous peoples into the body politic and enfranchise them once they were "civilized enough" to join Canada as citizens—once their "culture" had been disappeared. His histories of the Indian Acts ([1983] 1991, 2008) and sites of assimilation and deep brutality, such as Indian Residential schools (1999), align well with histories that account for the territorial dispossessions that accompanied these state-driven moves to eliminate Indigeneity.

23. People have repeatedly said that those who voted for this provision represent a statistically insignificant number of the community.

24. Rob Capriccioso, "Elizabeth Warren Finally Teaches a Lesson on Native Identity," *Indian Country Today Media Network*, May 7, 2012, indiancountrytoday medianetwork.com/2012/05/07/elizabeth-warren-finally-teaches-a-lesson-on -native-identity-111725.

25. Sean Sullivan, "The Fight over Elizabeth Warren's Heritage, Explained," *Washington Post*, September 27, 2012, accessed October 17, 2012, www.washingtonpost .com/blogs/the-fix/wp/2012/09/27/the-fight-over-elizabeth-warrens-heritage -explained/.

Chapter 3. Constructing Kahnawà:ke

1. See the description by Hauptman (2008) of Kahnawà:ke.

2. Here I understand desire as a hybrid form of Freudian "drive" and Foucauldian "discourse," both of which are an element of power and effect. See Ann Laura Stoler's discussion (1995) of desire in *Race and the Education of Desire*. For Stoler desire is a drive and a construction, a feature of power. She takes the premise of Foucault's analytical project "to trace how sexual desire is incited by regulatory discourses" as a job that is eclipsed in colonial studies literature by the focus upon the release and effects of desire, rather than its manufacture (167). Stoler argues there are points of convergence between Freudian and Foucauldian approaches to desire in their interest in boundary making, in the manufacture of identities, and in the recognition of an "internal enemy" (169). In the context of settler colonialism and colonial studies, in which the writing of the Iroquois is entrenched, the notions of effect, purpose, and boundary making are manifest in the project of ethnology and in particular in (a) writing

the past in particular ways, and (b) regulating that way through discursive practice and methodology.

3. This is true of Morgan's successors, the Boasian "culture patterns" school (of Franz Boas) in the United States (whose approach is very different than Morgan's) and then the structural-functionalists of the United Kingdom (and Australia). Karl Marx and Friedrich Engels were notably influenced by Morgan's work on property and kinship, and all were in different ways influenced by Johann Gottfried Herder's work on culture and language.

4. In their literature they refer to themselves as "annalists."

5. This notion of tradition as it manifests in Iroquois studies will be clarified shortly. The attendant question of authenticity will also be discussed with reference to how it has been played out in the context of Iroquois research along with research in other colonial contexts. Suffice it to say for now that within the frame of acculturative, assimilative, and colonialist processes at work among Indigenous peoples, tradition appears to some anthropologists as a matter of explicit pretense, a set of cultural practices and norms that are willful and, thus, insincere, contrived, and in some cases "inauthentic."

6. For a similar, but purely literary, approach to tradition, see Daniel Cottom 1996 and Alasdair MacIntyre [1981] 2007.

7. This is not language that Iroquois people use to describe their process of traditionalizing their culture or politics; it is a term I am using that inverts William Fenton's method of "upstreaming" (1998, 19). Here I am positing that the Iroquois are reading history forward to adapt to and address the political needs of the moment, specifically in the present.

8. My spelling of the Karihwí:io conforms to Mohawk spelling standards at Kahnawà:ke. This is also spelled "Gaiwiio," Gaihwiyo (Cayuga). Thanks to Tommy Deer and Rick Monture for help with this.

9. Nor is it to posit that the "Iroquois project" is entirely blind to process or that which resides in a contemporary web of meanings, self-consciously produced within historical conjuncture; on the contrary, traditional process and practices carry great meaning for many contemporary Iroquois people, whether they be "traditional" or "non-traditional" (Ciborski 1990; Jocks 1994; Alfred 1999). "Process" has been engaged by some scholars dealing with the Iroquois (Mathur 1973; Landsman 1988; Ciborski 1990; Landsman and Ciborski 1992; Jocks 1994; Alfred 1995, 1999).

10. Abu El-Haj has brought this very helpful book (and concept) to my attention.

11. Jameson's was a critique of the apolitical assumptions that guided Sigmund Freud's theorization of narrative and therapeutic process (1981).

12. Gail Landsman has written about the outright dismissal of particular Iroquois communities and people by these anthropologists on grounds of cultural impurity and political pathology (2006). There are shades of this approach in Laurence Hauptman's recent book on Iroquois leadership, where he attributes

the political actions of Kahnawa'kehró:non to the space of "cultural crisis" and diminishment, which was flagged and discussed in a review of the book (Simpson 2010).

13. These interpretations have diverged over issues of material heritage and property (NA 1970; Anonymous 1989; Fenton 1989; Tooker 1998); the influence of Iroquois political thought in relation to the American constitution (Wallace 1946; Tooker 1988, 1990; Hauptman 1988, 86–88; Landsman and Ciborski 1992); and the role of women in Iroquois society (Tooker 1984; Foster 1995).

14. This is more than a "strain." In the late 1990s I was told by a Seneca artist (now senior and well established) that anthropology was declared off-limits in Seneca territory after William Fenton betrayed the Seneca elders who allowed him to observe Longhouse ceremony and talked to him about ceremonial masks. He published this knowledge in his book on masks *after* they died (1987). For an account of this betrayal please consult Chief Irving Powless's narrative at the plenary session of the 1995 New York State Folk Arts Roundtable (Ward 1998, 68–71).

15. Indian ethnologists, linguists, and "informants" such as Ely Parker, Arthur Parker, and J. N. B. Hewitt have been involved in the process of writing the Iroquois past from "the go."

16. For a related discussion, but quite different position, see W. T. Hagan (1978) and Henrietta Fourmile's elaboration of similar issues (1996) in the context of Aboriginal Australia.

17. For an excellent departure from this canonical and authenticating mode of writing that uses some of the same primary sources please see Darren Bonaparte's *Creation & Confederation: The Living History of the Iroquois* (2006). Bonaparte's analysis of many first accounts lead him not so much to authentication but to a more dynamic framing of question of truth. Of the industry of trying to correctly date the foundation of the League, Bonaparte states, "the confederation epic gets more sophisticated as years go by, until it is as fully developed as the creation story and just as mythic. *How* this happened is much more intriguing than *when* this happened" (52).

18. For a review of research among the Iroquois and other Indians in the Northeast before 1978 see Elisabeth Tooker 1978a, "History of Research" in *The Northeast* (vol. 15). Tooker traces research back to explorer accounts of Giovanni da Verrazano, Jacques Cartier, and Samuel de Champlain; the drawings of John White; the records of Walter Raleigh; and Theodor de Bry's engravings (1978a: 4). The second wave of writing was that of colonial agents, missionaries, and traders who came to the "New World." Tooker's review of the literature goes up to the mid-twentieth century and ends with a consideration of more contemporary work being done among various peoples, such as the Kickapoo and Sauk and Fox. Her review cements the canonical basis of Iroquois, or northeastern, studies by ignoring or not including the work of early Iroquois writers on their

history and culture—among them, one of the first Iroquois histories written by a Tuscarora historian, David Cusick ([1828] 1848). This work forms a key component in Beauchamp 1892. Cusick's is an early work that was published close to the vision of Handsome Lake (1799). As a rare example of Iroquois history, we must wonder why his book has not enjoyed scholarly attention beyond that which places Cusick's date of the founding of the League as preposterous (Fenton 1998, 68). For another great exception to this trend in the literature see Bonaparte's analysis of Cusick's creation story and pre-creation world 2006, 40–44.

19. This process of domesticating space and naturalizing settler identities through the use of Iroquois signs and symbols was taken up by Landsman in a paper on white-settler suffragettes in the northeastern United States (1992, 247–84). Curtis Hinsley (1981) discusses the institutionalization of fetishized Native culture in his examination of the early history of the Smithsonian. For a consideration of these related processes from a literary perspective, see Cheryl Walker 1997. See the consideration by Helen Carr (1996) of the theoretical and discursive role that "the primitive" (and Indians as the representative of primitive) played in American anthropological and literary texts.

20. Ely Parker quoted in Arthur Parker, Ely Parker's nephew and, as will be apparent in the rest of this chapter, a significant figure in Iroquois studies (as well as Indigenous politics, more broadly defined) of the day. See Joy Porter 2001.

21. Abler and Tooker 1978, 511; Laurence Hauptman 1986, 18–20; 1988, 8–10; Joy Bilharz 1998.

22. Parker recorded Jemmy Johnson's ("Sosheowa") recitation of the Good Message, and this was reprinted with no modifications by Morgan in the *League* (Tooker 1978c: 23, 1983, 150; Parker 1913, 12).

23. Parker was from a "chiefly" lineage of the Seneca. Arthur Parker posits that Ely Parker's mother, Gaontgwuitwus, or known in English as "Elizabeth," was the great-granddaughter of Handsome Lake (1919, 20). Armstrong states that her father was Jimmy/Jemmy Johnson (whose recitation of the Gaiwi'io Parker transcribed for Morgan in 1845 and Morgan reprinted verbatim in the *League*), and Johnson is the descendant of Handsome Lake (Armstrong 1978, 8). Armstrong and Parker relate Parker's mother to Red Jacket through her mother's sister. Thus Ely Parker and Red Jacket shared the same clan, Wolf, which made Red Jacket welcome in the Parker home in spite of his difficult position vis-à-vis Handsome Lake and other Iroquois people at the time (Abler 1998, ix; Ely S. Parker to Bryant in Parker 1919, 216).

24. Pine Tree Chiefs are appointed, not hereditary chiefs. This title emerged after Europeans came here and was a position that accorded with the colonial scene. These men were bilingual and equipped to negotiate and translate concepts between hereditary chiefs, Clan Mothers, and Europeans. Most famous among them was Joseph Brant.

25. Morgan [1851] 1996; Stone 1866; Parker 1919; Parker [1952] 1998; Wallace [1969] 1972, 1978; Tooker 1978a; Fenton 1998.

26. Joseph Genetin-Pilawa 2012 has the most thorough account of this period in Seneca history to date—focusing on the Buffalo Creek Treaty and Parker's relationships with family that put him into the position to negotiate at age 16 for a repeal of the treaty (29–50).

27. Kurt Jordan has written a crucial archaeological history that significantly revises common understandings of this location and history as completely downtrodden and withouth productivity prior to the American Revolution (2008).

28. Robert Paine offers a philosophical elaboration of this process of "knowing the unknown" in ethnological and anthropological practice (1995). Bruce Trigger localizes and historicizes the process of representing Native people in his examination of ethnological, archaeological, anthropological, and ethnohistorical writing (1985b).

29. In spite of the documentation of deep history and governance in *The League of the the Iroquois* in 1851, the Iroquois along with many other Indian peoples in North America were placed in the global, temporal stage ("ethnical period") of "middle status barbarism" by 1877 in Lewis Henry Morgan's *Ancient Society*. Had they manufactured iron they could have joined Germanic and Italian tribes in the status of "upper status barbarism."

30. Tzvetan Todorov 1984; Gerald Sider 1987; Stephen Greenblatt 1991; Terry Goldie 1989; Walker 1997.

31. I problematize this simple formulation on "voice" and perspective in the following chapter but am using this line of argumentation to center the underexamined role of Ely Parker in the writing of the Iroquois Confederacy.

32. See, for example, Jeremy Beckett's "Walter Newton's History of the World—or Australia" (1993) for an Aboriginal oral history that brings Aboriginal and European myths and motifs into a unified frame of analysis for the Aboriginal narrator. See also the stories surrounding Captain Cook (Maddock 1988) and Ned Kelley (Rose 1994) in Aboriginal narratives of the past. These narratives deviate from the official record of the past, but are important circuits of knowledge. Isabel McBryde tells us that such stories "defy most Western canons of historical 'truth' and evidential 'objectivity,' yet they are still important and valid statements about the Aboriginal experience of European settlement" (1985, 10).

33. The search for a tradition of literary production has been on the research agenda for many minority scholars in critical and literary studies. For a similar process in African American studies, see the early work of Alice Walker (1983, 83–116) on the life of the anthropologist and writer Zora Neale Hurston. For another work in this vein, see the theoretically charged piece on African American Literary tradition by Henry Louis Gates Jr. (1989). A similar process is under way with the work of Ella Cara Deloria, the Dakota ethnographer and linguist who also worked under Boas. See Janet Murray 1974; Medicine's

article in *MELUS* (1980); and the recent works of Julian Rice (1992); Janet L. Finn (1995); and María Eugenia Cotera (2008). Like Hurston and George Hunt (Cannizzo 1983), other "Native" students/collaborators/informants of Boas, Deloria was responsible for the bulk of the ethnological material gathered on her own people and conducted her research at great personal expense. Unlike her contemporaries she trained with at Columbia—Margaret Mead and Ruth Benedict—Deloria struggled for most of her career to receive funding for her work.

34. There is evidence that suggests a much more nuanced relationship between Morgan and Parker than earlier chroniclers of Morgan and his work will allow. An article by Scott Michaelsen (1996) examines the various junctures at which the Morgan-Parker dialogues took place and maps out for us a more transactional set of relations (Resek 1960, 35–38, 41–44; Tooker 1984, 31; Trautmann 1987, 46; Fenton 1998, 108–9). "Morgan, at the time he most sought Parker's assistance, was holding over him the promise of various state posts as a civil engineer on the New York Canal system. More than one Morgan letter combines a request for detailed information with a report on progress toward Parker's postings" (Michaelsen 1996, 617). Obvious are the power differentials that shaped their relationship, but more compelling, perhaps, is what the fragments of Parker's writings suggest—that he may have had a much larger role in composing the *League* than even Morgan's warm inscription, or certainly the chroniclers that followed on his trail, have discussed (see Michaelsen 1996, 617; Parker, APS publications 497.3, 223). Such an exploration of his writing, prompted by the groundbreaking relational approach to ethnographic texts argued for by Michaelsen (conceived by Rosaldo and Clifford), if applied to further historiographical work in Iroquois studies, will pave the way for an understanding of Morgan and Parker that does more than merely elevate the discourse and life of Parker to another "level" (in the encompassing frame and name of "multiculturalism"). More important, perhaps, a relational approach would incorporate his knowledge into the canon of Iroquois studies or deconstruct it. Such a project lies beyond the horizon of this book and chapter, but is certainly worth further consideration.

35. One need only look to the debate sparked by Iroquois commemorations of the Kaswentha (two-row wampum) and the attempts by particular historians and anthropologists to presumably "correct the record" on Haudenosaunee interpretations of the treaty and cast aspersions on its actual veracity. Glenn Coin, "400 Years Later, a Legendary Iroquois Treaty Comes under Attack," *Syracuse Post Standard,* August 9, 2012, accessed August 20, 2013, www.syracuse .com/news/index.ssf/2012/08/400_years_later_a_legendary_ir.html. For a similar discourse of epistemic and pedantic arrogance regarding the veracity of Haudenosaunee history and how Haudenosaunee should interpret and use their treaty with the Dutch, see Kathryn Muller 2007. This piece ignores Dutch

sources attesting to the veracity of the treaty and claims a shaky provenance of Kaswentha, concluding, then, that what the Haudenosaunee normatively and strategically should do is assert the significance of another treaty in the present day.

36. Voget's articles on "Caughnawaga" do this sort of comparison—comparison with Morgan's *League* itself, but also with other kinship systems and Indigenous peoples in North America, see 1951 and especially 1953.

37. Arthur Parker 1916 (1967); Hewitt 1917, 429–38; Parker 1918, 120–24.

38. For the intimacies and representational practices of anthropology at Grand River (Six Nations), see Theresa McCarthy 2008.

39. See, for example, Fenton's discussion of the exact and approximate dates of the formation of the League (1998, 69).

40. The specificities of the legacy of this vision varies from community to community, whether they follow "Handsome Lake" or not, but may be generalized as a commitment to the ceremonial cycle; its attendant rituals; a refusal to participate in state elections or activities; in some cases to swear off alcohol; and, in some extreme forms, to not carry or use state-issued identification, to refuse health care if incumbent upon state-issued identification, for example, in Quebec, a Medicare card. I witnessed an elderly man from Kahnawà:ke refuse medical care in the Lachine General Hospital because he was asked to present such a card. In spite of his palpitations he stood with his wife and informed the medical doctor that he was a citizen of the Mohawk nation and would rather die of a heart attack than identify himself as a subject of any other nation.

41. For a full discussion of Fenton's book, consult Brian Deer 1999.

Chapter Four. Ethnographic Refusal

1. The emphasis here on the knowledge of Indigenous peoples is not to forgo the importance of that knowledge in Indigenous self-making or forms of either intersubjective recognition or institutional and political arrangements that speak to these formulations. "Indigenous" is a category of peoplehood that emerges formally in international politics in 1919 with a reference to Indigeneity in the League of Nations *Covenant of the League of Nations,* whereby the Greek government, after expropriating large landed estates, will give part of the land to "indigenous peasant proprietors, but the larger part is being used for the settlement of refugees" (418). There is also recognition (or identification) of Indigenous peoples as a subject of concern for the International Labor Organization in the 1957 C107 Indigenous and Tribal Populations Convention, which was concerned with those who were "tribal or semi-tribal," defined as groups/persons who "although they are in the process of losing their tribal characteristics, are not yet integrated into the national community." This definition gets revised through time (Neizen 2003). Key to both this definition of them and their construction (self or otherwise) is the consciousness of

the global experience of colonization, dispossession, and containment, which stretches this category to include those who are subjected to similar forms of power, force, and definition. A question then emerges as to whether Indigeneity would exist prior to settlement and anthropology and whether it is made only in these interstices. I would say that (a) politically it must know itself as having been in place prior to both, and (b) it is made in its present form through these matrices. As with blackness or queerness, it is made in its present form against whiteness or straightness but has its own varying, deeply differentiated, and sovereign histories away from both. I am indebted to Dawn Wells for research on the literature on Indigeneity that helped in the formulation of this definitional account.

2. See also John Smith 1624; Isaac Jogues 1655; Thomas Rowlandson 1682—all in Gordon Sayre 2000.

3. Colin Calloway 1992; John Demos 1994; Evan Haefeli and Kevin Sweeney 2003; Bruce Trigger 1985, 1991; Michelle Burnham 1997.

4. Bernard Cohn 1987; Nicholas Thomas 1994; Patrick Wolfe 1999; Mary Louise Pratt 1992.

5. Peter Pels and Oscar Salemink (1999, 19) trace the anthropological "culture" concept back to the eighteenth century, to Johann Gottfried Herder's notion of a nation that is necessarily differentiated from others, and possessing a history that was generated internally and shaped by language. Note that Patchen Markell 2003 has an entire chapter on the influence of Herder's version of culture on the Canadian political theorist, Charles Taylor.

6. I take up some of these issues in chapter 6.

7. This is not to say that all Indigenous peoples in Australia (or what is now the United States or Canada) remained in situ from first contact. Their histories of mobility (whether forced or voluntary) provide fodder for the question of land rights today, as the definition of "ancestral territory" often presumes fixity of place. For nuanced accounts of this territorial presumption as legal impasses, see Elizabeth Povinelli 2002; Paul Nadasdy 2005; Antonia Mills 1994. I am grateful to Nadia Abu El-Haj for pushing me on this.

8. For work on Locke in the historical context of colonization and Indigenous peoples in North America, see James Tully 1993, 137–76; and Barbara Arneil 1996.

9. Along with the Ghost Dance Religion, the vision and religion of Handsome Lake are cited as a paradigmatic case study of cultural "revitalization" in anthropological literature (Wallace 1956).

10. Warrior (1994) is also enunciating a literary critique that is particular to Native American and literary studies. In my analysis, intellectual and political traditions similarly inform the analysis of Native texts and thus shape the contemporary strategies of ethnography.

11. At the time that I started this research, in 1996, there was no research ethics

board in Kahnawà:ke. There is now a research ethics board for community-driven and outsider research.

12. Not nearly have all communities post-C-31 adopted blood-quantum requirements. See Joyce Green 2001 for discussion of the range of methods adopted by band governments for determining rights to membership across Canada.

13. Gerald Alfred 1995, 2005; Donna Goodleaf 1995; A. Simpson 2000; Kahente Horn-Miller 2005; Ryan Rice et al. 2008.

Chapter 5. Borders, Cigarettes, and Sovereignty

1. There are a few notable exceptions in the legal (O'Brien 1984; Evans 1995; Osburn 2000; Nickels 2001), anthropological (B. Miller 1996/97, 2012), historical (Carroll 2001; LaDow 2001; Taylor 2002), and Native American Studies literature (Luna-Firebaugh 2002).

2. The seminal piece on the U.S.-Mexican border is Gloria Anzaldúa 1987. Works that take off from her are José David Saldívar 1991; Ruth Behar 1993; and Héctor Calderón and José David Saldívar 1991. A critical essay that builds upon and critiques these works is Scott Michaelsen and David Johnson's introductory essay to *Border Theory* 1997, 3–4.

3. See Bruce Miller 2012 for an analysis of post-9/11 cross-border constriction in the northwest coast; and Sora Han 2006, 165–262 for post-9/11 racial profiling more generally.

4. Canadian Broadcasting Corporation's Witness television broadcast August 20, 1996 (transcript on file with author).

5. *Canada v. R.J. Reynolds Tobacco Holdings, Inc.,* 268 F.3d 103 (2d Cir. 2001).

6. Department of Justice Canada, "Government of Canada Launches Legal Action in Major Tobacco Smuggling Operation," accessed January 23, 2008, canada.justice.gc.ca/en/news/nr/1999/doc_24494.html.

7. Treaty of Amity, Commerce, and Navigation, art. 3, November 19, 1794, U.S.–Gr. Brit., 8 Stat. 116, 12 Bevans 13.

8. Canadian Broadcast Corporation's Fifth Estate television broadcast, September 28, 1993, transcript on file with author.

9. *The Smoke Ring* (Canadian Broadcasting Corporation's Fifth Estate television broadcast, January 20, 1998) was a very interesting and attempted corrective to the previous two documentaries that vilified Mohawk sovereignty.

10. Department of Justice Canada, "Government of Canada Launches Government of Canada Launches Legal Action in Major Tobacco Smuggling Operation."

11. See *Mitchell v. M. N. R.* [2001], s.c.r. 911.

12. See Canada Border Services Agency, "Summary of Allegations," accessed April 5, 2008, www.cbsa-asfc.gc.ca/media/release-communique/1999/0829ottawa-eng.html, for a chronology of cigarette taxation between 1989 and 1991.

13. U.S. Gen. Accounting Office Testimony, "Cigarette Smuggling: Information on Interstate and U.S.-Canadian Activity" (2007, 1).

14. *Troubled Waters,* October 4, 1994, CBC News: Fifth Estate.

15. The notion of "linking arms together" is more than mere imagery or a discursive device. It is the narrative of the League and reflected in the Hiawatha belt that represents the confederation of Six Nations. Mary Druke Becker extends this notion of linking arms together to the "covenant chain" agreed to between the Iroquois and the English, a chain of friendship that recognized and then elaborated alliances between nations for the purposes of trade. These are the understandings of friendship between equals that the Iroquois would bring to the treaty-making process itself (1998, 985–56). See also R. Williams 1999 for a book-length treatment of the interpretive space of treaty.

16. The Two-Row Wampum Treaty is a treaty of coexistence between the Dutch and Iroquois represented by a belt of purple and white wampum shells. There are rows of purple wampum parallel to each other, with white wampum between and around them. The white represents the sea of life that each row metaphorically shares. One purple row represents an Iroquois vessel and the other a European vessel. Although they share the same sea, they are separate and parallel; they should not touch or disturb each other or try to steer the other's vessel even though they share the same space. Between the vessels are chains that connect them to each other; these are to be shined and maintained by one or the other vessel.

17. Treaty of Amity, Commerce, and Navigation.

18. Treaty of Amity, Commerce, and Navigation.

19. For example, Francis M. Carroll quotes the northeast boundary as the following: "From the NorthWest Angle of Nova Scotia, vs. That Angle which is formed by a Line drawn due North from the Source of the Saint Croix River to the Highlands along the said Highlands which divide those Rivers that empty themselves in to the River St. Lawrence, from those which fall into the Atlantic Ocean, to the Northwestern-most head to the Connecticut River." He goes on to describe the ambiguities that attend these descriptions, that these geographic features were not commonly known by all, and that the boundaries remained into the 1800s with the Treaty of Ghent in 1815, providing for boundary commissions to survey and decide on the matter further. See Carroll 2000, 179, 181–82. This rendering of space and place that privileges boundaries over sites is critical to the disembodiment of territories from Indian grasp. A full discussion of the failures of cartography as a site-specific process and the implications of this for nation formation lies well beyond the horizon of this chapter; however, for an excellent discussion of this with reference to the predicament of Samuel Champlain's explorations in the St. Lawrence, see Kirby 1996.

20. Bryan Nickels 2001, 315, "However, to claim the free passage right in Canada, a U.S. Indian has to demonstrate a cultural or historical 'nexus' to the specific area in Canada he wishes to visit."

21. Treaty of Amity, Commerce, and Navigation.

22. Indian status cards are sometimes referred to in everyday speech of community members as "Indian cards."

23. 18 F.2D 282 (E.D. Pa. 1927). See Gerald Reid 2007, 61–78 for a recent historical reconstruction of this event.

24. The Indian Citizenship Act (Snyder Act) of 1924 granted citizenship to all Indians in the United States and was signed into law by President Calvin Coolidge on June 2 of that year. For a discussion of the effects of this act on the sovereignty of Native American nations in the United States and, in particular, for his discussion of the resistances against this act by Iroquois and other peoples, see Robert Porter 1999.

25. For a perspective on Mohawk citizenship, sovereignty, and borders from Ahkwesáhsne, see Michael Mitchell 1988, 105–36. For a treatment of the perspective of Native Americans generally, see Vine Deloria [1974] 1985; Alexandra Witkin 1995, 353, 379; and Eileen Luna-Firebaugh 2002, 159. For a discussion of the Iroquois perspective, see Robert Porter 1999, 127, 159–61.

26. See Beth LaDow 2001, which details the history of the U.S.-Canadian border from the Gros Ventre, Blackfoot, and Settler vantage points.

27. *Diabo v. McCandless*, 18 F.2d 282, 283 (E.D. Pa. 1927).

28. Ibid.; Sharon O'Brien 1984.

29. *Diabo*, 18 F.2d at 283, (emphasis added).

30. The Indian Advancement Act of 1884 replaced traditional governments with electoral systems understood as "band councils" on reservations. Reid 2004, 70.

31. "Deskaheh" is a hereditary chief of the Iroquois Confederacy. Levi General was a Cayuga from Six Nations who occupied the title of Deskaheh until his death.

32. Wampum belts are belts that are representations of law and agreements between parties that are made from wampum shell, a form of valued shell and in some cases, currency used by Indians and settlers in the sixteenth and seventeenth centuries. These belts are the authoritative basis for governance and treaty for some Indigenous people in the Northeast, and especially the Iroquois (for a brief history of wampum belts and Iroquois generally, see Tehanetorens 1983, 47–48). The Royal Canadian Mounted Police forcefully "seized the wampum [belts] used to sanction council proceedings and other council records," and the traditional government in place at Six Nations was forcibly disbanded. Weaver, quoted in Rogers and Smith 1994, 248.

33. For historical and personalized accounts of these struggles during and before the amendment to the act, see generally Janet Silman 1987; and Lynn Gehl 2000, 64–69.

34. *Goodwin v. Karnuth*, 74 F. Supp. 660 (W.D.N.Y. 1947).

35. *Karnuth v. United States*, 279 U.S. 231, 233 (1929) states that, though Antonio Danelon and Mary Cook both lived on the Canadian side of the border of Niagara Falls, "neither . . . [was] a native of Canada."

36. The Indian Reorganization Act (Wheeler-Howard Act) was enacted in Con-

gress on June 18, 1934. Section 19 defines "Indian" in three terms, the final term being related to blood quantum: "The term 'Indian' as used in this Act shall include all persons of Indian descent who are members of any recognized Indian tribe now under Federal jurisdiction, and all person[s] who are descendants of such members who were, on June 1, 1934, residing within the present boundaries of any reservation, and shall further include all other persons of one-half or more Indian blood."

37. 48 U.S.C. § 206 (1934).

38. Regarding "full-blooded," I am using the language of the legal decisions.

39. She was disenfranchised according to the Indian Act of Canada, which stated, "Any Indian woman who marries any person other than an Indian, or a non-treaty Indian, shall cease to be an Indian within the meaning of this Act." The Government of Canada at 661, quoting the Indian Act of Canada, R.S.C., ch. 98, § 14 (1927).

40. *Akins v. Saxbe*, 380 F. Supp. 1210 (D. Me. 1974).

41. For greater discussion of immigrant groups and notions of permissible citizenships in the United States, see Mae Ngai 2004. For the transnational project of fomenting whiteness in four settler countries through immigration regulations, see Marilyn Lake and Henry Reynolds 2008. For a treatment of the experience of Indigeneity at the border, see Smith 1997, 146–49, which provides a more nuanced account of the interpretive tensions between political forms of recognition at the border and more racialized interpretations between 1928 and 1952.

42. For a greater treatment of this subject, see generally Radhika Viyas Mongia 1999.

43. The Dawes Severalty Act of 1887 is much more complicated than this sentence indicates. Converting from communal forms of ownership (or stewardship) to individual forms of property required much more than a shift in territorial boundaries. The Dawes Severalty Act served to consolidate state power through its expropriation of massive amounts of land and the apportioning of land, based on Western notions of private property, appropriate ownership, and land tenure. The Dawes Severalty Act also instituted an astonishing twenty-five-year wait for allottees to "qualify" for ownership while they were required to pay rent on their land. After that time, they finally owned their land, or qualified, according to the civility standards of the local Indian agent, for the actual ownership of their land.

44. See Smith, 1997.

45. In the United States, there is no overarching form of policy regarding membership in an Indian tribe or nation, as in Canada. The process of determining membership occurs through the implementation of the Dawes Severalty Act, which first created membership lists for the allotment of land and did so according to the subjective tests of civility and, at times, the astonishing physical anthropology administered by Indian agents or by anthropologists,

who allotted Indians land based on their reading of Native peoples' bodily characteristics. These characteristics—curly hair, big feet, straight hair, and so on—were read as indexes of racial purity and, thus, cultural purity. The purer a person was in Indigenous culture, the more likely he or she was to be deemed less competent and less able to hold land in private ownership (Beaulieu 1984, 281, 281–314).

46. *Mosier v. United* States, 198 F. 54 (8th Cir. 1912).

47. *Mosier v. United States*, at 57.91.

48. During this qualifying period for allotment, individuals were assessed for their degree of aptitude and other evidence of civilization and "waited" for their certificates of competency and thus their possession of land. The recognition of blood over other identifying and recognizable criteria would be affirmed in the Citizenship Act of 1924, the Indian Reorganization Act of 1934, and in the INS immigration policy of 1952.

49. This extreme culturalist position was laid out in Canadian law in 2001. *Mitchell v. M.N.R.*, 1 S.C.R. 911 (2001). The legal strategy of Ahkwesáhsne had moved from a treaty rights argument to an aboriginal rights argument. The treaty rights approach failed with *Francis v. The Queen, S.C.C.* (1956), which denied Jay Treaty rights to the Ahkwesáhsne Mohawk Lewis Francis, who was transporting consumer goods from the United States to Canada for his own use. The court denied Francis's treaty rights, reasoning that Britain, not Canada, was a signatory to the Jay Treaty.

50. *R. v. Van der Peet*, 2 S.C.R. 507 para. 47 (1996): "In order to be an aboriginal right an activity must be an element of a practice, custom or tradition integral to the distinctive culture of the aboriginal group asserting the right." The court then determines whether that right is tied to distinctive cultural practices that were defined prior to contact. See Michael Asch 1999; and Dale Turner 2006 for trenchant critiques of this culture test.

51. *Attorney Gen. of Canada v. R.J. Reynolds Tobacco Holdings, Inc.*, 268 F.3d 103, 106 (2002) (overruled on other grounds).

52. Canada Border Services Agency, "Case Summary: Attorney Gen. of Canada v. R.J. Reynolds et al." (1999) (on file with author).

53. This term was first coined in the Hawthorn Report in Canada in 1966, "Indians should be regarded as 'citizens plus'; in addition to the normal rights and duties of citizenship, Indians possess certain additional rights as charter members of the Canadian community." See H. B. Hawthorn, ed., "A Survey of the Contemporary Indians of Canada: A Report on the Economic, Political, Educational Needs and Policies," accessed May 29, 2008, www.ainc-inac.gc.ca/pr/pub/srvy/sci3_e.html.

54. For an example of a perspective that is skeptical of aboriginal claims to tobacco trade, see John Thompson writing for the Mackenzie Institute (1994).

55. See Mishuana Goeman's *Mark My Words: Native Women Mapping Our Na-*

tions (2013) more generally but specifically p. 33 for an argument regarding the presumed criminality and degeneration of Native bodily form as it moves in or out side of sanctioned space.

Chapter 6. The Gender of the Flint

1. This interview is worked into Alanis Obomsawin's documentary, *Kanehsatake: 270 Years of Resistance* (1993).
2. Laurence Hauptman repeats this trope of "caretakers of the nation, mothers of the nation" in his recent book on Iroquois leadership (2010). See especially the chapter on Minnie Cornelius Kellogg.
3. Please consult the work of Sally Roesch Wagner (1996) on the discursive use of Iroquois women in the white women's movement for suffrage in the United States as well as the analysis by Gail Landsman and Sara Ciborski (1992) of their use for arguing for universal human rights based on the presumably savage exaltation of Iroquois woman in the Haudenosaunee political order.
4. The Provincial or state police force that literally means, Safety of Quebec; the abbreviation is "sQ."
5. See Dale Turner 2006 for an account of the Royal Commission and its mandate, specifically post-Oka Crisis.
6. See *At the Wood's Edge: An Anthology of the People of Kanehsata:ke* for a much more nuanced and pre-1721 account of their history as people who received the message of the Peacemaker prior to contact and whose claims to territory thus are profound in Iroquois and colonial terms (Gabriel-Doxtator and Van den Hende 1995, 2–23).
7. In *Sparrow* the Supreme Court of Canada considered for the first time the scope of section 35(1) of the Constitution Act of 1982, which recognizes and affirms the aboriginal and treaty rights of aboriginal peoples of Canada. Significantly, the court made it clear that the rights recognized and affirmed by section 35 are not absolute and outlined a test whereby the Crown may justify legislation that infringes on aboriginal rights. More recently, the Supreme Court of Canada, in a trilogy of cases dealing with commercial fishing rights (*R. v. Van Der Peet* [1996]; *R. v. Smokehouse* [1996]; and *R. v. Gladstone* [1996]), laid further groundwork on how aboriginal rights should be defined. In essence, the court decreed that a purposive approach must be applied in interpreting section 35 of the Constitution Act of 1982. In other words, the interests that section 35 was intended to protect must be identified. To define an aboriginal right, one must identify the practices, traditions, and customs central to aboriginal societies that existed in North America prior to contact with the Europeans. To be recognized as an aboriginal right, the practice, tradition, or custom must be an integral part of the distinctive culture of aboriginal peoples. The court reiterated that section 35 did not create the legal doctrine of aboriginal rights, but emphasized that they already existed under the common

law. The Crown can no longer extinguish existing aboriginal rights, but may only regulate or infringe upon them in a way consistent with the test laid out in the *Sparrow* decision.

8. Six Nations Mohawk Beverly Jacobs was the lead researcher and consultant to Amnesty International for the 2004 report.

9. Highway 16 stretches across Northern British Columbia. Eighteen women have been murdered between Prince Rupert and Prince George, rendering that stretch "the Highway of Tears" (Chinoy 2006). On September 12, 2012, it was reported that Bobby Jack Fowler murdered one of these women in British Columbia and died in an Oregon jail in 2006. See "Dead Oregon inmate linked to Highway of Tears case; RCMP to announce 'significant development' Tuesday," *Vancouver News*, accessed 08/22/2013, www.theprovince.com/news/Dead +Oregon+inmate+linked+Highway+Tears+case+RCMP+announce/7292547 /story.html. See also www.highwayoftears.ca/ for a family-driven memorialization to the victims and updates on investigations into the murders that ceased memorialization in 2005.

10. See Alan Cairns 2000 for an extended argument on the manner in which Indigenous (or "Aboriginal") "assimilation" of various sorts—urbanization, "intermarriage" (called such, rather than out-marriage) and self-identification—have in various ways compromised philosophically and politically based critiques of the state and the project of citizenship as a dispossessing and assimilating technique of white settler sovereignty. Time does not permit me to engage the central problem of this book—despite that the book is well researched—its weak theory of culture (as fundamentally depoliticized). Instead, see Dale Turner 2006 for a trenchant critique of Cairns's argument.

11. Peter and Trudy Jacobs, Canadian Human Rights Commission v. Mohawk Council of Kahnawà:ke 1998, accessed October 18, 2012, www.chrt-tcdp.gc.ca /search/view_html.asp?doid=440&lg=_e&.

12. Joanne Barker's analysis of similar issues of enrollment, disenrollment, and the burden of "authenticity" in meting out forms of recognition in her book *Native Acts* (2011) is an important U.S.-based account and analysis of similar issues unfolding across Indian country.

13. A "traditional woman" would be defined as someone who self-consciously practices "tradition," and rejects the authority of the settler nation-state to define her or accord her rights. She does not vote in federal or provincial elections, she does not pay taxes, she uses a "red card" (with her clan, not her band number) to cross the U.S.-Canadian border, she may refuse to use a provincially issued Medicare card to obtain health care. "Traditional" would entail a very adamant stance in terms of sovereignty, which is why much of the Iroquoianist literature on "culture" can exasperate contemporary ethnographers and ethnographic understandings of sovereignty. In 1997, way before I started formal fieldwork, I witnessed a "traditional" man refuse medical attention in a

hospital in Lachine because he did not recognize the Province of Quebec or Canada.

14. One man told me that his vision of community membership in Kahnawà:ke was predicated on recognition within the Longhouse; however, he had no problem personally with identifying as a Canadian, nor with concealing that he was Indian (as his mother had instructed) from kids that he played with in the Maritimes because they might beat him up if they knew. His willingness to "pass" as white in his youth was tied to fears surrounding the presence of the Ku Klux Klan and their violent attacks against visible minorities.

15. I have been told this, and women I interviewed told me that they also were told this.

16. People in Kahnawà:ke refer to the reserve community as "town."

17. A good part of this meeting was devoted to land requests from community members who have to go before the community and Council to request land. They have to put themselves on the agenda, attend three meetings, and answer questions from people in attendance, if asked.

18. He is referring to the locally controlled "band list."

19. A condensed form of this interview appears in chapter 4.

Conclusion

1. These conflicts are documented in Gerald Reid 2004.

2. Please note that this claim of an exclusionary tradition by the Mohawk Council of Kahnawà:ke was vigorously and immediately critiqued by then president of the Quebec Native Women's Association (QNWA), Ellen Gabriel, when the organization took public exception to the assertion that the evictions were being made according to "Mohawk custom." For the press release on behalf of the QNWA, see "Re: Evictions of Nonnative Residents," *Quebec Native Women, Inc.,* February 8, 2010, accessed August 20, 2013, www.faq-qnw.org/old/pressrel-en .html.

3. Kahnawà:ke was known in official correspondence as "Caughnawaga" (a French transliteration of the Mohawk word "on the rapids," or "Kahnawà:ke") until 1971. These pieces of correspondence may be found in "Record Group 10" (RG-10) in the National Archives of Canada.

4. There was extensive coverage in the United States and some coverage in the United Kingdom on the World Lacrosse Championships. See Associated Press, "No Trip for Iroquois Team," *New York Times,* July 17, 2010, accessed August 22, 2013, www.nytimes.com/2010/07/18/sports/18sportsbriefs-iroquois.html; Thomas Kaplan, "Bid for Trophy Becomes a Test of Iroquois Identity," *New York Times,* July 12, 2010, accessed, August 2013, www.nytimes.com/2010/07/18 /sports/18sportsbriefs-iroquois.html; Mike McAndrew, "Iroquois Nationals team stuck in New York another day despite US waivers on passport dispute," *Syracuse.com,* July 14, 2010, accessed, August 22, 2013, www.syracuse.com/

news/index.ssf/2010/07/us_agrees_to_let_us_born_membe.html; S. L. Price, "Pride of a Nation," *SI Vault*, July 19, 2010, sportsillustrated.cnn.com/vault /article/magazine/MAG1172077/index.htm; Ewan MacAskill, "Iroquois Lacrosse Team Caught in a Cleft Stick over Passports," *Guardian*, July 13, 2010, accessed August 22, 2013, www.guardian.co.uk/world/2010/jul/13 /iroquois-lacrosse-passport-world-cup; Ewan MacAskill, "Iroquois Lacrosse Team Cleared to Travel by America—Then Blocked by Britain," *Guardian*, July 15, 2010, accessed August 22, 2013, www.guardian.co.uk/world/2010/jul/15 /iroquois-lacrosse-team-passports-visa-us-uk.

Appendix

1. See also Joseph Tekaronhiake Lazare's Aboriginal People's Television Network show "By the Rapids" for animated narratives about return to the community from the city, accessed August 22, 2013, http://aptn.ca/pages/bytherapids/.

References

Abler, Thomas S. 1998. "Introduction," in *Red Jacket: Seneca Chief* [1952], by Arthur Caswell Parker. Lincoln: University of Nebraska Press.

Abler, Thomas S., and Elisabeth Tooker. 1978. "Seneca," in *The Handbook of North American Indians*, 505–17. Vol. 15: *Northeast*. Edited by Bruce G. Trigger. Washington, DC: Smithsonian Institution.

Abu El-Haj, Nadia. 2005. "Edward Said and the Political Present." *American Ethnologist* 32 (4): 538–55.

Agamben, Giorgio. 2005. *The State of Exception.* Chicago: University of Chicago Press.

Alfred, Gerald R. [Taiaiake] 1995. *Heeding the Voices of Our Ancestors: Kahnawake Mohawk Politics and the Rise of Native Nationalism.* Toronto: Oxford University Press.

Alfred, Gerald R. 1999. *Peace Power and Righteousness: An Indigenous Manifesto.* Toronto: Oxford University Press.

Alfred, Gerald R. 2002. "Sovereignty," in *A Companion to American Indian History*, 460–76. Edited by Phil Deloria and Neal Salisbury. New York: Blackwell.

Alfred, Gerald R.2005. *Wasáse: Indigenous Pathways of Action and Freedom.* Toronto: University of Toronto Press.

Amnesty International. 2004. *Stolen Sisters: Discrimination and Violence against Native Women in Canada.* Ottawa: Amnesty International Canada.

Amnesty International. 2009. *No More Stolen Sisters: The Need for a Comprehensive Response to Discrimination and Violence against Women in Canada.* Ottawa: Amnesty International Canada.

Andersen, Chris. 2008. "From Nation to Population: The Racialization of 'Metis' in the Canadian Census." *Nations and Nationalism* 14 (2): 347–68.

Andersen, Chris. 2011. "*Moya Timsook* ('The People Who Are Not their Own Bosses'): Racialization and Misrecognition of 'Mètis' in Upper Great Lakes Ethnohistory." *Ethnohistory* 58 (1): 37–63.

Andersen, Chris, and Brendan Hokowhitu. 2007. "Whiteness: Naivety, Void and Control." *Junctures* 8: 39–49.

Anderson, Benedict. 1991. *Imagined Communities: Reflections on the Origin and Spread of Nationalism.* London: Verso.

Anonymous. 1989. "Wampum Belts Returned to the Onondaga Nation." *Man in the Northeast* 38: 109–17.

Anzaldúa, Gloria. 1987. *Borderlands/La Frontera: The New Mestiza.* San Francisco: Aunt Lute.

Aristotle. [][350 B.C.E] 1995. *Politics.* Translated by Ernest Baker. New York: Oxford University Press.

Armstrong, William H. 1978. *Warrior in Two Camps: Ely S. Parker, Union General and Seneca Chief.* Syracuse, NY: Syracuse University Press.

Arneil, Barbara. 1996. *Locke in America: The Defence of English Colonialism.* London: Oxford University Press.

Asad, Talal. 1979. "Anthropology as the Analysis of Ideology." *Man* 14: 607–27.

Asch, Michael. 1999. "From Calder to Van der Peet: Aboriginal Rights and Canadian Law, 1973–96." In *Indigenous Peoples' Rights in Australia, Canada and New Zealand,* 428–45. Auckland: Oxford University Press.

Axtell, James. 1988. *After Columbus: Essays in the Ethnohistory of Colonial North America.* New York: Oxford University Press.

Backhouse, Constance. 1999. *Colour-Coded: A Legal History of Racism in Canada, 1900–1950.* Toronto: University of Toronto Press.

Baker, Lee D. 1998. *From Savage to Negro: Anthropology and the Construction of Race, 1896–1954.* Berkeley: University of California Press.

Baker, Lee D. 2010. *Anthropology and the Racial Politics of Culture.* Durham, NC: Duke University Press.

Barker, Joanne. 2008. "Gender, Sovereignty, Rights: Native Women's Activism against Social Inequality and Violence in Canada." *American Quarterly* 60 (2): 259–66.

Barker, Joanne. 2011. *Native Acts: Law, Recognition and Cultural Authenticity.* Durham, NC: Duke University Press.

Barker, Joanne, ed. 2005. *Sovereignty Matters: Locations of Contestation and Possibility in Indigenous Struggles for Self Determination.* Lincoln: University of Nebraska Press.

Beauchamp, William M. 1892. *The Iroquois Trail; or, Footprints of the Six Nations, in Customs, Traditions, and History, in which are included David Cusick's "Sketches of the Ancient History of the Six Nations."* Fayetteville, NY: H.C.

Beaulieu, David. 1984. "Curly Hair and Big Feet: Physical Anthropology and the Implementation of Land Allotment on the White Earth Chippewa Reservation." *American Indian Quarterly* 8 (4): 281–314.

Beauvais, Johnny. 1985. *Kahnawake: A Mohawk Look at Canada and Adventures of Big John Canadian, 1840–1919.* Kahnawake: Khanata Industries.

Becker, Mary Druke. 1998. "'We Are an Independent Nation': A History of Iroquois Sovereignty." *Buffalo Law Review* 46: 981–99.

Beckett, Jeremy. 1993. "Walter Newton's History of the World: Or Australia." *American Ethnologist* 20 (4): 675–95.

Behar, Ruth. 1993. *Translated Woman: Crossing the Border with Esperanza's Story.* Boston: Beacon.

Beiner, Ronald, ed. 1995. *Theorizing Citizenship.* Albany: State University of New York Press.

Ben-zvi, Yael. 2007. "Where Did Red Go? Lewis Henry Morgan's Evolutionary Inheritance and U.S. Racial Imagination." *New Centennial Review* 7 (2): 201–29.

Berkhofer, Robert F., Jr. 1978. *The White Man's Indian: Images of the American Indian from Columbus to the Present.* New York: Knopf.

Berlant, Lauren. 1997. *The Queen of America Goes to Washington: Essays on Sex and Citizenship.* Durham, NC: Duke University Press.

Bhabha, Homi. 1994. *The Location of Culture.* London: Routledge.

Bieder, Robert. 1986. *Science Encounters the Indian, 1820–1880: The Early Years of American Ethnology.* Norman: University of Oklahoma Press.

Bilharz, Joy. 1998. *The Allegany Senecas and the Kinzua Dam.* Lincoln: University of Nebraska Press.

Biolsi, Thomas. 2005. "Imagined Geographies: Sovereignty, Indigenous Space, and American Indian Struggle." *American Ethnologist* 32 (2): 239–59.

Biolsi, Thomas. [2001] 2007. *Deadliest Enemies: Law and Race Making on and off the Rosebud Reservation.* Minnesota: University of Minnesota Press.

Blackburn, Carole. 2000. *"Harvest of Souls": The Jesuit Missions and Colonialism in North America, 1632–1650.* Montreal: McGill-Queens University Press.

Blackhawk, Ned. 1997. "Julian Steward and the Politics of Representation: A Critique of Anthropologist Julian Steward's Ethnographic Portrayals of the American Indians of the Great Basin." *American Indian Culture and Research Journal* 21 (2): 61–81.

Blackhawk, Ned. 2006. *Violence over the Land: Indians and Empires in the Early American West.* Cambridge, MA: Harvard University Press.

Blanchard, David Scott. 1982. *Patterns of Tradition and Change: The Re-Creation of Iroquois Culture at Kahnawake.* PhD dissertation, University of Chicago.

Boas, Franz. 1889. "On Alternating Sounds." *American Anthropologist* 2 (1): 47–54.

Boas, Franz. 1911. *The Mind of Primitive Man.* New York: Macmillan.

Bonaparte, Darren. 2006. *Creation & Confederation: The Living History of the Iroquois.* Akwesasne: The Wampum Chronicles.

Brooks, Lisa. 2008. *The Common Pot: The Recovery of Native Space in the Northeast.* Minneapolis: University of Minnesota Press.

Bruyneel, Kevin. 2007. *The Third Space of Sovereignty: The Postcolonial Politics of U.S.-Indigenous Politics.* Minneapolis: University of Minnesota Press.

Burnham, Michelle. 1997. *Captivity and Sentiment: Cultural Exchange in American Literature, 1621–1861.* Hanover: University Press of New England.

Byrd, Jodi. 2011. *The Transit of Empire: Indigenous Critiques of Colonialism.* Minneapolis: University of Minnesota Press.

Cairns, Alan C. 2000. *Citizens Plus: Aboriginal Peoples and the Canadian State.* Vancouver: UBC Press.

Calderón, Héctor, and José David Saldívar, eds. 1991. *Criticism in the Borderlands: Studies in Chicano Literature, Culture and Ideology.* Durham, NC: Duke University Press.

Calloway, Colin G. 1992. *North Country Captives: Selected Narratives of Indian Captivity from Vermont and New Hampshire.* Hanover: University Press of New England.

Canada. 1858. *Report of the Special Commissioners to Investigate Indian Affairs in Canada.* Toronto.

Canada. 1989. *Indian Act.* Ottawa: Supply and Services Canada. Canadian Human Rights Tribunal (Decision).

Canada. 1998. Peter and Trudy Jacobs and Canadian Human Rights Commission and Mohawk Council of Kahnawake. March 11.

Canadian Broadcasting Corporation. 1993. Troubled Waters. "Fifth Estate" (weekly) television broadcast. Sept. 28, 1993. Transcript on file with the author.

Canadian Broadcasting Corporation. 1996. "The Dark Side of Native Sovereignty" "Witness" (weekly) television broadcast. August 20, 1996. Transcript on file with the author.

Cannizzo, Jeanne. 1983. "George Hunt and the Invention of Kwakiutl Culture." *Review of Canadian Sociology and Anthropology* 20 (1): 44–58.

Cannon, Martin. 1998. "The Regulation of First Nations Sexuality." *Canadian Journal of Native Studies* 18 (1): 1–18.

Cannon, Martin. 2005. "Bill C-31—An Act to Amend the Indian Act: Notes toward a Qualitative Analysis of Legislated Injustice." *Canadian Journal of Native Studies* 25 (1): 153–67.

Carr, Helen. 1996. *Inventing the American Primitive: Politics, Gender and the Representation of Native American Literary Traditions 1789–1936.* New York: New York University Press.

Carroll, Francis M. 2000. "Kings and Crises: Arbitrating the Canadian-American Boundary Dispute and the Belgian Crises of 1830–31." *New England Quarterly* 73 (2): 179–201.

Carroll, Francis M. 2001. *A Good and Wise Measure: The Search for the Canadian-American Boundary, 1783–1842.* Toronto: University of Toronto Press.

Carson, Nellie and Kathleen Steinhauer (as told to Linda Goyette). 2013. *Disinher-*

ited Generations: Our Struggle to Regain Treaty Rights for First Nations Women and Their Descendants. Edmonton: University of Alberta Press.

Cassidy, Frank, and Robert L. Bish. 1989. *Indian Government: Its Meaning in Practice.* Lantzville, BC: Oolichan Books.

Cattelino, Jessica. 2008. *High Stakes: Florida Seminole Gaming and Sovereignty.* Durham, NC: Duke University Press.

Cattelino, Jessica. 2010a. "Anthropologies of the United States." *Annual Reviews in Anthropology* 39: 275–92.

Cattelino, Jessica. 2010b. "The Double Bind of American Indian Need-Based Sovereignty." *Cultural Anthropology* 25 (2): 235–62.

Cattelino, Jessica. 2011. Thoughts on the U.S. as a Settler Society (Plenary Remarks, 2010 SANA Conference). *North American Dialogue: Newsletter of the Society for the Anthropology of North America* 14(1):1–6

Chinoy, Sharmeen. 2006. *Highway of Tears.* DVD. Al Jazeera International. 24 min.

Ciborski, Sara. 1990. *Culture and Power: The Emergence and Politics of Akwesasne Mohawk Traditionalism.* PhD dissertation, State University of New York at Albany.

Cohn, Bernard. 1987. *An Anthropologist among the Historians and Other Essays.* Delhi: Oxford University Press.

Colley, Linda. 2002. *Captives: The Story of Britain's Pursuit of Empire and How Its Soldiers and Civilians Were Held Captive by the Dream of Global Supremacy, 1600–1850.* New York: Pantheon.

Comaroff, John and Jean Comaroff. 1982. *Ethnography and the Historical Imagination.* Boulder, CO: Westview Press.

Cooper, Frederick, and Ann Stoler. 1997. "Between Metropole and Colony: Rethinking a Research Agenda." In *Tensions of Empire: Colonial Cultures in a Bourgeois World,* 1–56. Edited by Frederick Cooper and Ann Stoler. Berkeley: University of California Press.

Cornellier, Bruno. 2013. "The 'Indian Thing': On Representation and Reality in a Liberal Settler Colony." *Settler Colonial Studies* 3 (1): 45–60.

Cotera, María Eugenia. 2008. *Native Speakers: Ella Deloria, Zora Neal Hurston, Jovita Gonzalez and the Poetics of Culture.* Austin: University of Texas Press.

Cottom, Daniel. 1996. *Ravishing Tradition: Cultural Forces and Literary History.* Ithaca, NY: Cornell University Press.

Coulthard, Glen. 2007. "Subjects of Empire: Indigenous Peoples and the 'Politics of Recognition' in Canada." *Contemporary Political Theory* 6: 437–60.

Cusick, David. [1828]1848. *An Ancient History of the Six Nations.* Tuscarora, NY. Reprint: Lockport, NY.

Da Silva, Denise Ferreira. 2007. *Toward a Global Idea of Race.* Minnesota: University of Minnesota Press.

De Costa, Ravi. 2006. "Identity, Authority and the Moral Worlds of Indigenous Petitions." *Comparative Studies in Society and History* 48 (3): 669–98.

Deer, A. Brian. 1999. "La 'loi des condoléances' et la structure de la Ligue: Commentaire sur *The Great Law and the Longhouse: A Political History of the Iroquois Confederacy* de William N. Fenton." Review article, translated by Christian Ruel. *Recherches Amérindiennes au Québec* 29 (2): 63–76.

Deer, Tracey. dir. 2005. *Mohawk Girls.* DVD. Rezolution Pictures and National Film Board of Canada.

Deer, Tracey. 2008. *Club Native.* DVD. Rezolution Pictures and National Film Board of Canada.

Deloria, Philip J. 1998. *Playing Indian.* New Haven, CT: Yale University Press.

Deloria, Vine, Jr. [1974] 1985. *Behind the Trail of Broken Treaties: An Indian Declaration of Independence.* Austin: University of Texas Press.

Demos, John. 1994. *The Unredeemed Captive: A Family Story from Early America.* New York: Alfred A. Knopf Press.

Deskaheh, Levi General. 1991 (Akwesasne Notes, ed.). "An Iroquois Patriot's Fight for International Recognition," in *Basic Call to Consciousness*, 41–47. Summertown, TN: Book Publishing Company.

Dickson-Gilmore E. J. 1999a. "'This is my history, I know who I am': History, Factionalist Competition, and the Assumption of Imposition in the Kahnawake Mohawk Nation." *Ethnohistory* 46 (3): 429–50.

Dickson-Gilmore E. J. 1999b. "*Iati-Onkwehonwe:* Blood Quantum, Membership and the Politics of Exclusion at Kahnawake." *Citizenship Studies* 3 (1): 27–44.

Doxtator, Deborah. 1996. *What Happened to the Iroquois Clans?: A Study of Clans in Three Nineteenth Century Rotinonhsyonni Communities.* PhD dissertation, University of Western Ontario.

Duffy, Peter. 1999. "The Mohawks of Brooklyn." *Brooklyn Bridge* 4 (7): 48–57.

Eckstorm, Fanny Hardie. [1945] 1980. *Old John Neptune and Other Maine Indian Shamans.* Orono: University of Maine Press [A Marsh Island Reprint].

Evans, Denise. 1995. "Superimposed Nations: The Jay Treaty and Aboriginal Rights." *Dalhousie Journal of Legal Studies* 4: 215–30.

Fanon, Frantz. 1967. *Black Skin: White Masks.* Boston: Grove Press.

Fenton, William N. 1940. "Problems Arising from the Historic Northeastern Position of the Iroquois." In *Essays in Historical Anthropology of North America*, 159–252. Smithsonian Miscellaneous Collections 100. Washington, DC.

Fenton, William N. 1968. "Editors Introduction." In *Parker on the Iroquois*, 1–47. Edited by William N. Fenton. Syracuse, NY: Syracuse University Press.

Fenton, William N. 1978b. "Northern Iroquoian Culture Patterns." In *The Handbook of North American Indians.* Vol. 15: *Northeast*, 296–321. Edited by Bruce G. Trigger. Washington, DC: Smithsonian Institution.

Fenton, William N. 1987. *The False Faces of the Iroquois.* Norman: University of Oklahoma Press.

Fenton, William N. 1989. "Return of Eleven Wampum Belts to the Six Nations Iroquois Confederacy on Grand River, Canada." *Ethnohistory* 36 (4): 392–410.

Fenton, William N. [1962] 1996. "Introduction." In *League of the Iroquois*. By Lewis Henry Morgan. Secaucus, NJ: Citadel Press.

Fenton, William N. 1998. *The Great Law and the Longhouse: A Political History of the Iroquois Confederacy*. Norman: University of Oklahoma Press.

Finn, Janet L. 1995. "Ella Cara Deloria and Mourning Dove: Writing for Cultures, Writing against the Grain." In *Women Writing Culture*, 131–47. Edited by Ruth Behar and Deborah A. Gordon. Berkeley: University of California Press.

Flores, William V., and Rina Benmayor, eds., 1997. *Latino Cultural Citizenship: Claiming Identity, Space and Rights*. Boston: Beacon Press.

Fort, Kathryn. 2009. "The New Laches: Creating Title Where None Existed." *George Mason Law Review* 16 (2): 357–401.

Foster, Martha Harroun. 1995. "Lost Women of the Matriarchy: Iroquois Women in the Historical Literature." *American Indian Culture and Research Journal* 19 (3): 121–40.

Foster, Robert. 1991. "Making National Cultures in Global Ecumene." *Annual Review of Anthropology* 20: 235–60.

Fourmile, Henrietta. 1995. "'Who Owns the Past': Aborigines as Captives of the Archives." In *Terrible Hard Biscuits: A Reader in Aboriginal History*. Edited by Valerie Chapman and Peter Read. St. Leonards, NSW: Journal of Aboriginal History.

Fowler, Loretta. 2002. *Tribal Sovereignty and the Historical Imagination*. Lincoln: University of Nebraska Press.

Francis, Daniel. 1991. *The Imaginary Indian: The Image of the Indian in Canadian Culture*. Vancouver, BC: Arsenal Pulp Press.

Freilich, Morris. 1958. "Cultural Persistence among the Modern Iroquois." *Anthropos* 53 (3–4): 473–83.

Gabriel-Doxtator, Brenda Katlatont, and Arlette Kawanatatie Van den Hende. 1995. *At the Wood's Edge: An Anthology of the History of the People of Kanehsatà:ke*. Kanesatake, QC: Kanesatake Education Centre.

Garroutte, Eva. 2003. *Real Indians: Identity and the Survival of Native America*. Berkeley: University of California Press.

Gates, Henry Louis. 1989. *The Signifying Monkey*. New York: Oxford University Press.

Gehl, Lynn. 2000. "'The Queen and I': Discrimination against Women in the *Indian Act* Continues." *Canadian Woman Studies/Cahier de la Femme* 20 (2): 64–69.

Genetin-Pilawa, Joseph. 2012. *Crooked Paths to Allotment: The Fight over Federal Indian Policy after the Civil War*. Minneapolis: University of Minnesota Press.

Ghobashy, Omar Z. 1961. *The Caughnawaga Indians and the St. Lawrence Seaway*. New York: Devin-Adair.

Giddens, Anthony. 1991. *Modernity and Self Identity: Self and Society in the Late Modern Age*. Stanford, CA: Stanford University Press.

Ginsburg, Faye. 1988. *Contested Lives: The Abortion Debate in an American Community*. Berkeley: University of California Press.

Goeman, Mishuana 2013. *Mark My Words: Native Women Mapping Our Nations.* Minneapolis: University of Minnesota Press.

Goldie, Terry. 1989. *Fear and Temptation: The Image of the Indigene in Canadian, Australian and New Zealand Literature.* Montreal: McGill-Queen's University Press.

Goldstein, Alyosha. 2008. "Where the Nation Takes Place: Proprietary Regimes, Antistatism, and U.S. Settler Colonialism." *South Atlantic Quarterly* 107 (4): 833–61.

Goodleaf, Donna. 1995. *Entering the Warzone: A Mohawk Perspective on Resisting Invasions.* Penticton: Theytus Books.

Green, Joyce. 2001. "Canaries in the Mines of Citizenship: Indian Women in Canada." *Canadian Journal of Political Science* 34 (4): 715–38.

Greenblatt, Stephen. 1991. *Marvelous Possessions: The Wonder of the New World.* Chicago: University of Chicago Press.

Guillory, John. 1995. "Canon." In *Critical Terms for Literary Study*, 233–49. Edited by Frank Lentricchia and Thomas McLaughlin. Chicago: University of Chicago Press.

Guindon, Hubert. 1988. *Quebec Society: Tradition, Modernity and Nationhood.* Edited with an introduction by Roberta Hamilton and John L. McMullen. Toronto: University of Toronto Press.

Haefeli, Evan, and Kevin Sweeney. 1997. "Revisiting *The Redeemed Captive*: New Perspectives on the 1704 Attack on Deerfield." In *After King Phillips War: Presence and Persistence in Indian New England*, 29–71. Edited by Colin G. Calloway. Hanover: University Press of New England.

Hagan, W. T. 1978. "Archival Captive—The American Indian." *American Archivist* 41: 135–42.

Hagedorn, Nancy. 1988 "'A Friend to Go Between Them': The Interpreter as Cultural Broker during Anglo-Iroquois Councils, 1740–70." *Ethnohistory* 35 (1): 60–80.

Hale, Horatio, ed. 1883. *The Iroquois Book of Rites.* Philadelphia: D. G. Brinton.

Hall, Louis Karoniaktajeh. N.d. *Rebuilding the Iroquois Confederacy.* N.p.

Hall, Louis Karoniaktajeh. 1979. *Warrior's Handbook.* N.p.

Han, Sora. 2006. *Bonds of Representation: Race, Law and the Feminine in Post–Civil Rights America.* PhD dissertation: University of California, Santa Cruz.

Handler, Richard. 1988. *Nationalism and the Politics of Culture in Quebec.* Madison: University of Wisconsin Press.

Hanson, Alan. 1989. The Making of the Maori: Cultural Invention and Its Logic. *American Anthropologist* 91: 890–902.

Hardt, Michael, and Antonio Negri. 2001. *Empire.* Cambridge, MA: Harvard University Press.

Hauptman, Laurence M. 1983. *The Iroquois in the Civil War.* Syracuse, NY: Syracuse University Press.

Hauptman, Laurence M. 1986. *The Iroquois Struggle for Survival: World War II to Red Power*. Syracuse, NY: Syracuse University Press.

Hauptman, Laurence M. 1988. *Formulating American Indian Policy in New York State, 1970–1986*. Albany: State University of New York Press.

Hauptman, Laurence M. 2008. *Seven Generations of Iroquois Leadership: The Six Nations Since 1800*. Syracuse, NY: Syracuse University Press.

Havard, Gilles. 2001. *The Great Peace of Montreal 1701: French-Native Diplomacy in the Seventeenth Century*. Translated by Phyllis Aronoff and Howard Scott. Montreal: McGill-Queen's University Press.

Hertzberg, Hazel W. 1971. *The Search for an American Indian Identity: Modern Pan-Indian Movements*. Syracuse, NY: Syracuse University Press.

Hewitt, J. N. B. 1892. "Legend of the Founding of the Iroquois League." *American Anthropologist* 5 (2): 131–48.

Hewitt, J. N. B. 1929. "The Culture of The Indians of Eastern Canada." In *Explorations and Field-work of the Smithsonian Institution in 1928*, 179–82. Washington, DC: Smithsonian Institution Press.

Hinsley, Curtis, Jr. 1981. *Savages and Scientists: The Smithsonian Institution and the Development of American Anthropology 1846–1910*. Washington, DC: Smithsonian Institution Press.

Hobbs, Sandra. 2008. "Figures of the Native in 20th-century Quebec: The Subaltern and the Colonial Subject at the Intersection of Colony and Nation." *Journal of Postcolonial Writing* 44 (3): 307–18.

Hobsbawm, Eric, and Terrence Ranger, eds. 1983. *The Invention of Tradition*. Cambridge: Cambridge University Press.

Honneth, Alex. 1995. *The Struggle for Recognition: The Moral Grammar of Social Conflicts*. Cambridge: University of Massachusetts Press.

Horn O., H. Jacobs-Whyte, A. Ing, A. Bruegl, G. Paradis, and A.C. Macaulay. 2007. "Incidence and Prevalence of Type 2 Diabetes in the First Nation Community of Kahnawa:ke, Quebec, Canada, 1986–2003." *Canadian Journal of Public Health* 98 (6): 438–43.

Horn-Miller, Kahente. 2003. "The Emergence of the Mohawk Warrior Flag: A Symbol of Indigenous Unification and Impetus to Assertion of Identity and Rights Commencing in the Kanienkehaka Community of Kahnawake." Master's thesis, Concordia University, Montreal.

Horn-Miller, Kahente. 2005. "Otiyaner: The 'Women's Path' through Colonialism." *Atlantis* 29 (2): 57–68.

Hoxie, Frederick. 2008. "Retrieving the Red Continent: Settler Colonialism and the History of American Indians in the U.S." *Ethnic and Racial Studies* 31 (6): 1153–67.

"The Iroquois Wampum Controversy." 1970. *Indian Historian* 3 (spring): 4–14.

Isin, Engin, and Bryan Turner. 2003. "Citizenship Studies: An Introduction." In *Handbook of Citizenship Studies*, 1–10. Edited by Engin Isin and Bryan Turner. London: SAGE Publications.

Ivison, Duncan, Paul Patton, and Will Sanders. 2000. "Introduction." In *Political Theory and the Rights of Indigenous Peoples*, 1–21. Edited by Duncan Ivison et al. Cambridge: Cambridge University Press.

Jackson, Louis. 1885. *Our Caughnawagas in Egypt: A Narrative of What Was Seen and Accomplished by the Contingent of North American Indian Voyageurs Who Led the British Boat Expedition for the Relief of Khartoum up the Cataracts of the Nile.* Montreal: W. Drysdale.

Jameson, Fredric. 1981. *The Political Unconscious.* New York: Columbia University Press.

Jennings, Francis, et al. 1985. *The History and Culture of Iroquois Diplomacy: An Interdisciplinary Guide to the Treaties of the Six Nations and their League.* Syracuse, NY: Syracuse University Press.

Jocks, Christopher R. 1994. *Relationship Structures in Longhouse Tradition at Kahnawà:ke.* Doctoral dissertation, University of California, Santa Barbara.

Johansen, Bruce E. 1982 *Forgotten Founders: Benjamin Franklin, the Iroquois and the Rationale for the American. Revolution.* Ipswich, MA: Gambit Incorporated Publishers.

Johansen, Bruce E. 1990. "Native American Societies and the Evolution of Democracy in America, 1600–1800." *Ethnohistory* 37 (3): 279–90.

Johansen, Bruce E. 1996. "Debating the Origins of Democracy: Overview of an Annotated Bibliography." *American Indian Culture and Research Journal* 22 (2): 155–72.

Johnson, David E., and Scott Michaelsen. 1997. "Border Secrets: An Introduction." In *Border Theory: The Limits of Cultural Politics*, 1–42. Edited by Scott Michaelsen and David E. Johnson. Minneapolis: University of Minnesota Press.

Johnston, Darlene. 1986. "The Quest of the Six Nations Confederacy for Self Determination." *University of Toronto Faculty of Law Journal* 44 (1): 1–32.

Jordan, Kurt. 2008. *The Seneca Restoration 1715–1754: An Iroquois Local Political Economy.* Gainesville: University Press of Florida.

Jusdanis, Gregory. 2001. *The Necessary Nation.* Princeton, NJ: Princeton University Press.

Katzer, Bruce. 1972. *The Caughnawaga Mohawks: Occupations, Residence and the Maintenance of Community Membership.* Doctoral dissertation, Columbia University, New York.

Katzer, Bruce. 1988. "The Caughnawaga Mohawks: The Other Side of Ironwork." *Journal of Ethnic Studies* 15 (4): 39–55.

Kauanui, J. Kēhaulani. 2008. *Hawaiian Blood: Colonialism and the Politics of Sovereignty and Indigeneity.* Durham, NC: Duke University Press.

Kaunaui, J. Kēhaulani, and Patrick Wolfe. 2012. "Settler Colonialism Then and Now." A Conversation between J. Kēhaulani Kauanui and Patrick Wolfe. *Politica and Societa* (Settler Colonialism) 2: 235–58.

Kirby, Kathleen M. 1996. "Re-Mapping Subjectivity: Cartographic Vision and the

Limits of Politics." In *Bodyspace: Destabilizing Geographies of Gender and Sexuality*, 45–55. Edited by Nancy Duncan. London: Routledge.

Kip, William Ingraham. 1846. *The Early Jesuit Missions in North America*. New York: Wiley and Putnam.

Kojève, Alexandre. 1969. *Introduction to the Reading of Hegel: Lectures on the Phenomenology of Spirit*. Assembled by Raymond Queneau. Edited by Alan Bloom. Translated by James H. Nichols. Ithaca, NY: Cornell University Press.

Kuper, Adam. 1996. *Anthropology and Anthropologists: The Modern British School*. New York: Routledge.

LaDow, Beth. 2001. *The Medicine Line: Life and Death on a North American Borderland*. New York: Routledge.

Lake, Marilyn, and Henry Reynolds. 2008. *Drawing the Global Colour Line: White Men's Countries and the International Challenge of Racial Equality*. New York: Cambridge University Press.

Landsman, Gail H. 1988. *Sovereignty and Symbol: Indian-White Conflict at Ganienkeh*. Albuquerque: University of New Mexico Press.

Landsman, Gail H. 1992. "The 'Other' as Political Symbol: Images of Indians in the Woman Suffrage Movement. *Ethnohistory* 39 (3): 247–84.

Landsman, Gail H. 2006. "Anthropology, Theory, and Research in Iroquois Studies, 1980–1990: Reflections from a Disability Studies Perspective." *Histories of Anthropology Annual* 2: 242–63.

Landsman, Gail H., and Sara Ciborski. 1992. "Representation and Politics: Contesting Histories of the Iroquois." *Cultural Anthropology* 7 (4): 425–447.

Lawrence, Bonita. 2003. "Gender Race and the Regulation of Identity in the US and Canada." *Hypatia* 18 (2): 3–31.

League of Nations. N. d. *The Covenant of the League of Nations*. http://avalon.law .yale.edu/20th_century/leagcov.asp.

LeDuff, Charlie. 2001. "A Mohawk Trail to an Urban Skyline: Indian Ironworkers Return, Lured by Building Boom." *New York Times*, March 16, B1, B4.

Levin, Michael D., ed. 1993. *Ethnicity and Aboriginality: Case Studies in Ethnonationalism*. Toronto: University of Toronto Press.

Linton, Ralph. 1936. *The Study of Man*. New York: D. Appleton-Century Company.

Linton, Ralph, ed. 1940. *Acculturation in Seven American Indian Tribes*. New York: D. Appleton Century. Company.

Littlefield, Daniel F., Jr. 1996. "'They Ought to Enjoy the Home of their Fathers': The Treaty of 1838, Seneca, Intellectuals, and Literary Genesis." In *Early Native American Writing: New Critical Essays*, 83–103. Edited by Helen Jaskoski. Cambridge: Cambridge University Press.

Locke, John. [1797] 2003. *Two Treatises of Government and a Letter Concerning Toleration*. Edited by Ian Shapiro. New Haven, CT: Yale University Press.

Luna-Firebaugh, Eileen M. 2002. "The Border Crossed Us: Border Crossing

Issues of the Indigenous Peoples of the Americas." *Wicazo Sa Review* (spring): 159–81.

Lyons, Scott R. 2010. *X-Marks: Native Signatures of Assent.* Minneapolis: University of Minnesota Press.

MacIntyre, Alasdair. [1981] 2007. *After Virtue: A Study in Moral Theory.* Notre Dame, IN: University of Notre Dame Press.

MacLeod, D. Peter. 1996. *The Canadian Iroquois and the Seven Years' War.* Toronto: Dundurn Press.

Maddock, Kenneth. 1988 "Myth, History and a Sense of Oneself." In *Past and Present: The Construction of Aboriginality*, 11–30. Edited by Jeremy Beckett. Canberra: Aboriginal Studies Press.

Markell, Patchen. 2003. *Bound by Recognition.* Princeton, NJ: Princeton University Press.

Mathur, Mary Elaine Fleming. 1971. *The Iroquois in Time and Space: A Native American Nationalistic Movement.* Doctoral dissertation, University of Wisconsin, Madison.

Mathur, Mary Elaine Fleming. 1973. "The Case for Using Historical Data: Third Generation Tribal Nationalism." *The Indian Historian* 9 (4): 14–19.

McBryde, Isabel, ed. 1985. *Who Owns the Past?* Melbourne: Oxford University Press.

McCarthy, Theresa. 2008. "Iroquoian and Iroquoianist: Anthropologists and the Haudenosaunee at Grand River." *Histories of Anthropology Annual* 4: 135–71.

Mealing, S. R., ed. 1963. *The Jesuit Relations and Allied Documents: A Selection.* Ottawa: Carleton University Press.

Medicine, Beatrice. 1980. "Ella Deloria: The Emic Voice." *MELUS* 7 (4): 23–30.

Michaelsen, Scott. 1996. "Ely S. Parker and Amerindian Voices in Ethnography." *American Literary History* 8 (4): 615–38.

Miles, Tiya. 2005. *Ties That Bind: The Story of an Afro-Cherokee Family in Slavery and Freedom.* Berkeley: University of California Press.

Miller, Bruce G. 1996/97. "The 'Really Real' Border and the Divided Coast Salish Community." *B.C. Studies* 112 (winter): 63–79.

Miller, Bruce G. 2011. *Oral History on Trial: Recognizing Aboriginal Title in the Courts.* Vancouver: University of British Columbia Press.

Miller, Bruce G. 2012. "Life on the Hardened Border." *American Indian Culture and Research Journal* 36 (2): 23–45.

Milloy John S. [1983] 1991. "The Early Indian Acts: Developmental Strategy and Constitutional Change." In *Sweet Promises: A Reader in Indian-White Relations*, 145–54. Edited by J. R. Miller. Toronto: University of Toronto Press.

Milloy John S. 1999. *A National Crime: The Canadian Government and the Residential School System 1879–1986.* Winnipeg: University of Manitoba Press.

Milloy John S. 2008. *Indian Act Colonialism: A Century of Dishonour, 1869–1969.* Centre for First Nations Governance.

Mills, Antonia. 1994. *Eagle Down Is Our Law: Witsuwit'en Law, Feasts and Land Claims.* Vancouver: UBC Press.

Mitchell, Joseph. 1949. "The Mohawks in High Steel." Reprinted in *Apologies to the Iroquois* 3–36. [1959]. Edited by Edmund Wilson. New York: Vintage Books.

Mitchell, Michael [Grand Chief]. 1988. "Akwesasne: An Unbroken Chain of Sovereignty." In *Drumbeat: Anger and Renewal in Indian Country*, 105–36. Toronto: Summerhill Press and the Assembly of First Nations. .

Mongia, Radhika Viyas. 1999. "Race, Nationality, Mobility: A History of the Passport." *Public Culture* 11 (3): 527–556.

Montour, Louis T., and Ann Macaulay. 1985. "High Prevalence Rates of Diabetes Mellitus and Hypertension on a North American Indian Reservation." *Canadian Medical Association Journal* 132 (10): 1110, 1112.

Montour, Louis T., Ann Macaulay, and Naomi Adelson. 1989. "Diabetes Mellitus in Mohawks of Kahnawake, PQ: A Clinical and Epidemiologic Description." *Canadian Medical Association Journal* 141 (6): 549–52.

Moreton-Robinson, Aileen. 2000. *Talkin' up to the White Woman: Indigenous Women and Feminism.* Queensland: University of Queensland Press.

Moreton-Robinson, Aileen. 2004. "Whiteness, Epistemology and Indigenous Representation." In *Whitening Race: Essays in Social and Cultural Criticism*, 105–36. Edited by Aileen Moreton-Robinson. Canberra: Aboriginal Studies Press.

Moreton-Robinson, Aileen, ed. 2007. *Sovereign Subjects: Indigenous Sovereignty Matters.* New South Wales: Allen and Unwin.

Morgan, Lewis Henry. 1996 [1851]. *League of the Iroquois.* (Introduction by William N. Fenton). Secaucus, N.J.: Carol Publishing Book.

Morgan, Lewis Henry. Ancient Society. Introduction by Elisabeth Tooker. 1985 [1877]. Tucson: University of Arizona Press.

Morgensen, Scott. 2011. "The Biopolitics of Settler Colonialism: Right Here, Right Now." *Settler Colonial Studies* 1 (1): 52–76.

Muller, Kathryn. 2007. "The Two 'Mystery' Belts of Grand River: A Biography of the Two Row Wampum and the Friendship Belt." *American Indian Quarterly* 31 (winter): 129–64.

Murray, Janet. 1974. *Ella Deloria: A Biographical Sketch and Literary Analysis.* Doctoral dissertation, University of North Dakota, Grand Forks.

Nadasdy, Paul. 2005. *Hunters and Bureaucrats: Power, Knowledge and Aboriginal-State Relations in the Southern Yukon.* Vancouver: UBC Press.

Neizen, Ron. 2003. *The Origins of Indigenism: Human Rights and the Politics of Identity.* Berkeley: University of California Press.

Ngai, Mae. 2004. *Impossible Subjects: Illegal Aliens and the Making of Modern America.* Princeton, NJ: Princeton University Press.

Nichols Robert Lee. 2005. "Realizing the Social Contract: The Case of Colonialism and Indigenous Peoples." *Contemporary Political Theory* 4 (1): 42–62.

Nichols Robert Lee. 2013. "Indigeneity and the Settler Contract Today." *Philosophy and Social Criticism* 39 (2): 161–82.

Nickels, Bryan. 2001. "Native American Free Passage Rights under the 1794 Jay Treaty." *Boston College International and Comparative Law Review* 24 (spring): 313–39.

Niezen, Ronald. 2003. *The Origins of Indigenism: Human Rights and the Politics of Identity.* Berkeley: University of California Press.

Obomsawin, Alanis. dir. 1993. *Kanehsatake: 270 Years of Resistance.* DVD. National Film Board of Canada, Montreal. 119 min.

Obomsawin, Alanis. 1997. *Spudwrench: Kahnwake Man.* DVD. National Film Board of Canada, Montreal. 57 min., 46 sec.

O'Brien, Sharon. 1984. "The Medicine Line: A Border Dividing Tribal Sovereignty, Economies and Families." *Fordham Law Review* 53 (315): 315–50.

Ortner, Sherry B. 1995. "Resistance and the Problem of Ethnographic Refusal." *Comparative Studies in Society and History* 37 (1): 173–93.

Oliver, Kelly. *Witnessing Beyond Recognition.* Minneapolis: University of Minnesota Press.

Osburn, Richard. 2000. "Problems and Solutions Regarding Indigenous Peoples Split by International Borders." *American Indian Law Review* 24: 472–84.

Owen, Don, dir. 1965. *High Steel.* National Film Board of Canada, Ottawa. DVD. 13 min., 47 sec.

Pagden, Anthony. 1982. *The Fall of Natural Man: The American Indian and the Origins of Comparative. Ethnology.* Cambridge: Cambridge University Press.

Paine, Robert. 1990. "Our Authorial Authority." *Culture* 9:35–47.

Paine, Robert. 1995. "Columbus and Anthropology and the Unknown." *Journal of the Royal Anthropological Institute,* new ser. 1: 47–65.

Paine, Robert. 1999. "Aboriginality, Multiculturalism and Liberal Rights Philosophy." *Ethnos* 64 (3): 325–49.

Palmater, Pamela. 2011. *Beyond Blood: Rethinking Indigenous Identity.* Saskatoon, SK: Purich Publishing.

Parker, Arthur C. 1913. *The Code of Handsome Lake, The Seneca Prophet.* Albany: New York State Museum Bulletin 163.

Parker, Arthur C. 1918. "The Constitution of the Five Nations: A Reply." *American Anthropologist* 20 (1): 120–24.

Parker, Arthur C. 1919. *Life of General Ely S. Parker: Last Grand Sachem of the Iroquois and General Grant's Military Secretary.* Buffalo, NY: Buffalo Historical Society.

Parker, Arthur C. [1916] 1967. *The Constitution of the Five Nations or The Iroquois Book of the Great Law.* Ohsweken, ON: Iroqrafts.

Parker, Arthur C. [1952]. 1998. *Red Jacket: Seneca Chief.* Lincoln: University of Nebraska Press.

Parmenter, Jon. 2010. *The Edge of the Woods, Iroquoia 1534–1701.* Lansing: Michigan State University Press.

Pearce, Roy Harvey. 1953. *Savagism and Civilization*. Baltimore: Johns Hopkins University Press.

Pels, Peter, and Oscar Salemink. 1999. "Introduction: Locating the Colonial Subjects of Anthropology." In *Colonial Subjects: Essays on the Practical History of Anthropology*, 1–52. Edited by Peter Pels and Oscar Salemink. Ann Arbor: University of Michigan Press.

Phillips, Stephanie. 2000. *The Kahnawake Mohawks and the St. Lawrence Seaway*. MA thesis, McGill University.

Phung, Malissa. 2011. "Are People of Colour Settlers Too?" in *Reconciliation through the Lens of Cultural Diversity*, 289–99. Edited by Ashok Mathur, Jonathan Dewar, and Mike De Gagne. Ottawa: Aboriginal Healing Foundation.

Porter, Joy. 2001. *To Be an Indian: The Life of Iroquois-Seneca Arthur Caswell Parker*. Norman: University of Oklahoma Press.

Porter, Robert. 1999. "The Demise of the Ongwehonweh and the Rise of the Native Americans: Redressing the Genocidal Act of Forcing Citizenship upon Indigenous Peoples." *Harvard Blackletter Journal* 15: 107–83.

Postal, Susan Koessler. 1965. "Hoax Nativism at Caughnawaga: A Control Case for the Theory of Revitalization." *Ethnology* 4: 266–81.

Potvin, Louise, Margaret Cargo, Alex McComber, Treena Delormer, and Ann Macaulay. 2003. "Implementing Participatory Intervention and Research in Communities: Lessons from the Kahnawake Schools Diabetes Prevention Project in Canada." *Social Science and Medicine* 56: 1295–305.

Povinelli, Elizabeth A. 2002. *The Cunning of Recognition: Indigenous Alterities and Australian Multiculturalism*. Durham, NC: Duke University Press.

Pratt, Mary Louise. 1992. *Imperial Eyes: Travel Writing and Transculturation*. London: Routledge.

Ramirez, Renya. 2007. *Native Hubs: Culture, Community and Belonging in the Silicon Valley*. Durham, NC: Duke University Press.

Razack, Sherene. 2002. "The Murder of Pamela George." In *Race, Space and the Law: Unmapping a White Settler Society*, 121–47. Edited by Sherene Razack. Toronto: Between the Lines Press.

Reid, Gerald F. 1999. "'Un malaise qui est encore présent': Les origines du traditionalisme et de la division chez les *Kanien'kehaka* de Kahnawake au xx siècle." [translated from English by Christian Ruel]. *Recherches Amérindiennes au Québec* 29 (2): 37–50.

Reid, Gerald F. 2004. *Kahnawà:ke: Factionalism, Traditionalism, and Nationalism in a Mohawk Community*. Lincoln: University of Nebraska Press.

Reid, Gerald F. 2007. "Illegal Alien? The Immigration Case of Mohawk Ironworker Paul K. Diabo." *American Philosophical Society Proceedings* 151 (1): 61–78.

Resek, Carl. 1960. *Lewis Henry Morgan: American Scholar*. Chicago: University of Chicago Press.

Rice, Julian. 1992. *Deer Women and Elk Men: The Lakota Narratives of Ella Deloria*. Albuquerque: University of New Mexico Press.

Rice, Ryan, et al. 2008. *Oh So Iroquois*. Ottawa: Ottawa Art Gallery.

Richter, Daniel K. 1992. *The Ordeal of the Longhouse: The Peoples of the Iroquois League in the Era of European Colonization*. Chapel Hill: University of North Carolina Press.

Rickard, Jolene. 1995a. "Sovereignty: A Line in the Sand." *Aperture* 131: 51.

Rickard, Jolene. 1995b. "The Indian Defense League of America." *Akwesasne Notes* 1 (2): 48–57.

Rifkin, Mark. 2010. *When Did Indians Become Straight: Kinship, the History of Sexuality, and Native Sovereignty*. New York: Oxford University Press.

Rosaldo, Renato. 1994. "Cultural Citizenship and Educational Democracy." *Cultural Anthropology* 9 (3): 402–11.

Rosaldo, Renato. 1997. "Cultural Citizenship, Inequality and Multi-Culturalism." In *Latino Cultural Citizenship: Claiming Identity, Space and Rights*, 27–38. Edited by W. V. Flores and R. Benmayor. Boston: Beacon Press.

Rose, Deborah Bird. 1994. "Ned Kelley Died for Our Sins." *Oceania* 65 (2): 175–86.

Ross, Luana. 1998. *Inventing the Savage: The Social Construction of Native American Criminality*. Austin: University of Texas Press.

Russell, Peter H. 2005. *Recognizing Aboriginal Title: The Mabo Case and Indigenous Resistance to English-Settler Colonialism*. Toronto: University of Toronto Press.

Ryan, Simon. 1994. "Inscribing the Emptiness: Cartography, Exploration and the Construction of Australia." In *De-Scribing Empire: Post-Colonialism and Textuality*, 115–30. Edited by Chris Tiffin and Alan Lawson. London: Routledge.

Said, Edward. 1989. "Representing the Colonized: Anthropology's Interlocutors." *Critical Inquiry* 15 (2): 205–25.

Said, Edward. [1978] 1994. *Orientalism*. New York: Vintage Books.

Saldívar, José David. 1991. *The Dialectics of Our America: Genealogy, Cultural Critique, and Literary History*. Durham, NC: Duke University Press.

Sanjek, Roger. 2004. "Going Public: Responsibilities and Strategies in the Aftermath of Ethnography." *Human Organization* 63 (4): 444–56.

Sapir, Edward. 1927. "The Unconscious Patterning of Behavior in Society." In *The Unconscious: A Symposium*, 114–42. Edited by E. S. Dummer. New York: Alfred A. Knopf.

Saranillo, Dean Itsuji. 2008. "Colonial Amnesia: Rethinking Filipino 'American' Settler Empowerment in the U.S. Colony of Hawai'i." In *Asian Settler Colonialism: From Local Governance to the Habits of Everyday Life in Hawai'i*, 256–78. Edited by Candice Fujikane and Jonathan Okumara. Honolulu: University of Hawai'i Press.

Sawbridge, Tsuu T'ina, and Ermineskin First Nations. 1995. "The Other Side of the Story." Excerpted from a Press Release. *Windspeaker*. August 6, 1995, 6.

Sayre, Gordon. 2000. *American Captivity Narratives.* New York: Houghton Mifflin.

Schmitt, Carl. 2005. *Political Theology: Four Chapters on the Concept of Sovereignty.* Chicago: University of Chicago Press.

Scott, James. 1990. *Domination and the Arts of Resistance: Hidden Transcripts.* New Haven, CT: Yale University Press.

Seed, Patricia. 2001. *American Pentimento: The Invention of Indians and the Pursuit of Riches.* Minneapolis: University of Minnesota Press.

Sero, Peter. "Bloodlines Cross Mohawk Country." *Now* (October 6–12): 14–20.

Shimony, Annemarie Anrod. [1961] 1994. *Conservatism among the Iroquois at the Six Nations Reserve.* Syracuse, NY: Syracuse University Press.

Sider, Gerald. 1987. "When Parrots Learn to Talk, and Why They Can't: Domination, Deception and Self-Deception in Indian-White Relations." *Comparative Studies in Society and History* 29 (1): 3–23.

Silman, Janet [as told to]. 1987. *Enough Is Enough: Aboriginal Women Speak Out.* Toronto: Women's Press.

Silva, Noenoe. 2004. *Aloha Betrayed: Native Hawaiian Resistance to American Colonialism.* Durham, NC: Duke University Press.

Simpson, Audra. 2000. "Paths toward a Mohawk Nation: Narratives of Citizenship and Nationhood in Kahnawake." In *Political Theory and the Rights of Indigenous Peoples,* 113–36. Edited by Duncan Ivison, Paul Patton, and Will Sanders. Cambridge: Cambridge University Press.

Simpson, Audra. 2007. "On the Logic of Discernment." *American Quarterly* 59: (2): 479–91.

Simpson, Audra. 2009. "Captivating Eunice: Membership, Colonialism and Gendered Citizenships of Grief. "*Wicazo Sa Review* 24 (2): 105–29.

Simpson, Audra. 2010. "Review of Laurence Hauptman's 'Seven Generations of Iroquois Leadership: The Six Nations Since 1800.'" *American Indian Quarterly* 34 (2): 274–79.

Simpson, Audra. 2011. "Settlement's Secret." *Cultural Anthropology* 26 (2): 205–17.

Simpson, Cori. 2008. "'In the Eyes of the State': Memories of Indian Agents, Agency and Resistance in Kahnawake." Master's thesis, Trent University, Peterborough, ON.

Smith, Andrea. 2005. *Conquest: Sexual Violence and Native American Genocide.* Boston: South End Press.

Smith, Marian L. 1997. "The INS and the Singular Status of North American Indians." *American Indian Culture and Research Journal* 21 (1): 131–54.

Snow, Dean R. 1994. *The Iroquois.* Oxford: Blackwell.

Speck, Frank G. 1915. "The Eastern Algonkian Wabanaki Confederacy." *American Anthropologist* 15 (3): 492–508.

Spencer, Oliver M. 1836. *Narrative of O.M. Spencer: Comprising an Account of His Captivity among the Mohawk Indians of North America/Revised from the Origi-*

nal Papers by the Original Author of "Moral and Scientific Dialogues." London: J. Mason.

Stoler, Ann Laura. 1995. *Race and the Education of Desire: Foucault's History of Sexuality and the Colonial Order of Things.* Durham, NC: Duke University Press.

Stone, William L. 1866. *The Life and Times of Red Jacket, or Sa-go-ye-wat-ha; Being the Sequel to the History of the Six Nations.* Albany: Munsell.

Swanton, John R. 1938. "John Napoleon Brinton Hewitt." *American Anthropologist* 40 (2): 286–90.

TallBear, Kim. 2011. "The Political Economy of Tribal Citizenship in the US: Lessons for Canadian First Nations?" *Aboriginal Policy Studies* 1 (3): 70–80.

Tarbell, Reaghan, dir. 2008. *Little Caughnawaga: To Brooklyn and Back.* Mushkeg Media and National Film Board of Canada, Montreal. 48 min.

Taylor, Alan. 2002. "The Divided Ground: Upper Canada, New York, and the Iroquois Six Nations." *Journal of the Early Republic* 22 (spring): 55–75.

Taylor, Charles. 1994 "The Politics of Recognition." In *Multiculturalism: Examining the Politics of Recognition,* 25–73. Edited and Introduced by Amy Gutmann. Princeton, NJ: Princeton University Press.

Tehanetorens (Ray Fadden). 1983. *Wampum Belts.* Ohsweken: Iroqrafts Iroquois Reprint.

Thomas, Nicholas. 1994. *Colonialism's Culture: Anthropology, Travel, and Government.* Princeton, NJ: Princeton University Press.

Thompson, John. 1994. *Sin Tax Failure: The Market in Contraband Tobacco and Public Safety.* Toronto: The Mackenzie Institute.

Todorov, Tzvetan. 1984. (Translated by Richard Howard.) *The Conquest of America: The Question of the Other.* New York: Harper Perennial.

Tooker, Elisabeth. 1978a. "History of Research." In *The Handbook of North American Indians,* Vol. 15: *Northeast,* 4–13. Edited by Bruce G. Trigger. Washington, DC: Smithsonian Institution.

Tooker, Elisabeth. 1978b. "The League of the Iroquois: Its History, Politics and Ritual." In *The Handbook of North American Indians,* Vol. 15: *Northeast,* 418–41. Edited by Bruce G. Trigger. Washington, DC: Smithsonian Institution.

Tooker, Elisabeth. 1978c. "Ely S. Parker, Seneca, 1828–1895." In *American Indian Intellectuals: Proceedings of the 1976 American Ethnological Society,* 15–32. Edited by Margot Liberty. St. Paul, MN: West Publishing.

Tooker, Elisabeth. 1983. "The Structure of the Iroquois League: Lewis H. Morgan's Research and Observations." *Ethnohistory* 30 (3): 141–54.

Tooker, Elisabeth. 1984. "Women in Iroquois Society." In *Extending the Rafters: Interdisciplinary Approaches to Iroquoian Studies,* 109–23. Edited by Michael Foster, Jack Campisi, and Marianne Mithun. Albany: State University at New York Press.

Tooker, Elisabeth. 1988. "The United States Constitution and the Iroquois League." *Ethnohistory* 35 (4): 305–36.

Tooker, Elisabeth. 1990. "Rejoinder to Johansen." *Ethnohistory* 37 (3): 291–97.

Tooker, Elisabeth. 1998. "A Note on the Return of Eleven Wampum Belts to the Six Nations Iroquois Confederacy on Grand River, Canada." *Ethnohistory* 45 (2): 219–36.

Torpey, John. 2000. *The Invention of the Passport: Surveillance, Citizenship and the State.* Cambridge: Cambridge University Press.

Trautmann, Thomas. 1987. *Lewis Henry Morgan and the Invention of Kinship.* Berkeley: University of California Press.

Trigger, Bruce G. 1985a. *Natives and Newcomers: Canada's "Heroic Age" Reconsidered.* Montreal: McGill Queen's University Press.

Trigger, Bruce G. 1985b. "The Past as Power: Anthropology and the North American Indian." In *Who Owns the Past?*, 11–40. Edited by Isabel McBryde. Melbourne: Oxford University Press.

Trigger, Bruce G. 1988. *The Children of Aataentsic: The Huron People to 1660.* Montreal: McGill-Queen's Press.

Trigger, Bruce G. 1991. "Early Native and North American Responses to European Contact: Romantic versus Rationalistic Interpretations." *Journal of American History* 77 (4): 1195–215.

Tuhiwai-Smith, Linda. 1999. *Decolonizing Methodologies: Research and Indigenous Peoples.* London: Zed Books.

Tully, James. 1993. *An Approach to Political Philosophy: Locke in Contexts.* London: Cambridge University Press.

Turner, Dale. 2006. *This Is Not a Peace Pipe: Towards a Critical Indigenous Philosophy.* Toronto: University of Toronto Press.

Valaskakis-Guthrie, Gail. 2005. *Indian Country: Essays on Contemporary Native Culture.* Waterloo, ON: Wilfred Laurier University Press.

Vallières, Pierre. 1971. *White Niggers of North America: The Precocious Autobiography of a Quebec "Terrorist."* New York: Monthly Review Press.

Vennum, Thomas. 1994. *American Indian Lacrosse: Little Brother of War.* Washington, DC: Smithsonian Institution Press.

Verdery, Katherine. 1993. "Whither Nation and Nationalism?" *Daedalus* 122 (summer): 37–46.

Vernon, H. A. 1985 "Maris Bryant Pierce: The Making of a Seneca Leader." In *Indian Lives: Essays on Nineteenth and Twentieth-Century Native American Leaders*, 19–42. Edited by L. G. Moses and Raymond Wilson. Albuquerque: University of New Mexico Press.

Voget, Fred. 1951. "Acculturation at Caughnawaga: A Note on the Native-Modified Group." *American Anthropologist* 53 (2): 220–31.

Voget, Fred. 1953. "Kinship Changes at Caughnawaga." *American Anthropologist* 55 (3): 385–94.

Voget, Fred. 1984. "Anthropological Theory and Iroquois Ethnography: 1850 to 1970." In *Extending the Rafters: Interdisciplinary Approaches to Iroquoian Studies*, 343–58. Edited by Michael Foster, Jack Campisi, and Marianne Mithun. Albany: State University at New York Press.

Wagner, Roesch Sally. 1996. *The Untold Story of the Iroquois Influence on Early Feminists: Essays by Sally Roesch Wagner.* Fayetteville, NY: Sky Carrier Press.

Waldron, Jeremy. 1992. "Superseding Historic Injustice." *Ethics* 103 (1): 4–28.

Waldron, Jeremy. 2002. "Redressing Historic Injustice." *University of Toronto Law Review* 52: 135–60.

Walker, Alice. 1983. *In Search of Our Mother's Gardens: Womanist Prose.* San Diego: Harcourt Brace Jovanovich.

Walker, Cheryl. 1997. *Indian Nation: Native American Literature and Nineteenth Century Nationalisms.*. Durham, NC: Duke University Press.

Wallace, Anthony F. C. 1956. "Revitalization Movements." *American Anthropologist* 58: 264–81.

Wallace, Anthony F. C. [1969] 1972. *The Death and Rebirth of the Seneca.* New York: Vintage Books.

Wallace, Anthony F. C. 1978. "Origins of the Longhouse Religion." In *Handbook of North American Indians.* Vol. 15: *The Northeast*, 442–48. Edited by Bruce G. Trigger. Washington, DC: Smithsonian Institution.

Ward, Daniel Franklin, ed., with an introduction by Robert Baron. 1998. "Interpretation: Why? How? By Whom?" *New York Folklore* 24 (1–4): 31–76.

Warrior, Robert Allen. 1995. *Tribal Secrets: Recovering American Indian Traditions.* Minneapolis: University of Minnesota Press.

Weaver, Sally M. 1994. "The Iroquois: The Grand River Reserve in the Late Nineteenth and Early Twentieth Centuries, 1875–1945," in *Aboriginal Ontario: Historical Perspectives On The First Nations*, 213–57. Edited by Edward S. Rogers and David B. Smith. Toronto: Dundurn Press.

Welsh, Christine, dir. 2006. *Finding Dawn.* DVD. Distributed by Women Make Films, New York. 73 min.

Williams, Brackette F. 1989. "A CLASS ACT: Anthropology and the Race to Nation Across Ethnic Terrain." *Annual Review in Anthropology* 18: 401–44.

Williams, Robert A., Jr. 1999. *Linking Arms Together: American Indian Treaty Visions of Law and Peace 1600–1800.* New York: Routledge.

Witkin, Alexandra. 1995. "To Silence a Drum: The Imposition of United States Citizenship on Native Peoples." *Historical Reflections/Reflexions Historiques* 21 (2): 353–83.

Wolfe, Patrick. 1999. *Settler Colonialism and the Transformation of Anthropology: The Politics and Poetics of an Ethnographic Event.* London: Cassell.

Wolfe, Patrick. 2006. "Settler Colonialism and the Elimination of the Native." *Journal of Genocide Research* 8 (4): 387–409.

Wolfe, Patrick. 2011. "After the Frontier: Separation and Absorption in U.S. Indian Policy." *Settler Colonial Studies* 1 (1): 13–51.

Woo, Grace. 2003. "Canada's Forgotten Founders: The Modern Significance of the Haudenosaunee (Iroquois) Application for Membership in the League of Nations." *Law, Social Justice & Global Development* [An Electronic Law Journal]. Accessed August 22, 2013, elj.warwick.ac.uk/global/03–1/woo.html.

Index

borders: citizenship and, 116; exercising of rights at, 116–17, 131, 133–37, 193; international boundaries, 128; Mohawk experiences crossing, 117–23, 134; policies, 193; smuggling, 125, 128–29, 141; sovereignty and, 115, 125

boundaries, 128, 140, 166, 185; making, 212n2, 221n19

Bourassa, Robert, 152

Brant, Joseph, 203n15, 215n24

Brooks, Lisa, 203n15

Buffalo Creek Treaty, 79–80, 216n26

Byrd, Jodi, 22, 205n30

Canada-United States border. *See* United States-Canada border

Canada v. R. J. Reynolds, 126, 128–30, 141, 145

Canadian government, 3, 50, 57, 62; land appropriation, 52–53; taxation, 126, 129–30

canon, Iroquois, 217n34; acknowledgment and authorship in, 87–88, 90; culture and tradition in, 70, 73–74, 76; Fenton's contributions to, 88–89; texts, 86–92

canon, meaning, 86

capital accumulation, 17, 112, 126–27

Carroll, Francis M., 221n19

categorization, 31, 33, 95

Catholic Church, 49

Caughnawaga. *See* Kahnawà:ke

Cherokee, 64, 133

Chicano studies, 116

Christian Indians, 46

cigarette trade, 125–26, 128–29; lost revenue, 129–30, 141–42; research on, 142–43

citizenship: alien status, 134–35; ancestry and, 64; border crossing and, 119–21, 193; and civilization, 103, 169; cultural, 192; "feeling," 109, 172–75, 189–91; as a form of claiming, 35; Indian Citizen-

ship Act (1924), 134–37, 222n24; interviews on, 109–11, 171–74; Iroquois, 103; and membership distinction, 44, 171, 174–75, 188–89; Mohawk, 157; narratives of, 175–76; refusal of, 7, 116; state affiliation and, 116; taxation and, 138–39, 142; US, 121, 138–39; Warrior society and, 151–52

"citizens plus," 33, 142, 208n47, 224n53

civilization, 82, 212n22, 224n48; citizenship and, 103, 169; law and, 144

clan system, 48

collective rights, 153, 167, 168

Colley, Linda, 96

colonialism. *See* settler colonialism

Comaroff, John and Jean, 43

consciousness: citizenship and, 185; historical, 32, 185; Kahnawa'kehró:non, 33, 51, 53–55, 59–61, 106, 186–87

Constitution Act (1982), 225n7

containment, 97, 105, 127, 142, 144

contract theory, 204n23

Cook, Captain James, 100–101, 216n32

Coulthard, Glen, 24, 106, 206n33

cultural analysis, 93, 97, 209n3

cultural difference, 20–22, 139; in anthropological terms, 71, 78, 87, 101–2, 112; in colonial situations, 96–97

cultural loss, 48, 62

cultural practices, 140, 155, 213n5, 224n50

culture theory, 71, 74, 226n10

Danny, border-crossing experiences of, 120–25

Dark Side of Native Sovereignty, The (CBC), 125, 129, 141

Da Silva, Denise Ferreira, 13

Dawes Severalty Act (1887), 139, 223n43, 223n45

Death and Rebirth of the Seneca, The (Wallace), 86, 90–91

Deerfield Raid (1701), 47

Deloria, Ella Cara, 216n33

Deloria, Philip, 77, 103, 127
desire: anthropological, 69–71, 73, 190; Foucauldian and Freudian approaches to, 212n2; within narratives of citizenship, 176
Deskaheh (Levi General), 136–37, 222n31
detention, 18–19
diabetes, 6, 202n8
Diabo, Margaret K., 6
Diabo, Paul K., 135
diet, 6
disappearance: fear of, 14, 19, 25–26, 42, 181; of Indigenous peoples, 112, 204n18; refusing to, 22, 185; of women, 156, 226n9
dispossession: citizenship and, 25; and containment, 99; Indigenous, 16, 22, 74, 105; Iroquois, 82, 98; justification of, 101; land, 70, 76, 156; sovereignty and, 12, 108; territorial, 212n22; of women, 160
Doxtator, Deborah, 47, 192–93, 211n19

Eastern Door, The, 107–8
electoral participation, 54–55
elimination: fear of, 59, 181; refusal of, 22; settler logic of, 12, 19, 150, 205n28; of territory, 155
emergency, state of, 153–54
Empire, 97, 112, 155; anthropology and, 112; building, 130; citizenship and, 158; stories of captivity and, 95–96
Engels, Friedrich, 213n3
enslavement, 22–24
Equal Rights for Indian Women and the Native Women's Association of Canada, 56–57
ethnography, 94, 178, 190, 203n16; of Mohawk nationhood, 102; of Six Nations, 89–90
ethnology, 33–34, 65, 77, 93; American, 78, 85; definition of, 86; Iroquois, 70, 85–87; relational approaches to, 76, 217n34

evictions, 19, 23; of non-Natives from reserves, 13, 62, 180, 227n2
exclusion, 9, 13, 109, 176, 179; based on taxability, 138–39; from membership, 174; of women, 163–65, 168–69, 181–82
expropriation. *See* land expropriation

Fanon, Frantz, 24, 106, 206nn32–33
Fenton, William, 82, 85, 90, 214n14; *The Great Law and the Longhouse: A Political History of the Iroquois,* 86, 91–92; on Iroquois sense of time, 72–73; "Problems Arising from the Historic Northeastern Position of the Iroquois," 86, 88–89
fetishization, 163; of culture, 34, 71, 74, 99, 112, 124
Five Nations, 147, 184
Foucault, Michel, 212n2
Francis v. The Queen, s.c.c., 224n49
Frichner, Tonya Gonella, 1, 183

Ganienkeh, 38, 208n2
gender: bias, 56–57; border policies and, 193; exclusion by, 61, 168, 181; inequality, 175; membership and, 171; roles, 155, 168, 170. *See also* women
General, Levi (Deskaheh), 136–37, 222n31
Genetin-Pilawa, Joseph, 80, 216n26
"good Indian," notion of, 81
Goodleaf, Ida, 166–68
Goodwin v. Karnuth, 138
Gordian Knot, 77–79, 85
governance: Gayanerekowa, 27–28; Haudenosaunee, 7; Indigenous, 170; Iroquois Confederacy, 25, 32; Mohawk, 136, 179; settler, 11, 13, 20, 205n23; state, 16; white, 59
Great Law of Peace (Kaianere'kó:wa), 5, 32, 54, 91, 157, 179, 184; Parker's interpretation, 42, 88
Guillory, John, 86

Hale, Horatio, 90; *Iroquois Book of Rites*, 72–73, 85–88

Hall, Louis Karoniaktajeh, 29–31, 207n38; *Warrior's Handbook*, 26–28

Han, Sora, 153

Handsome Lake, 27, 29, 68, 81, 219n9; Code of (Karihwí:io), 72–73, 77, 84, 88, 91, 103

Haudenosaunee, 97, 112, 217n35, 225n3; assertions, 19, 24; governance, 7; identity, 14–15; legal and experiential history, 131; passports, 18, 25; rights, 117, 124; sovereignty, 177. *See also* Iroquois Confederacy

Hauptman, Laurence, 49, 80, 82, 213n12

Hegel, Georg Wilhelm Friedrich, 23–24, 205n26

Herder, Johann Gottfried, 213n3, 219n5

Hewitt, J. N. B, 88, 90; visit to Kahnawà:ke, 68–69, 94

Highway of Tears, 156, 226n9

Hinsley, Curtis, 215n19

historians, role of, 75

historical consciousness, 32, 42, 185

identity: American, 77–78; ancestry and, 41, 63; by blood quantum, 137, 139, 167–68; genealogical knowledge and, 15; Indian status and, 61; Indigenous, 63–64; Kahnawà:ke, 14, 55; Métis, 207n42; Mohawk, 45, 51, 53, 123–24, 162, 175; racialization of, 138–39; unprotected, 23; of women, 164

Immigration and Customs Enforcement (ICE), 193. *See also* Immigration and Naturalization Service (INS)

Immigration and Naturalization Service (INS), 137–38, 224n48

Indian Act (1850), 57–58

Indian Act (1876), 108, 136, 144–45; assimilation and, 212n22; Bill 267, 54; disenfranchisement under, 223n39; Kahnawà:ke acceptance of, 50–51,

56–58, 61; land rights, 152; membership and, 178–79; patrilineal/gender bias of, 10, 13, 55–57, 170; reservation system of, 155–56. *See also* Bill C-31

Indian Advancement Act (1884), 136, 222n30

Indian agents, 107, 127, 181, 223n45

Indian Citizenship Act (1924), 134–37, 222n24

Indian Defense League of America (IDLA), 136

Indian Reorganization Act (1934), 137, 222n36, 224n48

Indian status, 13, 15, 44, 53; cards, 113–14, 123, 137, 222n22; loss of, 56–57, 61, 211n16; of Métis, 207n42; for white men/women, 58, 60, 108

Indigeneity, 204n18, 212n22, 218n1; nationalism and, 17–18; settler colonialism and, 23, 98, 181; sovereignty and, 23

Indigenous peoples: anthropology and, 95, 99–100; assimilation, 212n22; of Australia, 100, 191, 219n7; colonial stories on, 95–96; disappearance, 112, 204n18; empowering/disempowering, 100; history, 83; identity, 63–64; politics, 11, 112; "problem" of, 19–21, 156–57; recognition of, 218n1; sovereignty, 11, 20, 129, 141, 193; term usage, 202n11

intercultural interactions, 83, 85

ironworkers, 2–5, 7, 65; interviews with, 168–69, 197

Iroquois: authority, 159; border crossers, 116–17, 131, 135–37; civilization and citizenship, 102–3; clan, 162, 192–93; culture and tradition, 10, 26, 29–31, 70–74, 91–93, 103; and ethnographer relations, 87; history and origins, 65, 75–76, 89, 215n18; kinship relations, 15, 47–48; land loss, 49; literature, 39, 69–76, 80, 226n13; membership,

162–63; notions of time, 72–73; politics, 34, 47, 203n15; self-perception, 131–32; sovereignty, 113, 132, 136, 177, 183; spatiality, 159, 203n15; trade friendships, 221n15. *See also* Iroquois studies

Iroquois Book of Rites (Hale), 72–73, 85–88

Iroquois Confederacy, 2, 15, 80; history, 91; member nations, 133, 207n45; passports, 11, 19, 21, 23, 25, 182–84; reformulation, 82; title holding system, 72. *See also* Haudenosaunee

Iroquois Nationals Lacrosse Team (INLT), 1, 25, 227n4

Iroquois studies, 29, 39, 190; canonical texts in, 74, 85–92; Fenton's contributions to, 88–89, 91, 93; formation of, 104

Jacobs, Peter, 161

Jameson, Fredric, 74, 213n11

Jay Treaty (1794), 32, 34, 115; border-crossing rights, 115, 122–23, 133, 137; trading rights, 126, 128–29, 140

Jesuits, 46–47, 95–96

Johnson, Jemmy, 215nn22–23

Jordan, Kurt, 216n27

jurisdiction, 68, 105, 179

Kahnawà:ke: anthropological report on, 68–69; and Canada relations, 50–53, 63, 210n11; "central fire" designation, 208n45; history and settlement, 38–39, 45–49, 188; lacrosse team, 4, 201n5; land loss, 49, 180; literature, 42, 209n3; modes of communication, 195–96; nationhood, 185–86; non-Natives residing in, 13, 57, 60–62, 107–8, 179–80; politics, 43–44, 46; "praying Indians" designation, 39, 65, 94, 190; reserve status, 50–51; as a single-nation community, 186–88, 190; sovereignty, 19, 61, 98; territory and community profile, 3–7, 31, 41–44, 65, 104

Kahnawa'kehró:non (people of Kahnawà:ke): clans, 15, 204n21; contemporary struggles, 33–34; culture, 47–48, 65, 209n3; expectation/ fear of disappearance, 25–26, 42, 59; historical recognition of, 32–33; labor, 2–3; legal status, 33, 53; membership, 7–10, 13–16, 40, 56–58, 159–61, 185; mistrust among, 41; political orientation, 54; refusal of the state, 106; scholars, 4, 201n6; spoken language, 6, 31; use of St. Lawrence River, 51–53

Kahnawà:ke Membership Law, 13–14, 44, 180, 202n12, 204n19

Kaianere'kó:wa. *See* Great Law of Peace

Kanehsatà:ke, Mohawks of, 39, 148, 158; Oka land protest, 39, 150–51; reservation configuration, 154–55; women, 149–50

Kanien'kehá:ka, 14, 27. *See also* Kahnawa'kehró:non

Karihwí:io, 72, 77, 84, 88, 91, 103

Karnuth, Dorothy, 138, 223n39

Kentaké, 46, 48

knowing, process of, 75, 83, 95, 100–101, 178

knowledge construction, 67, 75, 178

Kuper, Adam, 86

labor, 101, 206n32; Kahnawa'kehró:non, 2–3

lacrosse, 182; Iroquois Nationals Team, 1, 25, 184, 227n4; Kahnawake Mohawks, 4, 201n5

land claims, 49, 93, 100, 206n34, 210n10; cultural practice and, 155; Six Nations, 211n19

land expropriation: eliminatory logic of, 181; in Kanehsatà:ke (Oka Crisis), 147–48, 150–51, 154; in Mohawk history, 68; for St. Lawrence Seaway project, 52; territorial loss, 48–49, 82, 106, 179

100; settler colonial, 16, 24–25, 177; sovereignty and, 22

Nichols, Robert Lee, 204n23

Obama, Barack, 1, 12

objectivist history, 75

occupation: land, 179; naturalization of, 109; settler, 2, 19, 21, 26, 106

Of Property (Locke), 101

Oka Crisis (1990), 5, 34, 169; media coverage, 147–48; nationhood and, 39, 157; resolution, 153; role of women in, 148–50, 166; standoff, 152–53, 180

Onondaga, 72, 87, 90

oral history, 88, 181, 210n12, 216n32

Ortner, Sherry, 203n16

Ottawa, the (people), 208n45

Paine, Robert, 216n28

Parker, Arthur, 42, 90, 214n15, 215n20, 215n23; *The Code of Handsome Lake, The Seneca Prophet,* 86, 88; *The Constitution of the Five Nations or The Iroquois Book of the Great Law,* 86, 88

Parker, Ely S.: ancestry and family, 81, 93, 103, 215n23; biographies, 80; contribution to history, 83–84; on ethnographers, 90; as a mediator and interpreter, 81–82; relationship with Morgan, 70, 76–77, 79–85, 98, 217n34

Parmenter, Jon, 46, 192–93, 209n5

Parti Quebecoise, 206n37

passports: Iroquois Confederacy, 11, 19, 21, 23, 182–84; "red cards," 123, 226n13; refusal of, 1, 18, 25

patrilineal descent, 10, 57–58, 179

Pels, Peter, 219n5

Pine Tree Chiefs, 81, 203n15, 215n24

playgroups, 77–79

political membership, 11, 48, 160, 169; 176; Kahnawà:ke, 8, 159, 166

Povinelli, Elizabeth, 143, 159, 191

power: desire and, 212n2; of Empire, 95;

foreign, 158; Iroquois authoritative, 159; state, 16, 18, 160, 205n31, 223n43; of white men, 59–61; women's, 170–71

precariousness, settler, 22, 143

property. *See* landownership

public perception, 126, 128, 142

purity: cultural, 20, 34, 103, 204n18, 213n12, 224n45; racial/blood, 162, 175

Quebec, 3, 55, 206n37

Quebec Native Women's Association (QNWA), 227n2

R. J. Reynolds Tobacco Holdings, 126, 128–30, 141, 145

R. v. Van Der Peet, 140, 155, 224n50

race, 108, 161; affectability of, 13; purity, 175, 224n45; sex and, 48, 59–60

racialization, 138–40

racial mixing, 48, 54; "half-breeds," 107–8, 207n42

Racketeering Influenced and Corrupt Organizations (RICO), 126, 130

"radical Indigenism," 105

Ramirez, Renya, 243

Razack, Sherene, 156, 204n23

recognition: by blood quantum, 54–55, 57, 137–40, 167–68; Canadian forms of, 55, 57, 135–40, 182; challenges/ problems of, 63, 196; citizenship and, 134–37, 142, 189–90; "feeling side" of, 113, 191; formal, 15–16; of Indigenous peoples, 218n1; Iroquois space of, 159; of land rights, 154; of Métis, 207n42; misrecognition/nonrecognition and, 16, 22–24, 41, 100, 151; of non-Natives on reserves, 13, 108; political, 20, 23, 32, 64, 130, 143, 158, 205n31; racialized forms of, 137–38, 193; settler colonialism and, 20–21; sovereignty and, 11; terms of, 40; of women, 164

recovery, notion of, 83

Red Jacket, 81, 131, 215n23

refusal/refusing: to be eliminated, 22; ethnographic, 34, 102, 105–7, 113; the nation-state, 182; at Oka, 147–48; of recognition, 11, 16, 24, 128, 185; of state gifts, 1, 7, 12

registration lists: federal, 8, 56–57; local Indian, 56, 107, 202n12, 212n19

Reid, Gerald, 181

relatedness, 12, 15, 17, 40

religion: Catholic Church, 49; conversion, 46, 95–96; Indigenous saints, 5. *See also* Handsome Lake

representation, historical, 97–98, 144

research ethics, 34, 106, 198, 219n11

reservations, 127, 154–55, 192; space of, 187

residency rights, 21, 48, 61–62, 180

Richard, interview with, 37–38, 63–65, 111

Rifkin, Mark, 13

rights: aboriginal, 140, 169, 225n7; assertion of, 182; border, 116–17, 131, 133–37; collective, 14, 153, 167, 168; inequality of, 175; land/property, 58, 139, 154, 160, 182, 211n19; membership, 178, 198; residency, 21, 48, 61–62, 180; territorial, 140, 152, 155, 165; trade, 126, 128–30, 140; women's, 165–66, 190

rituals, 99

Ross, Luana, 153

Said, Edward, 72, 92, 178

Salemink, Oscar, 219n5

Sapir, Edward, 104

savagery, 141–42, 144–45

Seed, Patricia, 25

seigniorial land grants, 46, 188, 210n10; Kahnawà:ke, 3, 63, 210n12; Kanehsatà:ke, 154

self-consciousness, 24, 72, 107, 188

self-identification, 64, 123, 186, 196

self-perception, 24, 53, 131–32

Seneca, 79–82, 89, 214n14

settler colonialism: anthropology and, 95, 99; assimilation, 212n22; boundary making, 212n2; captivity stories, 96; failures, 7–8, 33; Indigenous governance and, 170; intercultural interactions, 83; justice/injustice, 23; knowledge and, 178; law, 124, 129; recognition and, 20–21; reservationization, 5–6, 187; sovereignty, 12, 130, 143, 148, 226n10; structure of, 40, 105, 114, 147–48, 153, 157, 205n30; successes, 177; territory and, 19, 71, 128–29, 155, 166

Seven Nations Confederacy, 207n45

Seven Years' War, 96

Shimony, Annemarie Anrod, 92; *Conservatism among the Iroquois at the Six Nations Reserve*, 86, 89–91

Six Nations, 26, 31, 87–88, 136; Hiawatha belt, 221n15; land claims, 211n19; Longhouse at, 89–90; sovereignty, 104; territorial loss, 49

slaves, 22–24, 206n32

Smith, Andrea, 156

social assistance, 4

social hierarchy, 103, 127

Sour Springs, 90

sovereignty: border politics and, 115, 125; colonialism and, 12, 130, 143, 148, 226n10; culture and, 20, 140; identity and, 64; of Indigenous peoples, 11, 20, 129, 141, 193; Iroquois, 113, 125, 132, 136, 183; Kahnawà:ke, 19, 61, 98; legal belonging and, 10; as a matter of importance, 104–5; Mohawk, 39, 126, 129, 141–42, 185; monarchical, 26; nested, 11–12, 116; Quebec, 206n37; representation and, 97, 104; Six Nations, 104

space: of boundaries, 128, 192, 221n19; domesticating, 215n19; Empire and, 95; Iroquois, 159, 203n15; material, 109, 112; membership and, 39; of mis/recognition, 22, 23, 40, 109, 182; of reservations, 16, 156, 179, 187, 192; settler, 78, 163; territory and, 102

Sparrow Case, 225n7

Speck, Frank, 207n45

Spencer, O. M., 42

St. Lawrence Seaway, 51–52, 63, 210n11

state, 115–16; apologies, 20, 204n23; and border rights, 136–37; dispossession, 150; homogeneity, 16, 18; nationalism and, 17; perception of the Iroquois, 131–32; power, 16, 18, 31, 160, 205n31, 223n43; recognition, 117, 140; refusal of the, 106, 194; sovereignty, 154, 159; surveillance, 127; violence, 180

state of exception, 151, 153

status Indians. *See* Indian status

Stoler, Ann Laura, 212n2

stories, Indian, 83, 96

Supreme Court of Canada, 140, 225n7

Tarbell, Reaghan, 196

taxation: on cigarettes, 126, 129–30, 141; citizenship and, 138–39, 142

Taylor, Charles, 20–21, 205n26

Tekakwitha, Kateri, 5

territory: Ahkwesáhsne, 116, 127–28; colonial/settler desire for, 19, 71, 128–29; identity and, 162; Iroquois, 131, 149; Kahnawà:ke, 3–7, 31, 41–44, 65, 104; loss of, 48–49, 82, 106; mapping of, 130–31, 166; membership and, 63; Mohawk, 9–10, 149, 162, 166, 179; rights, 140, 152–53, 155, 165; women and, 162–64, 169

texts, Native, 84. *See also* canon, Iroquois

Thompson, Loran, 127, 130–31

time, notions of, 72–73

tobacco companies: role in illegal trade, 125–26, 128–29, 141; taxation and, 129–30

tolerance, 21, 127, 180

Tonawanda, 49, 65, 84

Tooker, Elisabeth, 89, 214n18

totalitarianism, 153

trading rights, 126, 128–30, 140

treaties: Buffalo Creek (1838), 79–80, 216n26; of Ghent (1815), 221n19; signatories, 182–83; Two Row Wampum (1613), 32, 133, 221n16. *See also* Jay Treaty (1794)

Treaty of Amity. *See* Jay Treaty (1794)

Trigger, Bruce, 216n28

Troubled Waters (CBC), 127–29, 141

Twinn Case, 58–59, 211n16

Two-Axe Early, Mary, 61, 160

Two Row Wampum Treaty (1613), 32, 133, 217n35, 221n16

Tyendinaga, 48–49, 140, 192

United States-Canada border, 34; blood-quantum requirement at, 137–40; cigarette smuggling, 125–26, 128–30, 141; crossing rights, 116–17, 131, 133–37, 193; interrogations, 117–24, 134; sovereignty and, 115

United States ex rel. Diabo v. McCandless, 134–35

United States-Mexico border, 116, 220n2

Van Der Peet Case, 140, 155, 224n50

veterans, 5

Victorian ideals, 10, 138, 161, 180, 204n19

Voget, Fred, 88–89, 211n13, 218n36; Longhouse studies, 53–55

Wabanaki Confederacy, 207n45

Waldron, Jeremy, 154, 205n23

Wallace, Anthony F. C., 86, 90–91, 203n15

wampum belts, 136, 221n16, 222n32

Warren, Elizabeth, 64

Warrior, Robert Allen, 84, 105, 219n10